The Afro-American Periodical Press 1838-1909

The Afro-American Periodical Press

1838-1909

PENELOPE L. BULLOCK

Louisiana State University Press
Baton Rouge and London

Designer: Albert Crochet
Typeface: Linotype Caledonia
Typesetter: Service Typesetting Company
Printer and binder: Thomson-Shore, Inc.

Published with the assistance of a grant from the National Endowment for the Humanities.

Portions of this book were previously published in slightly different form in the *Atlanta Historical Bulletin* and are reprinted here with the gracious permission of the Atlanta Historical Society.

LIBRARY OF CONGRESS CATALOGING IN PUBLICATION DATA

Bullock, Penelope L.
  The Afro-American periodical press, 1838–1909.
  Bibliography: p.
  Includes index.
  1. Afro-American periodicals—History.
I. Title.
PN4882.5.B8   051   81-1712
ISBN 0-8071-0663-1   AACR2

Dedicated to
my parents
Penelope Burwell Bullock and B. F. Bullock, Sr.
and to
Clarence A. Bacote,
Professor of History, Emeritus
Atlanta University

Contents

Illustrations

Preface

One facet of the black experience in the United States that has received relatively little discussion in popular or scholarly literature is the Afro-American periodical press. The studies of Negro journalism that have been published concentrate on the newspaper press. This book is an effort toward filling that void. It presents a narrative history of the beginnings and the early development of periodical publishing among black Americans, discusses the individuals and the institutions responsible for the magazines, and suggests the circumstances in American history and culture that helped to shape this press.

These periodicals are not only a significant phase of Afro-American history and culture within themselves; they are also important sources of information on the black experience in general. For those Afro-Americans who had the opportunity to express themselves through written communication, the periodicals reflect life as they experienced and interpreted it. This work documents the current availability of these periodicals as a guide for researchers in black studies. Perhaps this can lead to an expanded record of files and periodicals not included here that may be in the possession of individuals and in the collections of libraries and other institutions.

If this book gives the general reader a broader knowledge of the history of black periodicals in the United States, if it serves the student of Afro-American history and culture by pointing to

potential source materials, and if it elicits more extensive identi-
fication and location of these periodicals, it will have achieved
its purpose.

Acknowledgments

To all those who have assisted and encouraged me in this project, I express my thanks. I am especially grateful to:

Members of my family;

The late Wallace J. Bonk, chairman of my doctoral committee at the University of Michigan School of Library Science, and the other members of the committee—Russell E. Bidlack, Joe Lee Davis, and Edmon Low—who guided the original study through its completion as a dissertation;

The University of Michigan Horace H. Rackham School of Graduate Studies, the United States Office of Education, and the Ford Foundation for financial assistance during the dissertation years;

The reference departments of the University of Michigan Graduate Library and the Trevor Arnett Library of Atlanta University for their interlibrary loan services;

The "anonymous" readers who saw in the dissertation the possibility of a book;

The personnel of the Louisiana State University Press who guided the dissertation through its transformation into this book;

The libraries and institutions that I have visited for access to their collections and for the generous and invaluable assistance of their staffs;

The many more libraries, institutions, and individuals who took the time to search for information and materials and responded to my inquiries;

And, finally, those scholars, librarians, archivists, and teachers whose concern and contribution in years past have sustained black studies, even when activity in this area was less widespread and popular than it is today.

ONE

Perspective

In order to assert and maintain their rank as
men among men, [black people in the United
States] must speak for themselves; no outside
tongue, however gifted with eloquence, can tell
their story; no outside eye, however penetrat-
ing, can see their wants.

—*Anglo-African Magazine*, January, 1859

⁕

Freedom's Journal is recognized and commemorated as the first
newspaper issued by black people in the United States. Less
familiar is the *Mirror of Liberty*. Yet that publication is of com-
parable significance, for it was the first black periodical published
in this country. It was established in New York City in July, 1838,
eleven years after *Freedom's Journal* was initiated in that city.
Two months later, another Afro-American periodical, the *National
Reformer*, was founded in Philadelphia. The appearance of the
Mirror of Liberty and the *National Reformer* in 1838 marked the
beginning of the black periodical press in the United States.

This book presents the history of the first seventy years of that
press. The individual periodicals are described, and trends in the
general development of the Afro-American periodical press between 1838 and 1909 are discussed. In 1910, W. E. B. Du Bois
founded *Crisis* magazine under the auspices of the newly organized National Association for the Advancement of Colored People. With the publication of *Crisis*, a new era in the history of
black periodicals began.

Ninety-seven titles have been included in this survey. A periodical has been defined as a black publication if the principal editor or editors can be identified as Afro-American. Newspapers and the following classes of periodicals have been excluded: publications issued by fraternal and beneficial societies, newsletters and student publications from educational institutions, magazines for children and young people, Sunday School literature, and church missionary journals. Other periodicals sponsored by religious denominations have been restricted to publications at the national level. Weekly and semimonthly publications have been considered only if at some point in their history they were issued as monthlies or as quarterlies. Within these limitations, all titles identified as Afro-American periodicals have been included. Some of the periodicals are obviously more outstanding than others. But however insignificant many of the titles may appear to be when examined individually, all of them are a part of the history of the Afro-American periodical press.

Of the ninety-seven titles between 1838 and 1909, eleven were founded or proposed in the twenty-five years preceding or during the Civil War. Only one periodical was issued during the Reconstruction era. Eighty-five were established or proposed in the three decades after Reconstruction. Of these eighty-five, fifteen were founded or proposed during the 1880s, twenty-eight were established in the 1890s, and forty-one began publication in the decade from 1900 to 1909.

In the entire period from 1838 to 1909, the greatest activity was in New York and Pennsylvania. New York had sixteen titles, with eleven in New York City and two in Brooklyn. Pennsylvania had fifteen titles, with eight in Philadelphia, three in Harrisburg, and three in Pittsburgh. During the pre-1865 era, periodicals were issued in New York, Pennsylvania, and Indiana, and in Baltimore, New Orleans, and San Francisco. The sole periodical of the Reconstruction era was published in Brooklyn in 1866. During the 1880s, periodical publication extended northward into Massachusetts, westward into Illinois, and southward into the District of Columbia, Virginia, North Carolina, Kentucky, Alabama, and Texas. In the decade of the 1890s, magazines appeared in South Carolina, Georgia, Tennessee, Ohio, Minnesota, Missouri, and the Oklahoma Territory. Between 1900 and 1909, periodicals were initiated in New Jersey, Connecticut, Delaware, Iowa, and Kansas. During the three decades between 1880 and 1909, the largest number of periodicals was published in Pennsylvania, with twelve titles, New York, with eleven titles, and the District of Columbia, with nine titles.

Some of the periodicals of the antebellum era were general magazines, containing a variety of material on many subjects and attempting to appeal to the public at large. Such a publication was the *Repository of Religion and Literature and of Science and Art*. Other periodicals concentrated on specialized interests. The *African Methodist Episcopal Church Magazine* was established primarily to transmit the proceedings of church conferences and other news of the denomination to the membership. During the last two decades of the nineteenth century and the first decade of the twentieth, specialized publications became a major part of the Afro-American periodical press. Of the eighty-five titles between 1880 and 1909, fifty-two were special interest periodicals. The two largest groups were the educational and religious journals. Several women's magazines were also issued. Other specialized publications were in the areas of music and the theater, business, medicine and health, trades and occupations, and agriculture.

In regard to the sponsorship of the periodicals, two types of magazines were published—those issued by established organizations and those carried on by individual enterprise without institutional support. The black church played a major role in the sponsorship of periodical publications. During the antebellum era, the African Methodist Episcopal Church was responsible for both the *African Methodist Episcopal Church Magazine* and the *Repository of Religion and Literature and of Science and Art*. In the decades after Reconstruction, the religious denominations continued to be important sponsors. Other organizations in both the antebellum and the postbellum periods also made their contribution. Significantly, the only black periodicals initiated before

1910 that are still issued today are those published by organizations. They are the *A. M. E. Church Review*, founded in 1884;
the *A. M. E. Zion Quarterly Review*, founded in 1890; *National
Notes*, founded in 1897 for the National Association of Colored
Women; and the *Journal* of the National Medical Association,
founded in 1909.

Longevity was not a general characteristic of the black periodical press between 1838 and 1909. None of the periodicals initiated
before 1865 were in existence when the Civil War ended. Only
three of the eleven titles of the antebellum period were published
for longer than five years, and the majority lasted no more than
one or two years. The sole periodical of the Reconstruction era
was also short-lived. For the eighty-five titles between 1880 and
1909, the pattern was the same. Only twenty-three were issued
for longer than five years, and forty-five periodicals apparently
folded in their first or second year.

Thus, for a large number of the periodicals, there are no extensive files to examine. Even for many of the titles that were
published for any length of time, complete files have not survived.
For many of the magazines, only scattered issues or a single "Vol.
I, no. 1" issue are available today. For some periodicals, no copies
can be found; brief notes in contemporary newspapers and other
sources are the only evidence of their publication. Nevertheless,
the Afro-American periodical press must be recognized as a significant institution in American history and culture.

Before presenting the history of this institution for the period
from 1838 to 1909, it is appropriate to outline the political and
social background of these years, for the status of the Negro in
American life played a major role in the creation and growth of
the Afro-American periodical press. When the first decennial census of the new American nation was taken in 1790, the total number of Negroes in the United States was recorded as 757,208. This
was 19.3 percent of the entire population of the country. By 1860
the Negro population had increased to 4,441,830, although the
proportion to the total population had decreased to 14.1 percent.

Although most Negroes were in bondage during these years, free persons comprised an appreciable segment of the Negro population. In 1790, 59,557, or 7.9 percent, of the Negroes in the country were classified as free persons. In 1830 free persons numbered 319,599, or 13.7 percent, of the Negro population. By 1860 the proportion had dropped to 11 percent, although the number had risen to 488,070. The majority of the free Negroes lived in the South throughout these years: 54.6 percent in 1790, 56.8 percent in 1830, and 52.9 percent in 1860.[1]

In both the North and the South, free Negroes concentrated in the urban areas. Between 1790 and 1860 their number in the city and county of New York increased from 1,101 to 12,574; in Brooklyn from 14 to 4,313; in Philadelphia from 1,420 to 22,185; and in Baltimore from 323 to 25,680. In the city and parish of New Orleans, free persons of color totaled 7,161 in 1820 and 19,226 in 1840. By 1860 their number had decreased to 10,939.[2] The exodus from New Orleans was prompted by the loss of civil rights resulting from disfranchisement and other legislation.

Free Negroes did not generally enjoy the same rights and opportunities as the white population. An example of the inferior status in which they increasingly found themselves was the suffrage legislation in Pennsylvania and New York. In the eighteenth century, the constitutions and laws of these states did not attempt to disfranchise Negroes. By the mid-nineteenth century, restrictive measures based on racial discrimination had been adopted. In Pennsylvania the Constitution of 1838 explicitly limited voting privileges to white men only; in New York a series of laws, culminating in the Constitution of 1821, effectively disfranchised most Negroes. The historian Leon F. Litwack points out that "by 1840, some 93 per cent of the northern free Negro population lived in states which completely or practically excluded them from the right to vote."[3]

Racial prejudice and the legal and extralegal discriminatory practices resulting from it extended into all phases of the life of free Negroes throughout the United States. Partly out of response to this situation, these individuals banded together and formed their own institutions—churches, schools, fraternal orders, mutual aid societies, state and national conventions, labor organizations, literary and educational societies, libraries, and newspapers and periodicals. In these institutions they sought to provide for themselves the opportunities and benefits that they were otherwise denied. At the same time, they utilized these agencies as instruments of protest in an effort to gain equal rights with other Americans. Even though free Negroes formed their own communities within the larger society, their ultimate objective was full participation in American life.

As the years passed, racial tension and discrimination mounted, and the federal government, attempting to bring about a political and peaceful resolution of the slavery controversy, took measures that eventually proved detrimental to the Negro. Under the provisions of the Compromise of 1850 enacted by Congress, the slave trade was abolished in the District of Columbia and California was admitted into the Union as a free state. However, other territory gained through the Mexican War was organized without Congressional provisions regarding slavery, a matter that was to be determined in the state constitutions drawn up by the residents of that territory. Also included as a part of the compromise was a more stringent fugitive slave law, which, in effect, endangered the security of free Negroes.

In 1854 Congress passed the Kansas-Nebraska Act. By providing that the question of slavery be decided by the territorial legislatures rather than by Congress, this act repealed the Missouri Compromise of 1820, which had prohibited slavery in these regions. In the 1857 *Dred Scott* v. *Sanford* case, the U.S. Supreme Court ruled that Dred Scott, as a slave and a Negro, could not be considered a citizen of the United States and therefore could not bring suit in a federal court. The decision handed down in this case not only denied citizenship to the Negro; it also denied Congress the power to regulate slavery in the territories. With this series of federal actions, the decade preceding the Civil War was a time of extremely depressed hopes for black people.

This mood of despair among both slaves and free Negroes was

replaced by an atmosphere of anticipation following the Union military victory. With the emancipation of the slaves and the enactment of certain legislative measures between 1865 and 1875, a promise of full citizenship came to all Negroes. The Thirteenth Amendment to the Constitution, ratified in 1865, legally abolished slavery. That same year, Congress created the Freedmen's Bureau to assist the emancipated Negroes in adjusting to their new way of life. In 1866 Congress passed the Civil Rights Act in an effort to nullify the Black Codes that had been enacted by southern legislatures to keep the Negro in a subordinate status. The Fourteenth Amendment, adopted in 1868, reaffirmed the rights granted by this act and also attempted to guarantee suffrage (although Negroes were not explicitly mentioned in the amendment). The Fifteenth Amendment, designed as a further safeguard of the right to vote, was ratified in 1870. When the reconstruction plan developed by the Radical Republicans was enacted by Congress in 1867, the way was opened for Negroes to become participants in the governments of the southern states.

At the same time, however, the South was waging a relentless campaign to subjugate the Negro through such extralegal measures as the activities of the Ku Klux Klan. In an effort to combat the Klan and other secret societies, Congress passed the Enforcement Acts of 1870 and 1871. In 1875 another Civil Rights Act was enacted to guarantee Negroes equal rights in public accommodations. Gradually, however, the southern white Democrats regained control of their state governments and removed black people from political participation. The Amnesty Act passed by Congress in 1872, which made it possible for ex-Confederates to return to political activity, was an important factor in this development. With the election of the Moderate Republican Rutherford B. Hayes in 1876 and the withdrawal of federal troops from South Carolina and Louisiana in 1877, political reconstruction came to an end.

With the return of the Democratic party to power in the South, disfranchisement and other restrictive measures were systematically instituted against the Negro. The black vote was eliminated through such techniques as the poll tax, the white primary provision (which made the Democratic party a private association with the right to decide who could participate in its primary elections), and the laws that required the ability to read and interpret sections of the state constitutions to the satisfaction of official examiners as a qualification for voting. Segregated public school systems with their inequities for black students became the pattern at all levels of education. Jim Crow laws legalized segregation in transportation and in other public accommodations.

During this period, the U.S. Supreme Court generally supported southern policy. A series of decisions invalidated legal gains that the Negro had made during Reconstruction. In the Civil Rights Cases of 1883, the 1875 Civil Rights Act was declared unconstitutional. Other decisions condoned the doctrine of "separate but equal" in public accommodations. In the *Plessy* v. *Ferguson* case of 1896, the majority opinion of the Supreme Court upheld a Louisiana law requiring segregated railroad coaches. Not only the Supreme Court but also the executive and legislative branches of the federal government and northern public opinion in general tacitly supported the southern point of view. As Benjamin Quarles has written, "by 1900 the South's white-supremacy doctrine met with little disapproval in other quarters. Increasingly there had been a merging of the southern and the national image of the Negro. At the turn of the century the idea that certain races were naturally inferior became more tenaciously held than ever. The belief that the Anglo-Saxons were superior to other races waxed in the 1890's."[4]

Economic hardships as well as political reverses were the fate of the Negro population during the latter part of the nineteenth century. Before the Civil War, many free Negroes in southern cities worked in the artisan and mechanical trades, in which they often held the monopoly. After the war they were gradually supplanted by white craftsmen. In the North, Negroes lost jobs in competition with immigrant labor, a trend that had started during the antebellum period. The urban Negro in both the North and the South found employment mainly in domestic and other personal services and in unskilled occupations. In the rural South, the former slave usually became an impoverished sharecropper. Thus, at the turn of the century, Negroes were generally receiving low wages and living in poverty.

In education, however, they made relatively more progress. First of all, there was a decrease in illiteracy. In 1870, 79.9 percent of the Negro population ten years of age and over was recorded as illiterate. By 1900 this figure had dropped to 44.5 percent and by 1910 to 30.4 percent.[5] Not only at the basic level of literacy, but at all stages of education, expanded opportunities were being provided. Numerous agencies and individuals—northern and southern, black and white, public and private, religious and secular—were making their contribution to the education of the Negro. The Freedmen's Bureau conducted schools throughout the southern states. Public school systems were created by the southern legislatures, and Negroes attended white state universities in the South during the Reconstruction period. Private societies organized to aid the freedmen also developed educational facilities. The Negro religious denominations, the white churches, and the American Missionary Association operated educational institutions. Two foundations were established by white philanthropists to assist Negro education, the George Peabody Fund in 1867 and the John F. Slater Fund in 1882.

The type of education that would be most beneficial for black people—industrial and vocational education versus liberal and higher education—became the subject of much debate. Two Negro leaders were regarded as the main protagonists in this controversy: Booker Taliaferro Washington and William Edward Burghardt Du Bois. The void in leadership caused by the death of Frederick Douglass in February, 1895, was soon filled by Washington's rise to national prominence. In September of that year, in a speech at the Cotton States Exposition in Atlanta, Washington stressed vocational training and economic self-reliance while renouncing social equality for Negroes in American society. Largely as the result of favorable white reaction to this speech in the North and the South, Washington moved into a unique position of leadership.

Booker T. Washington (1856–1915) had been educated at the Hampton Normal and Agricultural Institute in Virginia. In 1881 he was selected as the first principal for a new school that was opening at Tuskegee, Alabama. He continued as the head of Tuskegee Institute until his death. Hampton and Tuskegee developed into the leading institutions for the industrial training of Negroes, and Washington became the most widely known and respected advocate of industrial education for black people. In 1895, the young Negro scholar, W. E. B. Du Bois (1868–1963), received his doctoral degree from Harvard University. Du Bois became engaged in scholarly pursuits and was soon recognized as the chief spokesman for liberal education, particularly for those Negroes with exceptional intellectual ability whom he called the "Talented Tenth." Du Bois took a position of aggressive agitation for political and social equality for all Negro citizens—a stance that Washington did not openly assume.

The emphasis on manual training for Negroes was a phase of the industrial growth of the country and the resulting attention given generally to vocational education. The pattern of population movement among Negroes was also determined by economic developments. In the late nineteenth century, this population showed a trend toward urbanization, as did the total United States population. During the Reconstruction and early post-Reconstruction years, Negroes had tended to remain in the rural areas of the South. As new industry came to the urban South, they began to move into the towns and cities in search of employment. In 1900, 90 percent of the total Negro population of the country was still living in the South. In 1910, thirty-three of the forty-three American cities with 10,000 or more Negro residents were located in southern states.[6]

During the post-Reconstruction era, political and economic reverses prompted some Negroes to join the westward migration of Americans seeking better fortunes in the frontier lands. An exodus of thousands of Negroes from the South into Kansas took place in 1879, and in later years many all-Negro communities were established in the Oklahoma Territory. This westward movement, however, embraced less than 1 percent of the Negro population, and the mass migration of black people from the South into the urban areas of the North did not occur until the period of World War I.[7]

The overall development of the Afro-American periodical press was influenced by the status of Negroes in American society during the years between 1838 and 1909. This press began in the 1830s as a part of the organized activities of black people who were working for the emancipation of the slave and for the liberation of the free Negro from inequities and restrictions. As the status of free Negroes deteriorated during the 1850s and the early 1860s, they became increasingly alarmed about their situation. As a result, more periodicals were initiated than at any time previously. Thomas Hamilton of the *Anglo-African Magazine* spoke for most of the black periodical editors of these years when he said: "The wealth, the intellect, the Legislation, (State and Federal,) the pulpit, and the science of America, have concentrated on no one point so heartily as in the endeavor to write down the Negro as something less than a man. . . . This Magazine will have the aim to uphold and encourage the now depressed hopes of thinking black men, in the United States."[8] Between 1865 and 1879, when there were prospects of full citizenship for black people, the periodical press was dormant. But from 1880 to 1909, with the adverse course of events of the post-Reconstruction years, periodicals proliferated as they had during the 1850s and the early 1860s. Black people again used this press to serve their needs in segregated communities and to agitate for integration into American society.

In addition to the political and social circumstances that played such an important part in the history of the Afro-American periodical press, other factors also contributed to its genesis and growth, namely: the development of the magazine in general in the United States; the literary traditions of the Afro-American people; and the personalities, interests, and talents of the editors and publishers of the periodicals. These influences will be discussed in the chapters that follow, as the individual publications are described and the general history of the press is presented.

In this book the terms *periodical* and *magazine* are used interchangeably. The term *journal* is used in referring to both newspapers and periodicals. Although the word *Afro-American* can have a wider geographical connotation, it refers here to black people in the United States. The following terms are used interchangeably: *Afro-American, Negro, Negro-American, colored,* and *black.* Varying terms of designation have been a constant feature of the history of this ethnic group in the United States. Although certain terms may have been more prevalent in different periods, all of them have been used at practically all times throughout this history. In 1848 the black abolitionist Henry Highland Garnet, pleading for a united front in the struggle against slavery, made this observation:

> Let there be no strife between us, for we are brethren, and we must rise or fall together. How unprofitable it is for us to spend our golden moments in long and solemn debate upon the questions whether we shall be called *"Africans," "Colored Americans,"* or *"Africo Americans,"* or *"Blacks."* The question should be, my friends, *shall we arise and act like men, and cast off this terrible yoke?*[9]

TWO

Before Emancipation
The First Periodicals

Liberty is the word for me—above all, liberty.
—*Mirror of Liberty*, July, 1838

❧

Many years before the Civil War was fought and Emancipation proclaimed, the black periodical press had been established in the United States. In 1838 the first two Afro-American periodicals were founded: the *Mirror of Liberty* in New York City and the *National Reformer* in Philadelphia. In 1841 the *African Methodist Episcopal Church Magazine* appeared in Brooklyn, and in 1843 *L'Album Littéraire* began publication in New Orleans. These four periodicals were of brief duration, and their total pages constitute only slender volumes. Yet they are significant as the beginnings of a new minority periodical press in the United States.

Each of these publications served a different purpose. The *Mirror of Liberty* reported on the activities of the New York Committee of Vigilance. The *National Reformer* set forth the principles of the American Moral Reform Society. The *African Methodist Episcopal Church Magazine* was a medium of communication for that denomination, and *L'Album Littéraire* provided an outlet for the literary talents of free men of color in Louisiana. At the same time, the promoters of these four periodicals—David Ruggles and George Hogarth in New York, William

Whipper in Pennsylvania, and Armand Lanusse in Louisiana—were motivated by a common objective. Implicitly or explicitly, they all spoke for a single cause: the vindication of equal rights. Between 1838 and 1848, each in his own way was protesting not only the institution of slavery in the South but also the inferior status of free Negroes in both the North and the South.

After a short period of dormancy, the black periodical press became active again between 1854 and 1863. As one of the editors wrote, these were years of disillusionment for black men, "men who, for twenty years and more have been active in conventions, in public meetings, in societies, in the pulpit, and through the press, . . . yet see, as the apparent result of their work and their sacrifices, only Fugitive Slave laws and Compromise bills, and the denial of citizenship on the part of the Federal and State Governments."[1] Seven titles were initiated or proposed during these years: the *Afro-American Repository*, projected by the National Emigration Convention of Colored People in Cleveland in 1854, with James Monroe Whitfield designated as editor; the *New Republic and Liberian Missionary Journal*, launched in Harrisburg, Pennsylvania, in 1856 by John Wolff; the *Repository of Religion and Literature and of Science and Art*, established in Indianapolis in 1858 by literary societies of the African Methodist Episcopal Church under the leadership of Bishop Daniel Alexander Payne (and later transferred to Philadelphia, then to Baltimore); *Douglass' Monthly*, initiated by Frederick Douglass in Rochester, New York, in 1858; the *Anglo-African Magazine*, founded by Thomas Hamilton in New York City in 1859; the *Lunar Visitor*, started by John Jamison Moore in San Francisco in 1862; and the *Students' Repository*, issued by Samuel H. Smothers at the Union Literary Institute in Randolph County, Indiana, in 1863.

These periodicals reflected the diverse measures to which Negroes turned in an effort to change their oppressed status in American society. Some individuals considered emigration to foreign lands and initiated or supported movements for establishing settlements in Canada, Africa, the West Indies, and Central and South America. This attitude was shown in the *New Republic and Liberian Missionary Journal*. It was reflected by the writings of the emigrationists James Theodore Holly and Martin Robison Delany in the *Anglo-African Magazine* and by advertisements that appeared in *Douglass' Monthly* (although the publishers Hamilton and Douglass were not themselves proponents of emigration). Much more prevalent was the determination to combat racial prejudice by remaining in the United States and disproving the charges of Negro inferiority. Periodicals were established to present facts about the achievements of black people and to display the intellect and talent of black writers, as portrayed in the *Anglo-African Magazine* and the *Repository of Religion and Literature and of Science and Art*.

Many of the periodicals encouraged self-improvement among Negroes and urged them to take advantage of educational opportunities. Daniel A. Payne, who in the 1840s had utilized the *African Methodist Episcopal Church Magazine* for the educational advancement of the ministry, in the 1850s promoted cultural improvement for ministers and lay members of the church through the *Repository of Religion and Literature*. Samuel H. Smothers issued the *Students' Repository* in Indiana to stimulate an interest in education. On the West Coast, John J. Moore pointed out in the *Lunar Visitor* that it was the duty of editors and contributors "to discuss thoroughly and plainly every obstacle to . . . education, with the cause and remedy."[2]

As *Douglass' Monthly* demonstrated, editors also continued their campaign for the emancipation of slaves in the South and for the political liberation of free people throughout the United States. None of these themes were new to the black periodical. In its beginning years, this minority press had given attention to emigration, to education and self-improvement, to emancipation, and to equality before the law. With the establishment or proposal of these seven titles between 1854 and 1863, however, the decade witnessed the first concentration of periodical publication to take place among Afro-Americans. Such activity would not occur again until the decade of the 1880s.

Most of the antebellum periodicals were established in urban locations where free Negroes had developed their own community life. Some of the publications were sponsored by the churches, schools, and civil rights organizations. Others were issued through individual enterprise, without institutional support. The editors of these publications were often united by bonds of common interest and close ties of friendship. Ruggles and Whipper were agents in their communities for Douglass when he began publishing the *North Star* newspaper in 1847. The friendship between Ruggles and Douglass dated back to 1838 when young Douglass, a fugitive slave who had safely reached New York City, found refuge in Ruggles' home. When the *Anglo-African Magazine* was initiated in January, 1859, *Douglass' Monthly* commented that the new year had brought forth "nothing more gratifying and encouraging than this new publication."[3]

The men who edited and published these periodicals earned their livelihood in a variety of occupations. Many, of course, were ministers. Whitfield was a barber, Whipper a wealthy lumber and coal yard merchant. Lanusse and Smothers were school principals, Douglass was an antislavery lecturer. Ruggles and Hamilton were engaged in publishing and bookselling. Although some of the editors had attended institutions of higher education, others had acquired only a common school education. At least two—William Whipper and Frederick Douglass—had no formal schooling at all.

Certain periodicals—notably the *Mirror of Liberty*, the *National Reformer*, and *Douglass' Monthly*—contained primarily the writings of their editors, supplemented by material reprinted from other publications. Other periodicals attempted to serve as outlets for the literary talents of black men and women. In the *African Methodist Episcopal Church Magazine*, the contributors were mainly the ministers of that denomination. *L'Album Littéraire* printed the creative writings of Louisiana residents. In the *Repository of Religion and Literature* and the *Anglo-African Magazine* a broader spectrum of writers was represented. Contributions were printed from unknown persons as well as from the black leaders of the day. The *Anglo-African Magazine* had stated that writers were to be paid "according to the means of the Publishers." At the end of the first year Hamilton announced: "The contributors to this Magazine have performed a labor of love—the publisher has not yet been able to pay them—for which we present our loving thanks."[4]

In format the antebellum periodicals ranged from the four-page *Lunar Visitor* to the *Repository of Religion and Literature*, which began as a forty-eight-page quarterly. Most of the publications had only a few, if any, advertisements, usually for local services offered by individuals personally acquainted with the editors and publishers. Among these were William Still's boardinghouse in Philadelphia, John J. Zuille's printing shop in New York City, and the Bethel Church Academy conducted in Baltimore by George T. and John L. Watkins. The *Anglo-African Magazine* carried notices for the books and other publications sold by Hamilton. *Douglass' Monthly* had extensive advertising, including announcements of new books and the detailed circulars of James Redpath's Haytian Emigration Movement.

Only a few of these publications were illustrated. The pictures in the *African Methodist Episcopal Church Magazine* were mainly undistinguished portrayals of biblical scenes. In the *Anglo-African Magazine* and the *Repository of Religion and Literature*, the quality of the illustrations improved. Both of these periodicals had, as occasional frontispieces, portraits of outstanding black personalities engraved by John Sartain, a leading illustrator of American magazines of that period.

The subscription price to the antebellum periodicals, for both the quarterlies and the monthlies, was usually $1.00 a year. The *Lunar Visitor* in California had a higher rate, at 25¢ per month. During 1862 the *Repository of Religion and Literature* lowered its yearly rate from $1.00 to 60¢ to attract more readers. Too few subscribers, plus the problem of delinquent subscribers, plagued the antebellum periodicals and proved to be a major cause of their early demise. The publication issued regularly over the longest period of time was *Douglass' Monthly*. This was a testi-

mony to Frederick Douglass' reputation among white and black
abolitionists in the United States and abroad, but even this journal encountered financial difficulties. Appeals for new subscribers
and for the payment of overdue subscriptions appeared in the
pages of the *Monthly*, just as in other periodicals. Next in duration were the two publications from the A. M. E. Church, although the *Church Magazine* was published quite irregularly and
the *Repository of Religion and Literature* was temporarily suspended for almost a year.

All of the periodicals initiated between 1838 and 1863 ceased
to exist before the Civil War ended, but they all played a part
in establishing a new minority periodical press in the United
States. The outstanding Afro-American periodicals of the antebellum period were the *Mirror of Liberty*, the *National Reformer*,
the *African Methodist Episcopal Church Magazine*, the *Repository of Religion and Literature and of Science and Art, Douglass'
Monthly*, and the *Anglo-African Magazine*. Individual discussions
of these periodicals are presented at the end of this chapter.

The Louisiana periodical, *L'Album Littéraire: Journal des
Jeunes Gens, Amateurs de Littérature*, was a magazine of creative
writing. All of the contents—poetry, short stories, fables, essays,
and editorials—were in French. The majority of the writers were
young men of color living in Louisiana. Among them was Camille
Thierry, a New Orleans-born poet who eventually migrated to
France to escape race discrimination. The literary historian Edward L. Tinker, in commenting on the issues of the periodical,
gives this analysis: "They contain poems, short stories and a series
of anonymous editorials of a very radical slant for that time.
Reading between the lines it is easy to see that an attempt was
being made to instill in young colored readers the courage to
assert their rights, although of course, as a matter of precaution,
this advice was couched in the vaguest terms."[5] Thus *L'Album
Littéraire*, as different as it was from other Afro-American periodicals, still bore affinity to them in spirit.

The only issues of this periodical that have survived are those
of July, August 1, and August 15, 1843. The publication was

started in April of that year by J. L. Marciacq, a Frenchman who taught the children of free black families. In the periodical itself, Marciacq and J. L. Sollée, the printer, were indicated as the two persons responsible for the magazine, and the name of Armand Lanusse appeared only as a contributor. But Tinker is inclined to believe that Lanusse, rather than Marciacq, was the real promoter of the periodical.[6] A free man of color born in New Orleans in 1812, Lanusse was principal of a Catholic school for orphan children and was a frequent contributor to the Negro newspapers in the city. In 1845 he compiled *Les Cenelles*, an anthology of poetry by Louisiana authors.[7]

In other parts of the country, free Negroes were giving increasing attention to emigration as their status in society became less secure. The National Emigration Convention of Colored People held its first meeting in 1854 in Cleveland, Ohio, and Martin Robison Delany was elected president. This group met again in Cleveland in 1856. Two years later a third meeting was held in Chatham, Canada. The members of the organization were opposed to the American Colonization Society and its program for the settlement of Negroes in Liberia; they were interested in the possibilities of sponsoring their own emigration projects to the West Indies, Canada, and Central and South America.

One item on the agenda of the 1854 meeting was the establishment of a periodical. The report from a committee appointed to study this matter recommended that the organization issue a quarterly journal that would be its official publication and also serve as a literary periodical for black people in general. This document stated that the journal should be "open to a fair and impartial discussion of all questions connected with the welfare, progress and development of the Negro race." It urged that "the ablest colored writers in both hemispheres should be engaged as its regular contributors, and articles invited on the various branches of literature, science, art, mechanics, law, commerce, philosophy, theology, et cetera." The report anticipated that the quarterly would be a publication in which "solid will doubtless predominate over light matter."[8]

The members of the committee preparing this document were James Monroe Whitfield, James Theodore Holly, and William Lambert. The convention adopted the report and designated Whitfield as editor of the periodical. A delegate from the state of New York, Whitfield was a resident of Buffalo, earning his livelihood as a barber and writing poetry. His volume, *America and Other Poems*, had been published the year before. In previous years, Whitfield had used his literary talent to defend the merits of emigration in debates with Frederick Douglass and other black leaders.[9]

This proposal for an international black literary periodical remained a nebulous idea until 1856, when the second emigration convention drew up a blueprint for the publication. The periodical was given the title *Afric-American Repository*. The editor was to be assisted by eight corresponding editors, who, with the editor, would constitute a board of publication to manage the literary and business affairs of the quarterly. The board was charged with the responsibilities of securing contributions from qualified black writers, "wheresoever dispersed," and of building up "a world-wide circulation." Each issue would have about two hundred pages, and the periodical was to be sold at seventy-five cents a copy. A timetable was outlined for publication, with the first number scheduled for July, 1857.

The promoters were determined that the *Afric-American Repository* would be a solvent periodical, and they set a goal of one thousand subscribers for the first issue. If at least five hundred dollars were not raised by April 1, 1857, publication would be delayed until this amount was on hand. The editor's salary would be six hundred dollars a year, and the services of the corresponding editors would be compensated "by the discretionary action of the Board of Publication." Contributors were to be paid "according to the importance and value of their articles, and the available resources."[10]

Before the 1856 convention closed, the eight corresponding editors who would assist Whitfield had been appointed. Journalistic experience was well represented in the group. Martin R.

Delany had published the *Mystery* newspaper in Pittsburgh and then had associated with Frederick Douglass in launching the *North Star*. Mrs. Mary Ann Shadd Cary was issuing the *Provincial Freeman* newspaper in Toronto and Chatham. The other woman in the group, Mary E. Bibb, was the widow of Henry Bibb, who had founded the *Voice of the Fugitive* newspaper in Windsor, Canada. James Theodore Holly, an Episcopalian minister from New Haven, Connecticut, had formerly been associate editor of the *Voice*. The other corresponding editors named for the *Afric-American Repository* were William C. Munroe, a Detroit minister who presided over the 1856 convention; John N. Still of Shrewsbury, New Jersey; and Martin H. Freeman of Allegheny, Pennsylvania.

The Afric-American Printing Company was formed to publish the periodical and other literary productions from black authors. In August, 1857, the company announced that the first issue of the *Afric-American Repository*, originally scheduled for July, 1857, was postponed for one year, "in order to establish it upon a sounder basis."[11] No evidence has been found that any issues were ever published, but the documents relating to the *Afric-American Repository* indicate that it was the most ambitious periodical projected by Negroes during the antebellum period.

Although members of the National Emigration Convention opposed the American Colonization Society and its Liberia project, there were other Negroes who endorsed and supported the society's program. The *New Republic and Liberian Missionary Journal* reflected the sentiments of that segment of the black population. In December, 1855, a notice about this forthcoming publication in the *Colonization Herald* (published by the Pennsylvania Colonization Society) read as follows: "Under this title it is proposed to issue at $1 per annum a monthly publication from Harrisburg, Pennsylvania. Its editor and publisher, Mr. John Wolff, is represented as a colored man of pleasing address and considerable intelligence. . . . The journal is to be devoted to the cause of colonizing free people of color in the coast of Africa, and to the cause of Education and Temperance." In December,

1856, the *New York Colonization Journal* acknowledged receipt of the first number of the *New Republic and Liberian Missionary Journal* with this remark: "It commences its career in good style as the organ of an intelligent, and we trust an increasing portion of our colored brethren." Excerpts from the *New Republic* were printed in this issue of the New York journal and also in the January, 1857, number of the *African Repository* (published by the American Colonization Society).[12] No copies of the *New Republic* have been located.

During these years of emigration proposals and projects, Negroes were also migrating westward within the United States. The increase in the black population of California between 1840 and 1860 was largely the result of the gold rush, as Negroes moved to the West with other Americans to seek their fortunes. From less than one thousand in 1850, the number of nonwhites in the state rose to more than two thousand by 1852, and to four thousand by 1860. The city with the largest Negro population during those years was San Francisco. In the West, as in the East, Negroes formed their own churches and other institutions —schools, benevolent associations, literary societies, fraternal lodges, state conventions, and newspapers and periodicals. Although California entered the Union as a free state in 1850, blacks were still subjected to racial restrictions. Discouraged by this discrimination, hundreds of Negroes in that state migrated during the late 1850s and early 1860s to British Columbia and the Victoria Colony in Canada when gold was discovered in those regions.[13]

One prominent leader among the black people was John Jamison Moore, a minister in the African Methodist Episcopal Zion Church. Moore was born in West Virginia about 1804 and grew up in Pennsylvania. He came to San Francisco in 1852 as an itinerant preacher from the Philadelphia Conference of his church. In 1868 he was elected a bishop and moved back East, and until his death in 1893 he served the church in many capacities. His writings include an extensive history of the denomination. During his sixteen years in the West, Moore was involved in many activities: he was the teacher in the first school for Negro children in San Francisco (which was established privately), participated in the organization of a literary society and a fraternal lodge in that city, was elected chaplain of the first three state conventions held by Negroes to promote their civil rights, and was often the featured orator at programs held by black organizations. He later joined the exodus to Canada, where he became a contractor for wood-cutting and charcoal-burning among the gold miners and also invested in a mining company (which failed). When he returned to San Francisco, Moore initiated a periodical, the *Lunar Visitor*.[14]

The *Lunar Visitor* (so named because it was issued on a monthly basis) began publication in January, 1862. At that time, Negroes in San Francisco had no other journal, although a weekly paper had been issued during the late 1850s and another newspaper would start in the spring of 1862. The *Lunar Visitor* carried a few news items about the local community; it gave much more space, however, to editorial essays on larger issues. In this periodical, "devoted to the Moral, Intellectual and Social Improvement of the Colored Race," Moore discussed state and federal legislation pertaining to Negroes, the lack of unity among Negroes, and the education of their children.

On the subject of education, he stated that "proper and complete Education, is the harmonious development of man's *physical, mental,* and *moral* powers, giving them a high and happy mould. Perfect Education, furnishes man with clear and just perceptions of the varied relations he sustains to his Maker, his fellow-men and himself." Moore discussed the obstacles confronting the education of Negro children, citing not only the exclusion of these children from state school funds but also "the indifference of parents to the education of their children." On the topic of unity, Moore stated that Negroes had a "disinclination to copartnership in business." He believed that they "must feel an interest in assisting each other in common business; in rendering each other favors; supplying each other's wants as far as practicable, as do the whites." "Unity," he wrote, "is the source of strength, of power, operative or resistant."[15]

Education was also the concern of Samuel H. Smothers, who edited the *Students' Repository* in Indiana. This periodical was issued during 1863 and 1864 at the Union Literary Institute, a manual training school in Randolph County. The school, located in a farming community of Negro landowners near Spartanburg, was established during the 1840s by local members of the Society of Anti-Slavery Friends.[16] Its benefactors included persons in many parts of the country, among them Gerrit Smith of New York and Charles Eliot Norton of Massachusetts. The institute was organized primarily for the benefit of Negroes, who were excluded from the public schools, but it was to be conducted without "any distinction on account of color, rank or wealth."[17] Smothers was principal of the school.

In presenting his journal to the public, Smothers mentioned that he himself had "no collegiate education" and only "about nine months schooling, in a common district school." He was issuing this small quarterly publication in an effort "to build up *Union Literary Institute*, and awaken an interest among its Students and friends in the cause of education." Through the *Students' Repository* he also hoped "to cultivate the moral, intellectual, and religious character of the colored people, and to afford scope for their rapidly rising talents and aspirations."[18] The periodical contained mainly essays on education, morality, and self-improvement, most of them written by Smothers and by James Buckner and Samuel Peters, who assisted him in editing the publication. Two articles by Charles E. Norton also appeared in the magazine. The April, 1864, issue carried the minutes of the third annual meeting of the Ohio Colored Teachers' Association, with the text of the organization's constitution. Smothers was a member of this group. The *Students' Repository* was suspended in the fall of 1864 when Smothers enlisted as a volunteer in the Union army.

Mirror of Liberty

MIRROR OF LIBERTY. Such is the title of a new publication which has been commenced in New York by our indefatigable colored brother, DAVID RUGGLES, the enterprising and efficient Secretary of the N.Y. Committee of Vigilance.... For his untiring exertions in the cause of his oppressed brethren, Mr. Ruggles deserves their warmest gratitude; and we hope he will be encouraged to proceed in his noble efforts.

Such was the announcement that appeared in William Lloyd Garrison's Boston *Liberator* on July 20, 1838. On August 9, in an article in the New York *Gazette*, Ruggles was called a "scoundrel" and a "rascal." This writer suggested that Ruggles and the other "Ebony nuisances" associated with him should be compelled "to hammer stone for the rest of their lives upon Blackwell's island."

As a militant black leader in New York City during the 1830s and 1840s, David Ruggles was a controversial figure and his name was frequently in the newspapers. He did not shun this publicity but instead aggressively called attention to the causes for which he worked. Ruggles was thirty-nine years old when he died, but in his short life he achieved notoriety as a civil rights activist. As one of his admirers said, "truly, if life be reckoned by deeds, rather than years, then was his a *long* one."[19] Ruggles was secretary of the New York Committee of Vigilance, an interracial group that he helped organize to provide legal aid for free persons kidnapped as slaves; and he was active in the underground railroad, assisting runaway slaves in their escape to freedom. He served as corresponding secretary of the American Reform Board of Disfranchised Commissioners, an organization that agitated for voting privileges and other civil rights for free Negroes. And he published the *Mirror of Liberty* periodical.[20]

David Ruggles was born in Norwich, Connecticut, in 1810 and acquired a New England common school education. He came to New York City when he was seventeen years old. For a few years he was in the grocery business, advertising for sale such produce

MIRROR OF LIBERTY.

"LIBERTY IS THE WORD FOR ME—ABOVE ALL, LIBERTY."

Vol. I.	NEW-YORK, JULY, 1838.	No. 1.

The MIRROR OF LIBERTY is published quarterly, by David Ruggles, Editor, corner of Lispenard and Church streets, New York City.—Terms $1 per annum, payable in advance. Any person sending $5 shall be entitled to one copy gratis.

All letters and communications must be post paid.

INTRODUCTORY REMARKS.

This Journal enters the arena in behalf of the dumb—for the restoration of Equal Liberty, and the full enfranchisement of my down-trodden countrymen in this,

"Our own
Our native land."

But there are circumstances connected with the outset of this enterprize, which will necessarily diminish the merits of the present number.

We confidently hope, however, that all future numbers (which shall be filled and decked with a greater variety of subjects, many of which are excluded from this number for want of room,) shall maintain at least equal claims with the present one. The character of this periodical is expressed in the title chosen for its name. It will go for Truth and Equal Liberty. It will vindicate outraged human nature at all times, in season and out of season. It will never attempt to treat questions of public interest in a manner to avoid giving offence to men, when principle is involved; even if we possessed that art, we question the propriety of describing errors without showing the actors with them.

Unless we stab slavery through the conscience of the slave-holder, hope of its removal would be chimerical. The reader need not examine the Mirror for long and theoretical disquisitions on abstract questions, though it will present a retrospective view o the past, and contain a large amount of important intelligence connected with the history of my proscribed race, which has been for ages suffered to pass unnoticed.

It will contain facts and arguments, strictures and animadversions upon things as they are; strictures and disquisitions shall be applicable to existing persons and events.

The greedy appetite of scandal and abuse shall never be satisfied in the columns of this Journal, though Truth shall be decked in her natural habiliments of plainness, which will require no sacrifice.

The Mirror will endeavour to show, by its example, that there is nothing unusual in plain truth to the dignity of any good cause, and that Equal Liberty cannot exist without it. The Mirror is consecrated to the genius of liberty. It is trammelled by no sect, association or company of men; but is, in a word, a free and independent Journal. It will endeavour to avoid the fatal error of flattery at all times and on all occasions; but will vindicate right and expose error and the existing evils, which evidently obstruct the pathway to that consummation so long desired by a scattered, pealed and down-trodden people. It will never pay that fealty to men that is due to truth. It will fearlessly attack vice and immorality, in high places and in low places. We wish our readers to understand distinctly that we claim and shall maintain it too, come what will, the right to discuss and animadvert freely and frankly upon all subjects connected with the present well being and future destinies of my emaciated countryman.

Because there is no subject connected with the interest of mankind that is so delicate that it can, with conduciveness to our elevation, exist beyond the reach of investigation and comment before the open view of the world.

Therefore, we shall never hesitate to remark freely

and frankly upon the many blighting evils which are nurtured and cherished in the bosom of society.

It will be one of the primary objects of this periodical to point out the errors which have evidently proved snares to our feet, in the pathway to Equal Liberty. To show by every rational mode of reason and argument the perniciousness of the indifference, apathy and neutrality which exists upon all subjects connected with the present and future salvation of outraged Human Nature.

We have published no long and swelling prospectus to solicit subscribers for this paper; for them we depend, under God, upon its merits.

The Mirror will be published quarterly, on a super royal sheet of fine paper, in an octavo form, and shall contain 16 pages neatly covered; at the end of the volume the subscriber may possess 64 pages of valuable and interesting matter in a style for binding, which can be preserved.

Terms of subscription $1 per annum, payable in advance.

Any person sending $5 shall receive one copy gratis. All letters and communications must be post paid and addressed to the Editor, 36 Lispenard street, New York city.

DAVID RUGGLES, Editor.

New York, July 4th, 1838.

THE N. Y. GAZETTE AND THE BROOKLYN AFFAIR.

C. F. Daniels, the editor of this scurrilous print, a notorious pander for slaveholders, after some sympathetic remarks, and eulogizing the character of a certain man-stealing lordling who has for years held slaves in Brooklyn city, contrary to the laws of our state, half fed and half clothed; animadverts upon the editor of this Journal (who lately liberated one of the victims of oppression) in the following pathetic and laconic strain.

"One Ruggles, an insolvent black fellow, who holds some important office in the Anti-Slavery Society in this city, made his way into the house—managed to inveigle this unfortunate creature from her protectors, and has actually carried her off. She is entirely incapable of doing any thing to maintain herself, and will of course become a tenant of the Alms-house. This Ruggles is eminently entitled to the attention of the civil authorities, as a nuisance and a vagabond, and will at all events be treated as such if he ventures again into our friend's family; for he actually staid three hours on one occasion, to the great annoyance of the mistress of the mansion, who found it impossible to get him out of it, lone and unprotected as she was. Let the rascal try his impudence again, if he thinks it would be conducive to human liberty."

Well, I plead guilty to the charge of carrying the girl off, and admit that I remained in the house some time, discussing the matter with Dr. McClennan, as to who had the best right to remain in the house, he or the writer, who was on an errand of mercy, sustained by the laws of this state, while *he* (the doctor) was acting against law, conscience, and humanity. The affair was as follows:

Being informed that D. K. Dodge, a slaveholder from South Carolina, now residing with his family, at the corner of Atlantic and Henry streets, Brooklyn, where he has held three persons as slaves; one for four years and two for two years. I called to see Mr. D. relative to their rights as citizens of this state. He being absent, I inquired for Mrs. D. I was invited to walk into the basement, and Mrs. Dodge was sent for; as she approached me, I acquainted her of my errand as politely as I knew how. Mrs. D. united with me in deploring the evils of slavery,

Mirror of Liberty

as "free sugars . . . manufactured by free people, not by slaves."[21] In 1833 he gave up this livelihood to become a traveling agent for the New York *Emancipator* newspaper.

Reestablishing himself in business in New York City in 1834, Ruggles set up a bookstore and circulating library of antislavery publications. With this enterprise he also advertised services in job printing, picture framing, and bookbinding. Four years later he opened a subscription reading room where Negroes, "who are despised for their complexion and refused admission to public reading rooms generally, may enjoy the rich benefits which such an establishment furnishes."[22] The yearly membership fee of $2.75 gave subscribers access to the principal daily newspapers as well as to antislavery publications. Ruggles also took a leading part in the organization of literary societies for young black men during the 1830s. He was one of the founders of the New York Philomathean Literary Society; and he was on the governing board of the Phoenix Society and the New York Garrison Literary and Benevolent Society. These associations developed libraries, presented lecture series, and sponsored other activities for the educational and moral improvement of their members.

As secretary of the New York Committee of Vigilance, Ruggles engaged in the hazardous activity of rescuing free persons from abduction or arrest as slaves. He boarded ships in New York harbor and went to homes in the exclusive residential sections, seeking out such victims, and he took their cases to court in an effort to have their freedom restored. Ruggles also sheltered runaway slaves in his own home; among those whom he aided was Frederick Douglass. Because of these activities, Ruggles himself was jailed more than once. On one occasion, slave-catchers broke into his house in the middle of the night, although he managed to escape without harm. Ruggles was sometimes forced to change his place of residence in order to elude his enemies.

In 1839, Ruggles resigned as secretary of the vigilance committee after a dispute with some of the other officers concerning the financial records for which he was responsible. The following year, he became secretary of the American Reform Board of Disfranchised Commissioners. Whereas the vigilance committee saw the southern slaveholder as its chief enemy, the American Reform Board agitated against northern politicians who denied free black people their citizenship rights. Ruggles announced the objectives of the organization in a circular addressed to his fellow black Americans: "to vindicate equal human rights,—to take special cognizance of the oppressive legal or illegal customs under which we groan,—to unite and energize in securing our immediate relief and enfranchisement." Speaking at the group's first annual convention in 1841, Ruggles declared: "If we hope for redemption from our present condition, we must . . . UNITE in the hallowed cause of reform."[23]

In his crusade for equal rights, Ruggles personally defied the racial customs of the North. During the summer of 1841, he reported to the newspapers two incidents of discrimination in which he was involved. On a steamboat trip from New Bedford, Massachusetts, to Nantucket Island, Ruggles tried to purchase a ticket for first-class passage. He was refused, and when he insisted, he was beaten by the captain, and his hat and other personal belongings were taken from him. The second incident occurred less than a month later at the railroad station in New Bedford. After buying a ticket for Boston, Ruggles boarded the train and sat in a coach for white passengers. When he refused to leave this car at the order of the conductor, he was dragged from his seat and thrown off the train. Ruggles brought charges of aggravated assault against the railroad company but lost his case; later, he appeared and spoke before public meetings that were held to protest these incidents. In New Bedford, Frederick Douglass chaired a meeting at which a resolution was passed condemning Ruggles' treatment.[24]

It was during these years of abolitionist and civil rights activity that Ruggles published the *Mirror of Liberty*. The journal was issued quite irregularly between 1838 and 1841. Throughout this period, Ruggles was burdened with failing eyesight and generally poor health, with the entanglements of legal suits and court cases, and with poverty. In the January, 1839, issue he explained to his readers: "It is the opinion of our physician, that the infirmity which affects our eyes is nurtured and encouraged by seasons of mental anxiety, frequently caused by interesting scenes of action in which we have been called to participate, in this SLAVEHOLDER'S HUNTING GROUND."[25] Ruggles consulted a number of physicians for relief from his illnesses and tried, unsuccessfully, to raise enough money to go to Europe for treatment by eye specialists. Finally, in 1842, penniless and practically blind, he gave up his activities in New York.

With the assistance of Lydia Maria Child he went to Northampton, Massachusetts, for rest and recuperation and there became a member of the Northampton Association for Education and Industry, a utopian community settled by abolitionists. During this time, Ruggles learned about the water cure method of treating diseases. He treated himself in this manner, and his health was partially restored. He began to minister to others and soon became a skilled and widely known practitioner of hydropathy. Through the patronage of wealthy friends Ruggles developed his own sanitarium, an institution of several buildings located on more than one hundred acres in the vicinity of Northampton. He remained in Massachusetts, operating this water cure establishment, until his death in 1849.

Ruggles' periodical, the *Mirror of Liberty*, made its initial appearance in July, 1838, as an eight-page publication. This was actually only one-half of the first number. Ruggles announced that he was distributing it at that time to make the annual report of the vigilance committee immediately available, with the remaining pages to be published later. Thus, the next issue, dated August, 1838, was also volume one, number one. It contained sixteen pages, the first eight of which were mainly a reprinting of the July issue.

The *Mirror of Liberty* was originally planned as a quarterly, but number two of the first volume did not appear until January, 1839. The third number was issued in August, 1840, and the fourth in May, 1841. Ruggles apologized to his readers for these delays, referring to the "rough and inclement season of adversity" that had beset him; yet he was "neither destroyed nor discouraged."[26] In the August, 1840, issue he announced that the *Mirror of Liberty* would become a monthly; then, in an "Extra" issue dated July, 1841, he stated that the periodical would be published semimonthly. These plans apparently did not materialize, for no copies of the *Mirror of Liberty* and no record of publication after July, 1841, have been found.

Before he began publishing his periodical, Ruggles had contributed articles to antislavery newspapers and had utilized the pamphlet press to put forth his ideas. In 1834, when the procolonizationist David M. Reese criticized the American Anti-Slavery Society, Ruggles responded by writing and publishing a pamphlet entitled *The "Extinguisher" Extinguished: or David M. Reese, M. D. "Used Up."* He denounced colonization and attacked Reese's argument that emancipation would result in intermarriage between whites and blacks and lead to amalgamation. Four years later, when an anonymous publication again took issue with the American Anti-Slavery Society, Ruggles suspected Reese as the author and again wrote a rebuttal. This pamphlet was entitled *An Antidote for a Poisonous Combination Recently Prepared by a "Citizen of New-York," Alias Dr. Reese.* Another pamphlet, *The Abrogation of the Seventh Commandment, by the American Churches*, was published by Ruggles in 1835. This document, signed "A Puritan," called upon northern white churchwomen to help rid the Christian church of its hypocrisy in tolerating slavery and the licentiousness of white men toward female slaves. The proposal was made that these women should refuse to attend services whenever their churches were visited by southern slaveholders, so that the officials of the churches would be influenced to condemn rather than condone slavery and its practices.

Another force that Ruggles believed could help end slavery was "the mighty power of the American press." Declaring that all Negroes in the United States, North and South, were slaves in one way or another, he called upon black people to subscribe to newspapers such as the *Emancipator* and the *Liberator*. His plea for support of the antislavery press was made in a series of six essays published in the *Emancipator* in 1835. Ruggles set forth this reasoning in his appeal:

> It may be urged that the press cannot alter the laws of our country which make us *slaves*; this I admit. It cannot directly, but it can indirectly, changing the public opinion which creates the laws. What is the public opinion? It is the opinion of the majority of the intelligent people who inhabit our country, who are of the opinion that *we* ought to be banished to that Sepulchre, LIBERIA, for the crime of wearing a sable skin. It is the opinion of those who repudiate us as being by nature inferior to themselves.[27]

Ruggles was described by a contemporary, the black author William Wells Brown, as possessing "those qualities of keen perception, deep thought, and originality, that mark the critic and man of letters." "As a writer," Brown observed, "Mr. Ruggles was keen and witty,—always logical,—sending his arrows directly at his opponent." These characteristics definitely marked the *Mirror of Liberty*. Ruggles, who identified himself as the publisher and the editor, declared that the *Mirror of Liberty* "is a free and independent journal—its editor is an unmuzzled man, who goes for *freedom of speech and the liberty of the press*." The motto of the publication was "Liberty is the word for me—above all, liberty." In an editorial statement, Ruggles described the policy of the periodical: "It will never attempt to treat questions of public interest in a manner to avoid giving offence to men, when principle is involved; even if we possessed that art, we question the propriety of describing errors without showing the actors with them."[28]

Ruggles' periodical, like his activities with the vigilance committee, met with either approbation or furious attack; and Ruggles, true to his nature, took pleasure in reporting both types of reactions. Editorial comments on the *Mirror* by other publications were reprinted in the August, 1838, and January, 1839, issues. These excerpts indicated that the *Mirror* had reached towns in New York, Massachusetts, Vermont, Maine, Ohio, Pennsylvania, and Virginia. A paper in Ohio was quoted as saying that the editorial department of the *Mirror* showed "an ability and talent seldom to be found, even among those who call themselves the better part of creation." A paper in Virginia was quoted as calling the *Mirror* "an incendiary periodical" with "a disposition to encourage lynch law" and the editor a "poor deluded negro."[29]

The *Mirror of Liberty* documented in detail Ruggles' activities with the New York Committee of Vigilance. The reports of the committee, records of its financial receipts, and proceedings of meetings held in its behalf were carried. Accounts of kidnapping incidents and related court cases were featured. Ruggles promised to publish in one issue a slaveholder's directory, "furnishing the names and residences of all members of the bar, police officers, city marshals, constables, and other persons who lend themselves in the nefarious business of kidnapping; and the names of slaveholders residing in [New York] and in Brooklyn."[30] The *Mirror of Liberty* also served as a medium of communication for the American Reform Board of Disfranchised Commissioners.

Much of the material in the periodical was organized into departments: the "Poet's Mirror," "Correspondence Mirror," "Ladies Mirror," "Political Mirror," "Death's Mirror," and "Reform's Mirror." The "Death's Mirror" in August, 1840, carried the eulogy that Ruggles had delivered at the funeral of John Brown, a Negro physician in New York. The "Reform's Mirror" of that issue printed the texts of two laws passed by the New York state legislature, an act extending the right of trial by jury to fugitive slave cases and an act to protect free citizens from abduction into slavery.

The August, 1838, number of the *Mirror of Liberty* gave six pages to the text of a speech by William Lloyd Garrison commemorating the emancipation of slaves in the British West Indies. The front page of the "Extra" of July, 1841, was devoted almost entirely to a poem by John Greenleaf Whittier entitled "Our Countrymen in Chains!" In contrast, the *Mirror of Liberty* did not feature such contributions from Ruggles' black contemporaries. Occasionally, however, their names did appear in the periodical as officials of organizations from which reports were being published.

Although black leaders generally did not write for the *Mirror of Liberty*, many of them did rally to Ruggles' support when he appealed for aid. They organized public meetings—in New York, Hartford, New Bedford, and Boston—to solicit subscriptions and donations. These efforts did not succeed in maintaining the periodical, but they did show the regard in which Ruggles was held. Two special occasions were further testimony to Ruggles' standing among both black and white abolitionists. A soirée was organized in his honor in New York in 1840; a similar affair was held in Boston the following year.

Among those who spoke words of praise for Ruggles at the Boston soirée were William Lloyd Garrison, Wendell Phillips, William C. Nell, Thomas S. Jinnings, Samuel J. May, and Samuel Snowden. Snowden, a local black Methodist minister, gave this testimonial: "Success attend the abolition cause—success attend the Vigilance Committee. . . . May conviction cut the throat of pro-slavery doctrine, and truth dry it up, like Jonah's gourd vine. May our friend David Ruggles be as willing to lose his head in the good cause, as he was to lose his hat at New-Bedford." When Ruggles died in 1849, Frederick Douglass, then a newspaper editor in Rochester, New York, wrote that those "who have escaped the yoke of slavery by his aid . . . will never cease to remember this faithful friend of the slave, and lover of mankind—with grateful admiration."[31]

National Reformer

On February 7, 1866, a delegation of Negroes called upon the president of the United States and voiced concern about his refusal to recommend voting privileges for black people. They were representatives from a national convention of colored men meeting in Washington at that time. The spokesmen at this conference with President Andrew Johnson were Frederick Douglass and

George Downing. Among the other members of the delegation were Douglass' son Lewis; John Jones, a tailor with a prosperous business in Chicago; and William Whipper, a wealthy lumber merchant from Pennsylvania.

In 1866 William Whipper was an elder statesman among Negroes, for he had been in the forefront of activities since the 1820s. He had been a key figure in the operation of the underground railroad, a promoter of cultural societies in the Philadelphia area, and a delegate to the national conventions of colored people. He was a founder of the American Moral Reform Society and the editor of its periodical, the *National Reformer.*

Even though certain ideological differences existed between Whipper and other black leaders, he was respected for his long years of service, and his contemporaries spoke highly of him. William Still of Philadelphia, in a history of the underground railroad published in 1872, wrote of Whipper:

> Although an unassuming man, deeply engrossed with business— Anti-slavery papers, conventions, and public movements having for their aim the elevation of the colored man, have always commanded Mr. Whipper's interest and patronage. In the more important conventions which have been held amongst the colored people . . . perhaps no other colored man has been so often called on to draft resolutions and prepare addresses, as the modest and earnest William Whipper. He has worked effectively in a quiet way, although not as a public speaker. He is self-made, and well read on the subject of the reforms of the day.

William Wells Brown praised Whipper as "one of the deepest thinkers of which the black man can boast." Brown described him as an individual "of fine personal appearance, above the middle size, stoops a little,—that bend of the shoulders that marks the student. He is remarkably well read, able to cite authority from the ancients, and posted in all the current literature of the day."[32]

William Whipper was born in 1804 in Columbia, Pennsylvania, a town in Lancaster County on the eastern banks of the Susquehanna River. His mother was a Negro domestic servant, and his father was her white employer. Whipper grew up in his father's household, where he was tutored along with a white half-brother. When his father died, Whipper inherited a lumber business in Columbia. He formed a partnership with Stephen Smith, another black resident of the area who also operated a successful lumber-yard. Smith and Whipper opened a coal and wood business in Philadelphia and built up one of the largest wholesale enterprises in the city, with branches in other locations in the state. (Stephen Smith was reputed to be the wealthiest Negro in the United States at the time of his death in 1873.) During the Reconstruction period, Whipper was appointed cashier of the federal Freedmen's Bank in Philadelphia. In the last years of his life, he made his home in New Brunswick, New Jersey. He died in 1876 and was buried in Philadelphia.[33]

During his residence in Columbia, Whipper was active with the underground railroad. This town was one of the first stops in the free states for slaves escaping from Virginia and Maryland, and Whipper's home was a station on the route. Whipper also made substantial financial contributions to the abolitionist movement. In later years, when Still requested information from him for the history of the underground railroad, Whipper responded: "I never kept any record of those persons passing through my hands. . . . I can only refer to the part I took in it from memory, and if I could delineate the actual facts as they occurred they would savor so much of egotism that I should feel ashamed to make them public." He briefly summarized his activities: "In a period of three years from 1847 to 1850, I passed hundreds to the land of freedom. . . . I know that I speak within bounds when I say that directly and indirectly from 1847 to 1860, I have contributed from my earnings one thousand dollars annually, and for the five years during the war a like amount to put down the rebellion."[34]

Following the passage and aftermath of the Fugitive Slave Act of 1850, Whipper considered migrating to Canada with the hundreds of other Negroes leaving Columbia. But with the outbreak and progress of the Civil War, he saw the prospect of a better society in the United States and decided to remain in Philadelphia, where over the years he had developed not only his business but also other affiliations that he was reluctant to leave.

He had participated in the founding of literary societies among black people in Philadelphia and was the first secretary of the Reading Room Society, organized in 1828. A notice from Whipper published in *Freedom's Journal* indicated that the library of the society would include books on ancient, modern, and ecclesiastical history; volumes on the laws of Pennsylvania; and antislavery newspapers. Whipper was also a charter member of the Philadelphia Library Company of Colored Persons, established in 1833. In addition to maintaining a library, this society sponsored lectures, debates, and reading courses for its members.[35]

Whipper was active in the national convention movement that developed among Negroes during this period. He was a delegate to the first of these conventions, held in Philadelphia in 1830. At this meeting, the American Society of Free Persons of Colour was organized. Bishop Richard Allen of the African Methodist Episcopal Church was elected president and Whipper the corresponding secretary. Whipper was the only person who was a delegate attending all five of the annual meetings held from 1831 through 1835.[36]

During the 1834 meeting he offered a resolution to establish an association for moral reform. This organization, the American Moral Reform Society, was established at the 1835 convention. James Forten was elected president and Whipper the corresponding secretary. Whipper was on the committee that drafted the constitution and was also a member of the committee that prepared an address to the public explaining the principles of the society. Before the 1835 convention closed, Whipper offered a resolution that the new society should "establish as soon as possible a press, to be the organ through which [its] principles . . . shall be made known to the world."[37]

Three years passed before this journal, the *National Reformer*, began publication. Edited by Whipper from his home in Columbia, it was published in Philadelphia by the Board of Managers of the American Moral Reform Society. Twelve monthly issues were published between September, 1838, and December, 1839. No numbers appeared for May, June, July, and August, 1839. In the December, 1839, number, Whipper indicated that he would continue as editor, although he did allude to the difficulty of editing the periodical eighty-two miles distant from the site of publication. The American Moral Reform Society was in existence until at least 1841,[38] but no more issues of the periodical seem to have been published after 1839.

The *National Reformer* developed from the general spirit of reform that characterized this era in American history, from the convention movement among Negroes in the 1830s, and from the intellectual interests of William Whipper. Only a few black writers contributed to the periodical—notably Daniel Alexander Payne, William Watkins, and Henry Highland Garnet. Garnet, a young ministerial student in upstate New York, was becoming known as an antislavery lecturer. Payne and Watkins were active in the American Moral Reform Society. Payne, a pastor in Troy, New York, was an agent for the society and its periodical. Watkins, who conducted a school for Negro children in Baltimore, was a vice-president of the organization. For the most part, the *National Reformer* carried Whipper's own lengthy discourses and reprinted material relating to the movements he supported.

Whipper espoused a diversity of causes. Not only the freedom and equality of black people, but also moral reform and moral persuasion, temperance, nonviolence, economics, education, the equality of women, and justice for all people were the concerns of Whipper and of the *National Reformer*. The periodical reprinted essays on these topics from contemporary journals and carried news articles and discussions of current events, such as the Amistad case. It also contained reports of the American Moral Reform Society and the Philadelphia Vigilance Committee; an extract from Sarah Grimké's *Conditions of Slaves*, which had been published by the American Anti-Slavery Society; a speech by John Jay on "The Dignity of the Abolition Cause as Compared with the Political Schemes of the Day"; and the declaration of sentiments of the New England Non-Resistance Society. Nonviolence was one of Whipper's major concerns. Among the essays that he had contributed to other publications, before the *National Reformer* was founded, was a series on "Non-Resistance to Offensive Aggression" in the *Colored American* newspaper in 1837. Whipper believed that the philosophy of nonresistance to physical aggression was "not only consistent with reason, but the surest method of obtaining a speedy triumph of the principles of universal peace."[39]

For Whipper, the most important and the all-embracing concern was moral reform, which he believed was "the corner stone of the temple of universal freedom and eternal justice." The prospectus for the *National Reformer* stated: "We design to occupy a sphere in the moral reformation of this age and country that has but partially claimed the attention of those that have preceeded us." In an address to the public, Whipper declared: "Our country is rich with the means of resuscitating her from moral degeneracy. She possesses all the elements for her redemption; she has but to will it, and she is FREE."[40]

Whipper pleaded for justice for all men: "We have been of *no* sect, creed, or complexion, for the sake of all *sects, creeds*, and *complexions*. . . . The rights for which we are contending are the rights of universal man, and we shall not wait to inquire whether the oppressed are white, red, black, or brown, before we have bestowed on them our sympathy. . . . We here publicly renounce all COMPLEXIONAL ALLEGIANCE." Each issue of the *National Reformer* carried this biblical quotation in the masthead: "God hath made of one blood all nations of men for to dwell on all the face of the earth. *Acts*, xvii, 26." Whipper criticized institutions among Negroes that were racially exclusive; and he opposed the use of the words *colored* and *African* in the names of these organizations. The editor of the *Colored American* responded by accusing Whipper of sponsoring a racially segregated organization in the American Moral Reform Society. Whipper assured him that in this society "no complexional distinctions have ever been tolerated." "We could mention the names of several early and distinguished abolitionists that have been members ever since its formation," he pointed out, "and for the past three years there have always been white persons in the Board."[41]

The *National Reformer* carried an advertisement for Lydia White's free labor grocery and dry goods store in Philadelphia. One phase of the American Moral Reform Society's program was the boycott of products of slave labor and the patronage of stores selling products made by free people. The free produce movement had originated in England in the late eighteenth century, and in the United States it was developed during the 1820s as an antislavery measure by members of the Society of Friends and other abolitionists. Whipper himself had operated a free labor and temperance grocery store in Philadelphia, on South Sixth Street next door to the Bethel A. M. E. Church. The notice of Lydia White's store was the only advertisement to appear in the *National Reformer*, and there were no illustrations in the publication. The twelve numbers of this periodical were primarily a series of tracts on issues of the day, reflecting the mind and the intellectual interests of William Whipper.

African Methodist Episcopal Church Magazine

Toward the close of the eighteenth century, many free Negroes in the North who were affiliated with white churches began to withdraw their membership and form their own congregations. Then, during the early nineteenth century, these local churches organized into independent denominations. The beginning of the African Methodist Episcopal Church dates back to 1787. In that year, a group led by Richard Allen started a separate church in Philadelphia. In 1816, delegates from similar churches in Pennsylvania, Delaware, Maryland, and New Jersey convened in Philadelphia, where they founded the African Methodist Episcopal Church and chose Richard Allen as bishop.

One of Bishop Allen's first acts was the establishment of a publishing house, the A. M. E. Book Concern. He supervised this concern himself until the church conference created the position of general book steward to manage the publishing business. Before 1840, the main publications of the church were hymnals, editions of the discipline, and minutes of the conferences. For many years, interest had been expressed in the publication of a magazine. Finally, in 1841, the New York Annual Conference initiated a periodical for the entire denomination, to take the place of separately published conference minutes. The *African Methodist Episcopal Church Magazine* began publication in September of that year.[42]

The *Church Magazine* was issued in Brooklyn by George Hogarth, the general book steward. Hogarth was a merchant and pastor of a church in Brooklyn. Previously he had been a missionary for the A. M. E. denomination in Haiti and a minister in the Baltimore conference.[43] The periodical was announced as a monthly, but it was only after two and a half years, in May, 1844, that the twelfth number of the first volume was published. In an attempt to increase circulation, the 1844 General Conference appointed Molliston Madison Clark as an agent to travel throughout the constituency and solicit support for the magazine and other literature issued by the book concern. This additional effort still did not raise enough funds for regular publication, and by May, 1848, the *Church Magazine* had ceased to exist. The 1848 General Conference ordered the reestablishment of the magazine on a quarterly basis, but no evidence has been found that the periodical ever resumed publication.

The 1848 General Conference also ordered publication of a weekly newspaper, which was initiated that year as the *Christian Herald*. The *Herald* was edited by Augustus R. Green, who succeeded Hogarth as the general book steward. In 1852, the name of the weekly was changed to the *Christian Recorder*, the publication office was moved from Pittsburgh to Philadelphia, and Molliston M. Clark succeeded Green as editor. The *Christian Recorder* has continued publication to the present day. The early volumes of this newspaper contained much of the same type of material that had been printed in the *African Methodist Episcopal Church Magazine*.[44]

The *Church Magazine*, as the official journal for the denomination, gave the major portion of its space to church affairs: proceedings of the annual district conferences and the quadrennial General Conference, the financial reports of the general book steward, listings of all the ministers in the church, editorials on church matters and on religious subjects in general, news items about individual churches, and obituaries of parishioners. The periodical was also an outlet for literary expression by members of the church, especially those who chose to write poetry or essays on religious topics.

Among the contributors were John Mifflin Brown, Morris Brown, Jabez P. Campbell, Willis Nazrey, Daniel Alexander Payne, Stephen Smith, Austin Steward, Alexander W. Wayman, and William Whipper (editor of the *National Reformer* periodical). All but two of these persons (Steward and Whipper) were A. M. E. ministers, and of the ministers, all but one (Smith, the lumber merchant in Pennsylvania) became bishops in the church. Clark, the book agent, was the author of a series of essays on life among black people, based on information gleaned during his travels for the book concern.[45]

The most prolific contributor to the *Church Magazine* was Daniel Alexander Payne, who had entered the ministry of the A. M. E. Church in 1841. Among his writings were numerous essays discussing the need to raise the educational level of the denomination's ministers. In spite of opposition from many of the clergy, the 1844 General Conference adopted his proposal for a course of studies administered by the church.[46] Payne, then in his early thirties, soon became a leader of great influence in the A. M. E. denomination: in 1848 he was appointed church historian, and in 1852 he was elected bishop.

In his first history of the church, published in 1866, Payne recorded this opinion of the magazine: "The truth compels us to say that the character of this literature is *inferior*, and consists chiefly in letters about subjects interesting to but a few, if any, outside of the pales of the African M. E. Church. The editor himself *was destitute* of what *is now considered* a good, common school education. . . . In thought, he never rises above mediocrity, in composition, he evinces an absolute ignorance of rhetoric." As harsh as Payne was in his criticism of the literary aspects of the *Church Magazine*, he commended Hogarth for exhibiting fortitude and business acumen in efforts to keep the publication alive. Payne realized that the magazine was trying to survive against insurmountable odds, noting that "for eight years it was on the wing—though its motions were irregular."[47]

A foreboding of the fate of the *Church Magazine* could be detected in Hogarth's prospectus, printed in the first issue: "In embarking upon this laudable enterprise, it becomes our duty, in the onset, to inform our friends that such a work cannot be conducted with dignity and honor to our people unless it meets with an ample supply of pecuniary and intellectual means." Hogarth estimated that 900 subscriptions at $1.00 per year would insure regular monthly publication. When the periodical was initiated, the responsibility for its circulation was placed on the ministers, who were to act as subscription agents. Hogarth's report for the year ending in June, 1843, showed only 150 yearly and half-yearly subscribers. In May, 1844, he reported 213 subscribers.[48]

It was at this point that the General Conference designated Clark as the traveling book agent for the A. M. E. Book Concern. During the first months, Clark was enthusiastic about his work, expressing optimism in a letter to Hogarth: "I feel confident that I can get . . . one thousand subscribers out of ten or fourteen thousand members, within one or two years. . . . Do not be discouraged: our people are awaking up on the subject. I am now more than ever encouraged in the work. I only want good health, the blessing of God, and the spring and summer to come, to make great progress in my business." At the end of one year, a despondent Clark concluded that he had been "of little or no use to the book concern" and tendered his resignation. In his annual report he pointed out that "such is the want of interest on the subject, such is the want of taste for reading among our people, except perhaps one-tenth part of them, that the books cannot be sold, or subscriptions obtained to the magazine, except at a very sparing rate."[49]

In his 1891 history of the church, Payne made similar observations regarding the *African Methodist Episcopal Church Magazine*:

> The chief reasons which might be assigned for the failure of the magazine are the almost total want of learning among the laity of the Church, the limited education of the ministers, and the small number who were sufficiently educated or had the time either to contribute to its support by writing or to appreciate the efforts put forth for its sustenance. Low as the price was, it was too high for the majority of both ministers and laity who could read, owing to the extreme poverty of the great mass of those to whom the magazine naturally addressed itself.[50]

Repository of Religion and Literature and of Science and Art

Ten years after the *African Methodist Episcopal Church Magazine* ceased publication, the A. M. E. denomination started another periodical. In contrast to the *Church Magazine*, the *Repository* was a general periodical, addressed to the public at large, and it was published by the literary societies organized within the district conferences. These societies were promoted by Bishop Daniel Alexander Payne for the educational and cultural growth of the ministers and lay members of the church. The periodical was initiated by the Indiana Conference. A prospectus issued in 1857 announced that the journal was designed "first, to diffuse useful knowledge among our people—second, to cultivate and develop their latent talents, and elevate their intellectual, moral, and religious character."[51]

The *Repository* began publication in April, 1858, as a quarterly. For the first three years it was issued in Indianapolis and sponsored by the literary societies of the Baltimore, Indiana, and Missouri conferences. By January, 1861, the site of publication had moved to Philadelphia; and the New England conferences had also become sponsors. With the January, 1862, number, the *Repository* became a monthly, the publication office was transferred to Baltimore, and the periodical was issued as "the organ of all the Literary Societies that will contribute the annual sum of $24 for its support."[52]

The *Repository* had ended its first year of operation with five hundred subscribers and a cash balance of thirty-five dollars. By 1862, however, the periodical was experiencing financial difficulties. Appeals were constantly issued for more subscribers and for the payment of delinquent dues, and a special plea was made to the church members and the general Negro population in Baltimore, because the constituents in the Midwest were no longer supporting the periodical. Only eight dollars had been received from that area in 1861, with three hundred dollars outstanding in unpaid subscriptions. By April, 1864, the periodical had ceased to exist. The proceedings of the Baltimore Annual Conference of that month recorded that the publication had "failed to be issued for want of means" and that efforts were being made "towards liquidating the debt on the Repository." A resolution urged that "each minister indebted for the Repository be compelled to settle such bills by the 1st of June, 1864."[53]

The 1857 prospectus had stated that the periodical would be conducted by a corps of seven editors, with Bishop Payne as the chief editor. In the course of publication, the size of this editorial board was increased and a publishing and finance committee was added. Although Payne was the titular head of the *Repository* throughout its existence, one person from the editorial board functioned as the executive editor. This position was held successively by Molliston Madison Clark, Elisha Weaver, Aneas McIntosh, and John Mifflin Brown.

Daniel Alexander Payne was born in Charleston, South Carolina, in 1811. His parents were free Negroes, and he attended a private elementary school. After additional tutoring, Payne opened his own school in 1829; he closed the school six years later when the state legislature passed laws directed against the

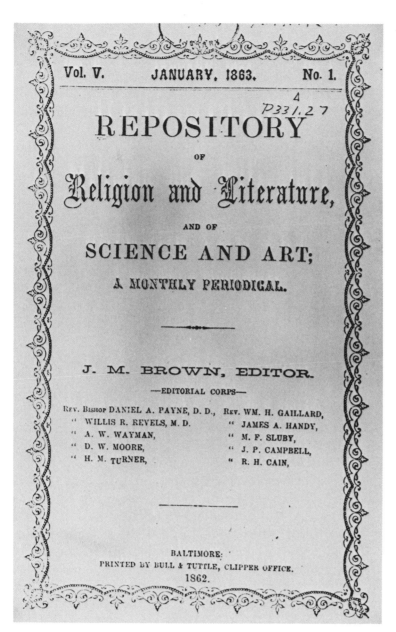

Vol. V.   JANUARY, 1863.   No. 1.

$P331.27$

REPOSITORY

OF

Religion and Literature,

AND OF

SCIENCE AND ART;

A MONTHLY PERIODICAL.

J. M. BROWN, EDITOR.

—EDITORIAL CORPS—

Rev. Bishop DANIEL A. PAYNE, D. D.,   Rev. WM. H. GAILLARD,
"   WILLIS R. REVELS, M. D.   "   JAMES A. HANDY,
"   A. W. WAYMAN,   "   M. F. SLUBY,
"   D. W. MOORE,   "   J. P. CAMPBELL,
"   H. M. TURNER,   "   R. H. CAIN,

BALTIMORE:
PRINTED BY BULL & TUTTLE, CLIPPER OFFICE.
1862.

Repository of Religion and Literature and of Science and Art

teaching of black people. Payne then left Charleston and went North to further his education. After studying at a theological seminary in Gettysburg, Pennsylvania, he accepted the call to a Presbyterian church in Troy, New York. He eventually moved to Philadelphia, where he joined the A. M. E. denomination.

At the 1848 General Conference, Payne was appointed church historian, and four years later he was elected bishop. He played a leading part in the reorganization of Wilberforce University as an A. M. E. institution in 1863. This school had been founded seven years earlier for the education of Negroes by the Methodist Episcopal Church. Payne served as president from 1863 until 1876, resigning voluntarily to devote more time to the history of the church and other writing. As historian and bishop, he traveled extensively in the United States and Canada in the interest of the denomination, attended the quadrennial General Conferences from 1844 to 1892, and was very influential in the formulation of church policies. Payne was bishop for forty-one years—serving as senior bishop for twenty of those years—until his death in 1893. His major concerns and achievements were related to the education of the ministry and constituency of his church.[54]

Molliston M. Clark, executive editor of the *Repository* for the first two issues, had attended Jefferson College in Pennsylvania. He had been traveling agent for the A. M. E. Book Concern and the *African Methodist Episcopal Church Magazine*, and he had edited the *Christian Recorder* newspaper for the church. Clark was succeeded as executive editor of the *Repository* by Elisha Weaver. Weaver, who had studied briefly at Oberlin College, was pastor of a church in Indianapolis. In 1859, after publication of the second volume, he resigned from the *Repository* because of his election as general book steward and editor of the *Recorder*. The January, 1860, number was issued by Aneas McIntosh, also a minister in the Indiana Conference.[55] The *Repository* was then suspended for the rest of the year. Publication resumed in January, 1861, with John Mifflin Brown as executive editor. He served until at least January, 1863 (the date of the last known issue). Brown had studied at the Wesleyan Academy in Wilbraham,

Massachusetts, and at Oberlin College, and he had been principal of Union Seminary, the school operated in Ohio by the A. M. E. Church before it acquired Wilberforce University. In 1864, Brown was elected a bishop of the church.[56]

Daniel A. Payne was not only the promoter of the *Repository*; he was also the most prolific writer in the magazine. His signed contributions appeared in all but five of twenty-six issues, with some numbers carrying two or three articles by him. The executive editors Molliston M. Clark, Elisha Weaver, and John M. Brown also contributed many of the feature articles. Other members of the editorial corps who wrote for the periodical were Willis R. Revels, Alexander W. Wayman, Henry McNeal Turner, Richard H. Cain, Thomas Strother, W. H. Gaillard, and Jabez P. Campbell. Many well-known persons outside the editorial staff also contributed: Solomon G. Brown, Robert Campbell, W. T. Catto, Sarah M. Douglass, Frances Ellen Watkins (Harper), William E. Matthews, Isaac Myers, Hiram R. Revels, Maria W. Stewart, Benjamin Tucker Tanner, George T. Watkins, John L. Watkins, and William J. Wilson, who wrote under the pen name "Ethiop." The editors also encouraged young and unknown writers (many of them women) by printing the speeches and papers they had given before the literary societies of the church and at meetings of secular organizations.

The contents of the *Repository of Religion and Literature and of Science and Art* were as varied as the title promised. The material was organized into departments for religion, literature, science, natural science, the arts, music, biography, and poetry. The periodical also had a "Mothers' Department," a "Young Ladies' Lecture Room," and a "Children's Room." Brief reviews of books and magazines appeared in the "Monthly Book Table." News of individual churches and ministers, as well as announcements and reports from the annual conferences, were given in the "Church's Monthly Record." Marriage and obituary notices were also included. Occasionally the periodical carried the texts of historical documents, such as the 1791 correspondence between Benjamin Banneker and Thomas Jefferson.

Many of the feature articles in the *Repository* were presented in series format. Among the series written by Payne were "Religion and Sanctification," "Matrimony," and "Letters to Children About God." Benjamin T. Tanner wrote a series on "God's Existence and Attitudes, as Seen in the Solar System." In two articles, Molliston M. Clark described his 1846 trip to London as delegate to a religious conference. Elisha Weaver wrote a number of articles on the subject of economy. John M. Brown contributed a biographical series on Bishop Richard Allen and his associates, and he also presented a group of instructional letters entitled "To a Young Brother in the Ministry." Willis R. Revels wrote several essays on hygiene and on the natural sciences. A series of articles on natural history—describing insects, birds, and other animals—was contributed by Solomon G. Brown.

From the point of view of the editors, the seemingly disparate topics in the *Repository* were actually interrelated. The editors believed that "man cannot fully understand the Bible without a familiar knowledge of nature." They pointed out that the writers in both the Old and the New Testaments had a knowledge of the natural sciences, and that "the sublimest imagery of Moses, Job, and Isaiah are drawn from the works of nature."[57] Thus Professor Robert Campbell's article on the aquarium (a new method of sustaining aquatic animals in a water tank with the use of plants) appeared on the same page with Bishop Payne's essay on religion and piety.

The *Repository* attempted to promote an appreciation of the fine arts among its readers. In the first article of a projected series on Negro artists, Payne presented a biographical sketch of Robert Seldon Duncanson and described some of his paintings. Payne, an occasional visitor in Duncanson's Cincinnati studio, called him "the finest landscape painter that has yet appeared among colored men, and one of the finest America has as yet produced."[58] Payne also sought to enhance the aesthetic appeal of the *Repository* with special illustrations and engaged the services of John Sartain. Portraits engraved by Sartain appeared as frontispieces in at least two issues of the periodical—Richard Allen in the January, 1861, number, and Daniel Coker (who, with Allen, was one of the founders of the A. M. E. Church) in the July, 1861, issue.

Articles on music were a regular feature of the *Repository*. William H. Gibson, a teacher in Louisville, Kentucky, discussed music as a science to be developed among the church constituency. He felt that congregations should be taught to sing "by note and system." "Many benefits are derived from the use of this science to church members," he observed. "It enables them to sing with accuracy; it brings about an order in our churches, that singing at random cannot produce." "Lastly," he indicated, "where there is good church music, you will . . . find a large congregation."

Gibson also recommended the use of instrumental music in worship services. On this point Thomas Strother, a minister in Richmond, Indiana, sharply disagreed. Strother felt that "too much artificial assistance in religious operations is apt to spoil all." He noted that "instrumental music where it is used in churches, has invariably to be laid aside in revival season, in order to keep up the revival spirit any given length of time." "The reason is obvious," he contended, "because there is nothing. . . that is capable of reaching the finer sensibilities of the human soul, and affecting it religiously, to the same extent that the human voice will."[59]

Throughout the five years of publication, the *Repository of Religion and Literature and of Science and Art* presented a variety of reading, and special sections of the periodical were addressed to different interests and age groups. At the same time, the editors emphasized the general, overall value of the periodical: "It improves the minds of our people, as well as it encourages those of the white people, who are subscribers and well wishers to the colored people, and who know that education among any society of people, [makes] them fit for society, better neighbors in any community, wherever God permits their lot to be."[60]

Douglass' Monthly

In 1838 a young slave in Maryland named Frederick Augustus Washington Bailey escaped to freedom. After reaching New York

City, he sent for his fiancée, Anna Murray, a free woman living
in Baltimore. They were married and traveled on to New Bedford, Massachusetts. Once settled in his new home, this twenty-
one-year-old fugitive changed his name to Frederick Douglass.[61]
The person who assisted Douglass during his first days of freedom in New York—and in whose home he was married—was
David Ruggles, secretary of the Committee of Vigilance and publisher of the *Mirror of Liberty* periodical. Douglass recorded
these events in an autobiography published seven years after his
escape:

> On the third day of September, 1838, I left my chains, and suc-
> ceeded in reaching New York. . . . There I was in the midst of
> thousands, and yet a perfect stranger; without home and without
> friend. . . . I was afraid to speak to any one for fear of speaking to
> the wrong one, and thereby falling into the hands of money-loving
> kidnappers. . . .
>
> Thank Heaven, I remained but a short time in this distressed
> situation. I was relieved from it by the humane hand of Mr.
> DAVID RUGGLES, whose vigilance, kindness, and perseverance, I
> shall never forget. I am glad of an opportunity to express, as far
> as words can, the love and gratitude I bear him. . . . I had been in
> New York but a few days when Mr. Ruggles sought me out, and
> very kindly took me to his boardinghouse at the corner of Church
> and Lespenard Streets. . . .
>
> Very soon after I went to Mr. Ruggles, he wished to know of
> me where I wanted to go; as he deemed it unsafe for me to re-
> main in New York. I told him I was a calker, and should like to
> go where I could get work. I thought of going to Canada; but he
> decided against it, and in favor of my going to New Bedford,
> thinking I should be able to get work there at my trade.[62]

Because of race prejudice, Douglass could not find employment
as a calker in New Bedford and earned his livelihood as a day
laborer.

Douglass soon became involved in the antislavery movement.
He attended meetings sponsored by the black community and
subscribed to the Boston *Liberator*. In 1841 he met the editor,

William Lloyd Garrison, for the first time. A close friendship developed, a relationship that lasted until an open breach between them occurred ten years later as a result of ideological differences. Also in 1841, the Massachusetts Anti-Slavery Society employed Douglass as a traveling agent to lecture and solicit subscriptions for the *National Anti-Slavery Standard* and the *Liberator*. Douglass worked in this capacity for four years, associating with Garrison, Wendell Phillips, and other New England abolitionists. During the winter of 1844–45, he was also busy writing his autobiography, the *Narrative of the Life of Frederick Douglass, an American Slave*. The book was published in 1845, and Douglass, still a fugitive, left the United States for his own safety. He remained abroad for two years, lecturing and promoting the sale of the autobiography in the British Isles. During this time, his freedom was purchased from his American owner with funds raised by British friends.

When Douglass was preparing to return to the United States, his friends wanted to give a testimonial affair in his honor. He suggested that he would rather use the money to buy a printing press and start a newspaper. He believed that "a tolerably well conducted press, in the hands of persons of the despised race, by calling out the mental energies of the race itself; by making them acquainted with their own latent powers; by combining and reflecting their talents—would prove a most powerful means of removing prejudice, and of awakening an interest in them."[63]

Douglass returned to Massachusetts in the spring of 1847. Some of his white abolitionist friends, including Garrison and Phillips, tried to dissuade him from this publishing venture, but he decided to go ahead with his plans. In September of that year Douglass issued a prospectus for a weekly newspaper, in November he moved to Rochester in upstate New York, and in December he began publishing his paper. The prospectus stated that the objectives were "to attack Slavery in all its forms and aspects" and to promote the moral and intellectual improvement of black people.[64] For sixteen years, from 1847 to 1863, Douglass carried on his journalistic enterprise, despite inadequate financial re-

sources and frequent absences from the office for lecture tours
and other trips in the United States and abroad. His weekly
newspaper began publication on December 3, 1847, as the *North
Star*. In June, 1851, the *North Star* merged with the *Liberty Party
Paper*, a weekly issued in Syracuse and financed by the white
abolitionist Gerrit Smith. The title was changed to *Frederick
Douglass' Paper*, and publication continued at Rochester with
Douglass as editor. He issued the weekly under that title until
the summer of 1860, when he discontinued this publication because of the problem of delinquent subscribers.

Meanwhile, in 1858, Douglass announced plans to publish a
monthly antislavery periodical for European circulation. "The
first number," he stated, "will be published for the month of
June 1858, and will be sent to all the British subscribers, in lieu
of the weekly which they now receive."[65] The earliest issue of
Douglass' Monthly that has been found is that of January, 1859,
which is designated as volume one, number eight. (No complete
files of *Douglass' Monthly* or of the *North Star* and *Frederick
Douglass' Paper* are available today. Douglass' own volumes were
lost in the fire that destroyed his Rochester home in 1872.) In
August, 1860, the weekly newspaper ceased publication; and the
monthly periodical began to list prices for both American and
British subscribers, whereas previously only a British rate had
been given.

The *Monthly* was published until the summer of 1863, when
Douglass decided to discontinue it and go South to recruit Negro
soldiers for the Union army. In his "Valedictory" as an editor,
Douglass observed that his journalistic enterprise "ends its existence in the same room on the same street where it began." "It
has been during these sixteen years," he reflected, "immovable
in its principles as it has been permanent in its local habitation."
Douglass now felt that he could better serve the cause of abolition as a recruiter for the military forces, thus taking "some hum-
ble part in the physical as well as the moral struggle against
slavery."[66] When Douglass did not receive the federal military
commission he had expected, he abandoned his recruiting plans.

He did not, however, resume publication of the periodical, but instead became a full-time lecturer in the cause of emancipation and civil rights.

During the Reconstruction period, Douglass was associated with a weekly newspaper published in Washington. When this paper, the *New Era*, started in January, 1870, under the sponsorship of a group of stockholders, it was edited by J. Sella Martin with Douglass as the corresponding editor. Later that year, Douglass moved to Washington and became editor and owner of the paper. He changed the title to the *New National Era*. In 1873 he turned the newspaper over to his sons Lewis and Frederick, Jr., who published the weekly until it went out of existence the following year. In 1889 Douglass was appointed by President Benjamin Harrison as minister to Haiti. He resigned two years later but continued to write and to lecture until the day of his death, February 20, 1895. Active in public life for more than fifty years, Douglass was regarded in his time as the leading spokesman for the Negro people.

Douglass' Monthly, with its predecessors, was a major channel for the expression of Douglass' beliefs and for the advocacy of causes that he supported.[67] In political matters, coverage was given to the national election, legislation before Congress, and the messages and speeches of President Abraham Lincoln (some of them reprinted in full). News was reported about meetings and activities of antislavery groups in the United States and Great Britain, such as the Rochester Ladies Anti-Slavery Society, the Ohio State Convention of Colored Men, the Irish Ladies Anti-Slavery Society, and the American Tract Society. Material was reprinted from the London *Anti-Slavery Reporter* and other British papers as well as from American abolitionist publications. Eulogies of Gamaliel Bailey, Theodore Parker, Joseph Sturge, and other white abolitionists were presented. A column captioned "Southern Gems" reprinted the announcements of Negroes for sale and rewards for runaway slaves that had appeared in proslavery publications. John Brown's raid at Harper's Ferry and his trial and execution were reported in detail. Historical accounts were given of the Amistad case, the Oberlin-Wellington rescue, and the insurrections of Denmark Vesey and Nat Turner.

Occasionally, signed contributions from black writers appeared in *Douglass' Monthly*. Essays by James McCune Smith were reprinted from the *Anglo-African Magazine*. Smith was also engaged to write the editorials during Douglass' absence for a lecture tour in 1859.[68] Bishop Daniel A. Payne wrote an open letter to the ministers of the African Methodist Episcopal Church, in which he raised questions about the management of the denominational newspaper the *Christian Recorder*.[69] Others from whom communications were printed in *Douglass' Monthly* were Alexander Crummell, Jermain Wesley Loguen, J. Sella Martin, John Willis Menard, Martin Robison Delany, Henry Highland Garnet, and George B. Vashon.

More frequently, though, *Douglass' Monthly* carried the writings of white abolitionists such as Gerrit Smith, Lewis Tappan, Wendell Phillips, and Charles Sumner. A regular feature of the periodical was a series of "Letters from the Old World," sent from England by Mrs. Julia Griffith Crofts. Douglass had been assisted in both the literary and business aspects of his publication by this Englishwoman whom he had met during his first trip abroad. Unmarried at that time, she came to the United States and lived in Rochester for six years. After her return to England in 1855, she continued to advise Douglass concerning his publication and to contribute material to it. Another white friend who assisted Douglass was Abram Pryne of Williamson and McGrawville, New York. Pryne was a minister, an antislavery lecturer, and later a member of the New York state legislature.[70] He served as editor during a six-month period that Douglass spent in England during 1859–60.[71]

Most frequently of all, this periodical presented Douglass' own speeches and writings. Editorials and other discourses reflected his philosophy, which moved from a stance of moral suasion and nonresistance to the support of political and military measures against slavery. When Douglass discontinued his monthly publication, he issued this statement:

I have lived to see the leading presses of the country, willing and ready to publish any argument or appeal in behalf of my race, I am able to make. So that while speaking and writing are still needful, the necessity for a special organ for my views and opinions on slavery no longer exists. To this extent at least, my paper has accomplished the object of its existence. It has done something towards battering down that dark and frowning wall of partition between the working minds of two races, hitherto thought impregnable.[72]

Anglo-African Magazine

Thomas Hamilton, publisher of the *Anglo-African Magazine*, was a member of a pioneering family of journalists and civil rights activists. He was born in New York City on April 20, 1823; when he died in Jamaica, Long Island, on May 29, 1865, a victim of typhoid fever in his forty-third year, he had worked for almost thirty of those years in journalism and publishing.[73] From his boyhood days, his one ambition was to be a publisher, to be an independent voice representing Negroes in the "fourth estate." At least three influences converged to bring him to this decision: he was growing up in a family endowed with literary talent, active in civic and religious affairs, and dedicated to the struggle for freedom and equality for black people; he was growing up in New York City at a time of considerable journalistic activity among Negroes; and he was growing up in a city in which outstanding white newspapers of antislavery sentiment were being issued. With these circumstances helping to mold his life, it is not strange that "to become a Publisher, was the dream of his youth . . . and the aim of his manhood."[74]

Thomas Hamilton was the youngest son of William Hamilton, who was a native of New York and a house carpenter by trade. William Hamilton was in the forefront of activities among free Negroes for forty years. In 1796 he sent a letter to the New York state governor, John Jay, deploring slavery and the oppression of black people. Hamilton beseeched the governor to use his influence to change these conditions: "Is it not high time that the scandal of this country should be taken away that it might be called a free nation? ... May you open your mouth and jude [judge] righteously and plead the cause of the poor and needy."[75] That same year, Hamilton was among the persons who, under the leadership of James Varick, withdrew from the Methodist Episcopal Church to hold their own worship services. Hamilton became one of the original trustees of the African Methodist Episcopal Zion denomination when it was organized by this group.

On January 1, 1808, a program was held at the Zion Church to celebrate passage of the federal law abolishing the importation of slaves. Varick preached the sermon, and Hamilton composed the hymns for this program. The celebration became an annual observance; and, on at least one occasion, Hamilton delivered the main oration. Also in 1808, Hamilton helped organize the New York African Society for Mutual Relief, and he was chosen its first president. This pioneering beneficial society provided financial assistance for members who were ill or unemployed and for the widows and orphans of deceased members. In 1827, when domestic slavery was legally abolished in New York State, he chaired a committee to plan a celebration; and he delivered the oration for this occasion.

Between 1831 and 1835 William Hamilton attended four of the national conventions held annually by black people and was elected president of the 1834 convention. In his opening address at this meeting, he articulated the attitude of the majority of blacks toward the American Colonization Society and the American Anti-Slavery Society: "Cheer up my friends! Already has your protest against the Colonization Society shown to the world that the people of colour are not willing to be expatriated.... That hitherto strong-footed, but sore-eyed vixen, prejudice, is limping off, seeking the shade. The Anti-Slavery Society and the friends of immediate abolition, are taking a noble, bold, and manly stand, in the cause of universal liberty."[76]

When William Hamilton died in 1836, he was eulogized as "a man of correct and upright deportment, a cultivated mind, of a sound and discriminating judgment, and also an active and efficient member of our Benevolent and Literary Societies, and of every other institution, whose object was the moral, and intellectual elevation of our people."[77] Hamilton himself did not publish any newspapers or periodicals, but he was the father of three sons who became active in journalism—William, Robert, and Thomas.

As a boy, Thomas worked in the newspaper district of New York City and became acquainted with many publications. In 1837 the *Colored American* (at first called the *Weekly Advocate*) was established, and he was employed as a carrier for the paper. The following year David Ruggles began publishing the *Mirror of Liberty*. In 1841 three other black journals were started in the metropolitan area: the weekly *Zion's Wesleyan*, the *Journal of Education and Weekly Messenger*, and the monthly *African Methodist Episcopal Church Magazine*. Other journals of antislavery persuasion were issued in the city by white organizations, and Thomas was employed by some of these publications. He worked as the mailing clerk for the *Evangelist* and for the *National Anti-Slavery Standard*. He was probably familiar also with out-of-town journals circulating in New York, such as the Boston *Liberator* and the two black publications from Philadelphia, the monthly *National Reformer* and the weekly *Demosthenian Shield*.

In the fall of 1841, Thomas Hamilton began his career as a publisher with the founding of the weekly *People's Press*. This newspaper replaced the *Colored American*, which had been discontinued that spring. When the *People's Press* ended after several months, he returned to the *National Anti-Slavery Standard* and also found employment with the New York *Independent*. In 1859 Thomas Hamilton inaugurated the two publications that established his reputation as a journalist: the monthly *Anglo-African Magazine* and the *Weekly Anglo-African* newspaper. He was now married and living in Brooklyn. His publication office was in New York City at the same address as the *National Anti-Slavery Standard*, 48 Beekman Street.

The monthly periodical began in January, 1859, and the first issue of the newspaper appeared on July 23, 1859. In launching the newspaper, Hamilton announced: "We hope to supply a demand too long felt in this community. We need a Press—a press of our own. . . . Our *cause* (for in this country we have a cause) demands our own advocacy."[78] The motto of the publication was "Man must be Free!—if not through Law, why then above Law." Thomas Hamilton issued the weekly until March, 1861, when he gave up his ownership and the paper was taken over by George Lawrence, Jr.[79] Lawrence was associated with James Redpath, the white abolitionist in Boston who worked as an agent for the Haitian government to promote emigration of Negroes to that republic. The newspaper, with the new title *The Pine and Palm*, became a medium of publicity for that movement.

By August, however, the Hamilton family was again publishing a newspaper at 48 Beekman Street, with the same name and motto as before. Thomas Hamilton's brother Robert assumed the position of publisher; but Thomas managed the daily business operations. During the war years, the *Anglo-African* built its reputation as a chronicler of military events and other national affairs and as a carrier of personal news between the black Union soldiers and their families and friends back home. Robert Hamilton continued to publish the *Anglo-African* newspaper until December, 1865, when it went out of existence. His son Robert H. Hamilton eventually became a journalist also, writing for the San Francisco *Elevator* (published by Philip A. Bell), the New York *Progressive American* (published by John J. Freeman), and for white newspapers in New York and Brooklyn.

Thomas Hamilton, in addition to his activities with the magazine and the newspaper, was also a book publisher and bookseller. He advertised for sale a number of books and pamphlets written by and about black people. At least two of these he published himself: *A Pilgrimage to My Motherland: An Account of a Journey Among the Egbas and Yorubas of Central Africa, in 1859–60*, by Robert Campbell, in 1861; and *The Black Man: His Antecedents, His Genius, and His Achievements*, a collection of biographical sketches by William Wells Brown, in 1863.

A quiet and modest person, Thomas Hamilton was not in the

limelight as his father had been and as his brother Robert came to be. Robert, a musician by avocation, was the chorister for the A. M. E. Zion Church in New York and also a private voice instructor. He organized musical programs to raise funds for the newspaper. One of these presentations was a concert by one hundred and fifty juvenile singers, in which six of his children were among the soloists. At various times, Robert served on executive committees in such organizations as the African Civilization Society and the American League of Colored Laborers.[80]

Yet Thomas Hamilton, in spite of his unassuming manner, became widely known and respected. When he died, his friends in New York eulogized him as "one of those untiring heroes, who, however quietly they labor, lift the people as they lift themselves." Messages of condolence came from an equal rights league in Adrian, Michigan; from a fraternal lodge in Columbus, Ohio; and from Philip A. Bell in San Francisco, who remembered Thomas Hamilton as the first newsboy for the *Colored American*, which he had established in New York in 1837.[81]

Hamilton had initiated the *Anglo-African Magazine* in January, 1859. The periodical appeared monthly until March, 1860, when it was suspended. After Hamilton's death, his brother William (who had become the general business agent for the family newspaper) announced plans for reviving the magazine. A prospectus was printed in the newspaper during November and December, 1865, but no issues or evidence of publication have been found for this period. During its brief existence, the *Anglo-African Magazine* quickly established its reputation as an outstanding black periodical. In the latter part of 1859, an anonymous donor gave ten dollars to start a fund for placing the magazine in all the public libraries in the country. This person believed that the publication was effectively combating race prejudice and should be put "within the reach of the masses." A list of donations and pledges was published in the November issue; among the contributors were the abolitionists Gerrit Smith and Benjamin Coates.[82]

When Thomas Hamilton inaugurated the *Anglo-African Magazine*, he announced that his objectives were to print accurate information about the educational, economic, social, and legal status of Negroes in the United States; to present biographies of prominent black people throughout the world; to review publications by black authors; and to provide an outlet for "the rapidly rising talent of colored men in their special and general literature."[83] The fifteen issues of the periodical contained much of the type of material that was promised. A series of articles analyzed data from the federal census and other sources regarding the Negro population between 1790 and 1850. The magazine gave a detailed account of John Brown's raid when it occurred in Virginia in 1859, "made up from the daily papers, for future reference." The 1831 confessions of Nat Turner were also carried at that time. The editor's note explained that these confessions were being published for two reasons: "first, to place upon record this most remarkable episode in the history of human slavery . . . and secondly, that the two methods of Nat Turner and of John Brown may be compared."[84] A biographical sketch of the actor Ira Aldridge was presented as an inspiration to young people. The author of the article reminded readers of the background of this person, who had left the United States in the 1820s because of racial prejudice and made his reputation in England and Europe: "Let young Anglo-Africans, when they feel the weight and the manifest nature of the barrier in their way to eminence, remember that, in 1858, the first living tragedian in the world was Ira Aldridge, an American black man, who was once a pupil in Colored School No. 1, Mulberry street, New York City."[85]

The roster of contributors to the *Anglo-African Magazine* was a veritable roll call of the black scholars of that day. One of the most prolific writers for the periodical was Martin Robison Delany. He was the author of essays on scientific subjects; but his most extensive contribution was a portion of a novel, which had not yet been published in book form, entitled "Blake, Or, The Huts of America: A Tale of the Mississippi Valley, the Southern United States, and Cuba." The editor's note accompanying the first installment described this as a "new work of thrilling interest," which "not only shows the combined political and commercial interests that united the North and South, but gives in the most familiar manner the formidable understanding among the slaves throughout the United States and Cuba." This note also gave the setting of the story: "The scene is laid in Mississippi, the plot extending into Cuba; the Hero being an educated West India black, who deprived of his liberty by fraud when young, and brought to the United States, in maturer age, at the instance of his wife being sold from him, sought revenge through the medium of a deep laid secret organization."[86] When the *Anglo-African Magazine* discontinued the novel after the July, 1859, issue, only one-third of the chapters had been printed. During 1861 and 1862 the complete work was serialized in the *Weekly Anglo-African* newspaper. This novel was not published in book form until 1970.[87]

In addition to Martin R. Delany, other frequent contributors to the magazine were James Theodore Holly, Frances Ellen Watkins Harper, James W. C. Pennington, and James McCune Smith. Holly wrote two series of articles: "Thoughts on Hayti," promoting emigration to that republic, and "Musings on the Kingdom of Christ." Mrs. Harper contributed fiction and nonfiction as well as the poetry that was establishing her reputation as a writer. (All of her contributions were under her maiden name; she married Fenton Harper in the fall of 1860.) The articles by Pennington dealt with slavery and the slave trade. Smith wrote on a variety of subjects, such as the influence of climate and geography on civilization, the German immigration into the United States, and the Dred Scott decision by the U.S. Supreme Court. Also appearing in the *Anglo-African Magazine* were Amos Gerry Beman, Edward Wilmot Blyden, Robert Campbell, Mary Ann Shadd Cary, Frederick Douglass, Sarah M. Douglass, John Mercer Langston, J. Sella Martin, William C. Nell, Daniel Alexander Payne, Charles B. Ray, and George B. Vashon. With this roster of contributors, serious matter tended to dominate the publication.

Yet, the *Anglo-African Magazine* was not without its lighter moments. Most of these were furnished by William J. Wilson, who wrote under the pen name "Ethiop."[88] Wilson contributed the "Afric-American Picture Gallery," a series of imaginative vignettes on the landing of the slave ship at Jamestown, the underground railroad, Toussaint L'Ouverture, Crispus Attucks, and other facets of black history. The February, 1860, issue also carried a satirical essay by Wilson entitled: "What Shall We Do with the White People?" which posed and partly answered this question:

> What then shall we Anglo-Africans do with these white people? *"What shall we do with them?"*....
>
> This people must be saved; quiet and harmony must be restored. Plans for the removal of these white people, as all such schemes are—such for example as these people have themselves laid for the removal of others out of their midst—would be wrong in conception, and prove abortive in attempt; nor ought it be desirable on our part were it even possible to forcibly remove them. It is their right to stay, only they have no right to jeopard the interest or the peace of the country if permitted to remain....
>
> We give them also high credit for their material progress. Who knows, but that some day, when, after they shall have fulfilled their mission, carried arts and sciences to their highest point, they will make way for a milder and more genial race, or become so blended in it, as to lose their own peculiar and objectionable characteristics? In any case, in view of the existing state of things around us, let our constant thought be, *what for the best good of all shall we do with the White people?*[89]

Thomas Hamilton republished the twelve issues of the *Anglo-African Magazine* for 1859 in a bound edition. This volume featured, as frontispiece, a portrait of Alexandre Dumas engraved by John Sartain. An advertisement for the volume maintained that the periodical was fulfilling the objectives for which it had been established: "It contains more facts and statistics of the colored race than any other publication extant: as well as numerous articles which are specimens of the best writings yet produced by colored Americans. The Magazine is thus of service in two important directions: it elicits the talents of colored writers of both sexes, and affords useful information in regard to this class, which is daily becoming of more importance in the country."[90] The editors of certain antislavery journals might have challenged the claim that the *Anglo-African Magazine* provided more information about black people than any other publication. Nevertheless, Thomas Hamilton had made an outstanding contribution. He had played a significant role in the journalistic activity of his day and in the development of the Afro-American periodical press.

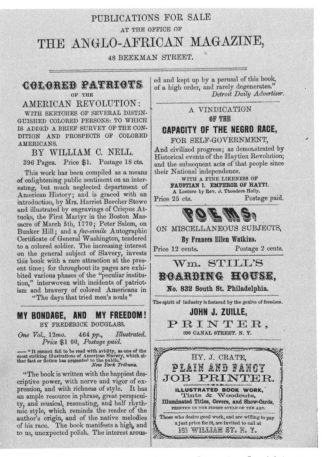

Advertisement page from the *Anglo-African Magazine*

Courtesy American Antiquarian Society

THREE

After Reconstruction
General Periodicals

> At present this [Negro] scholarship is practi-
> cally hedged in. The white Magazines and
> Reviews stand in no need of it, and are in no
> humor or condition to try experiments. . . .
> Nothing remains but for the Negro to open a
> channel for himself. The men of this organiza-
> tion are prepared to lead off in the work of
> cutting the ditch.
> —*A. M. E. Church Review*, July, 1884

When Frederick Douglass issued his valedictory statement as publisher of *Douglass' Monthly*, he spoke for all the black maga-zine editors of the antebellum period. None of the periodicals initiated before 1865 were still in existence when the Civil War ended, and the publishing of black periodicals did not begin again until the decade of the 1880s. This hiatus can be attributed largely to the optimism that pervaded the black population. Ne-groes anticipated that legal measures taken by the federal gov-ernment would guarantee first-class citizenship and place them in the mainstream of American life. Thus the periodical, as an agent for the vindication of equal rights, was no longer needed.

This expectation of a new society was destroyed by the turn of events of the post-Reconstruction era. Before the end of the nineteenth century, black people generally had been cast into second-class citizenship by custom and law throughout the coun-try. Once again, as in the crucial years preceding the Civil War, the Afro-American periodical proliferated to protest injustices, to agitate for equality before the law, to offer solutions for resolving racial conflict, to encourage Negroes in their efforts toward advancement, to chronicle the activities and achievements of black people, and to provide an outlet for their literary talent. Once again, these periodicals were promoted by black institutions as well as by individual entrepreneurs.

The general periodicals published between 1880 and 1909 reflected the spectrum of attitudes that existed among Negroes regarding their status in American society. The *Paul Jones Monthly Magazine* maintained—although ambivalently—that racial problems were nonexistent for Negroes who proved themselves worthy of respect. John C. Dancy said of the journal that he edited, the *A. M. E. Zion Quarterly Review*: "while it has always assumed an attitude of conservatism, it has been a conservatism which believes that there are other triumphs to be won and other liberties to be assured." In unequivocal words, W. E. B. Du Bois shunned the financial support and possible influence of advertisers and published his periodical "not as a matter of business but as a matter of spiritual life and death." The *Horizon*, he declared, "is a demand for democracy—spiritual freedom for ten millions of people, and not for these only but for all men the world over."[1]

The *Colored American Magazine* was edited by Walter W. Wallace and Pauline E. Hopkins as a publication through which Negroes could "demonstrate their ability and tastes, in fiction, poetry, and art."[2] When Frederick R. Moore assumed management of the periodical, he announced that the purpose of the magazine would be "to record the doings of the race along material lines."[3] He promoted economic self-reliance among Negroes as a leverage for gaining respect and equality. *McGirt's Magazine* advocated the exercise of political power as the means of obtaining justice in the United States. Somewhat at the center of the spectrum was the *Voice of the Negro*, attempting to reconcile the conflicts and divergent points of view that existed not only between white and black people, but also among Negroes themselves.

Although none of the black antebellum periodicals continued after the war, there were fifteen or more writers in these early publications who lived to contribute to the magazines of the post-

Reconstruction decades. Four A. M. E. ministers wrote for all three of the periodicals of their denomination—the *African Methodist Episcopal Church Magazine* established in 1841, the *Repository of Religion and Literature and of Science and Art* established in 1858, and the *A. M. E. Church Review* established in 1884. These individuals, all of whom became bishops in the church, were John Mifflin Brown, Jabez P. Campbell, Daniel Alexander Payne, and Alexander W. Wayman. John Jamison Moore, the A. M. E. Zion minister who issued the *Lunar Visitor* in San Francisco during the early 1860s, returned East after the war, became a bishop in his church, and contributed to the *A. M. E. Zion Quarterly Review*. Solomon G. Brown, who wrote articles on natural science for the *Repository of Religion and Literature*, contributed poetry to the *National Baptist Magazine*.

Other writers in this group were A. M. E. bishops Benjamin Tucker Tanner and Henry McNeal Turner, scholars Alexander Crummell and Edward Wilmot Blyden, congressmen John Mercer Langston and Richard H. Cain (also an A. M. E. bishop), and capitalist and labor organizer Isaac Myers. The most extensively published writers who spanned the antebellum and post-Reconstruction years were Frederick Douglass and Frances Ellen Watkins Harper. Douglass wrote primarily for his own *Monthly* among the black periodicals before 1865, but in the decades following Reconstruction he was a widely sought and frequently reprinted author in the Afro-American press. The writing career of Frances E. W. Harper extended from the mid-1840s, when her first collection of poems was published, until her death in 1911.[4] During this time her poetry, fiction, and nonfiction appeared in many periodicals.

The antebellum *Afric-American Repository* (which was never published) had proposed paying its contributors and editors. The *Anglo-African Magazine* had made a promise of remuneration to writers, which it was not able to fulfill. In the post-Reconstruction period, however, some editors did give token payments to individuals whom they felt would enhance their publications. Jesse Max Barber paid Charles W. Chesnutt ten dollars for an article contributed to the *Voice of the Negro*. Responding to a request from Barber for material, William Stanley Braithwaite offered him six poems for twenty dollars. In an autobiography published in 1940, Mary Church Terrell reminisced about her association with the *Voice of the Negro*: "I thoroughly enjoyed writing for the Voice, although the remuneration I received was small. At that, it was more than was usually given me for an article." James E. McGirt offered Chesnutt three dollars each for short stories for his magazine. Pauline E. Hopkins instituted the practice of paying writers for their contributions to the *Colored American Magazine*.[5]

During the post-Reconstruction period, salaries were paid to the editors of two of the church-sponsored general periodicals. When the *A. M. E. Church Review* was established in 1884, the church conference set an annual salary of $1,000 for the editor. In 1900 John C. Dancy, editor of the *A. M. E. Zion Quarterly Review*, pointed out in his report that he had received "$886.93 for the four years without complaining while the Editor of the sister Church Review received $1,350 per year." Dancy also mentioned that he had personally paid a debt of $360 owed the printer. He hastened to add, however, that he placed concern for the church above personal financial interest: "It is needless for me to say that I stick to this work because I really like it. I am deeply absorbed in the work and growth of the Church and feel that I should always do something for its help and development." In contrast to these periodicals, the *National Baptist Magazine* began publication "with a debt and an empty treasury," and there is no indication that the editor received a salary.[6]

In addition to the ministers who edited the periodicals issued by denominations, other clergymen were associated with general magazines published independently. Among these men were Jesse S. Woods, S. Douglass Russell, and John W. E. Bowen, who was both a minister and an educator. Other educators editing general periodicals were Simon Green Atkins and W. E. B. Du Bois. Men in other professions who edited or published magazines were physician Miles V. Lynk, lawyers Archibald H. Grimké and

Thomas A. Church, and businessmen Frederick R. Moore and James H. W. Howard. These individuals had already become well known in their main fields of endeavor. There were also young and unknown persons who attempted to issue periodicals. One of the most ambitious was Walter W. Wallace, the drugstore prescription clerk in Boston who launched the *Colored American Magazine*. Although most of the editors and publishers were journalists by avocation, a few individuals sought to earn their living in writing and publishing. Among these were Charles Alexander and Timothy Thomas Fortune. Pauline E. Hopkins and Carrie A. Bannister were the women editors of general magazines during these years.

In the decade before 1910, the two periodicals with the largest circulation were the *Voice of the Negro* and the *Colored American Magazine*. The *Voice of the Negro* was backed with the funds and other resources of a nationally operated white publishing company. Within a few months of its founding, the periodical was reporting a circulation of 15,000. One year after that publisher withdrew from the enterprise, the *Voice* ceased publication. The *Colored American Magazine* was the main periodical benefiting from the financial subsidy of Booker T. Washington. He supported others, such as *Alexander's Magazine*, but his major interest was in the *Colored American Magazine*. This publication had a reported circulation of 17,840.[7] After Washington stopped subsidizing the *Colored American Magazine*, it soon went out of existence.

These two magazines solicited advertisements from national firms as well as from black businesses and educational institutions in an effort to broaden their financial base. The *Voice of the Negro* carried advertisements for Coca-Cola, Underwood typewriters, and for railroad companies across the country—Southern Railway, the Louisville and National Railroad, Southern Pacific, and the Rock Island system. The *Colored American Magazine* had advertisements from the Atlantic and Pacific Tea Company (now familiarly called A and P); the Doubleday, Page and Company book publishers; and the Century Manufacturing Company

Advertisement from the *Voice of the Negro*

(which sold buggies, harnesses, pianos, and sewing machines).
Other relatively successful periodicals also solicited national advertisements. In *Howard's American Magazine*, advertisements
appeared for Fels-Naptha soap, Runkel Brothers breakfast cocoa,
and the Garner detachable bicycle, "the wheel of the 20th century," that could be "taken apart or reassembled in 3 and 6
seconds by any person."[8]

The magazines published by individuals who were not able to
secure national advertising, or did not choose to solicit it, were
generally short-lived. Other factors also led to the early demise
of most of the periodicals. The methods of distribution were inadequate, and publishers had to depend primarily upon persons
whom they appointed as subscription agents in various cities.
Another problem was that of delinquent subscribers, as well as
too few subscribers. The majority of the periodicals were issued
at an annual subscription of $1.00, the same rate that had pre-
vailed during the antebellum years. This low price still did not
attract enough subscribers or encourage prompt payment. Among
the general periodicals published without the support of established black institutions, only a few lasted as long as ten years,
notably the *Colored American Magazine* and the combined *Howard's Negro-American Magazine* and *Howard's American Magazine*. Others endured for at least three or more years, including
McGirt's Magazine, *Alexander's Magazine*, the *Voice of the Negro*, and the *Horizon*. The majority, however, lasted only one or
two years, and sometimes for only one or two issues.

The church-supported general periodicals achieved more sustained publication, but they too had to contend with delinquent
subscribers. In 1895, Dancy of the *A. M. E. Zion Quarterly Review* announced: "We have indulged some of our readers for
full three years, and must insist now that they MUST PAY their
subscriptions." In the August, 1901, issue of the *National Baptist
Magazine*, editor William B. Johnson made this appeal: "We
hope all persons who owe us will come to the Convention and
pay up." The *A. M. E. Church Review* alone was solvent. At the
close of the first four years of publication, editor Benjamin T.

Advertisement from the *Colored American Magazine*

Courtesy Moorland-Spingarn Research Center, Howard University

Tanner reported that this venture had been a success. Although many of the subscribers had not been prompt with their payments, the *Review* had a cash balance of $288.46. Tanner stated that the *Review* had a circulation of 2,500.[9]

The black churches took the leadership in sponsoring general magazines during the post-Reconstruction period. The African Methodist Episcopal Church, with the establishment of the *A. M. E. Church Review* in 1884, made the outstanding contribution, just as it had during the antebellum years. A separate discussion of this review is given at the end of the chapter. The *A. M. E. Zion Quarterly Review* (founded in 1890) and the *National Baptist Magazine* (founded in 1894) also served as general periodicals. The two Methodist reviews have continued publication to the present day, although they ceased to function as general periodicals early in the twentieth century when other magazines were established by secular organizations and commercial publishing ventures.

The history of the African Methodist Episcopal Zion Church dates back to 1796 when a group of Negro parishioners of the Methodist Episcopal Church in New York City began to hold their own worship services. Under the leadership of James Varick, they withdrew from the white church and eventually organized an independent denomination in the early 1820s. Varick was elected bishop of the new church. The first journalistic effort of this denomination was *Zion's Wesleyan*, a weekly paper started in New York City in 1841, which failed after a year or two. In 1860 the church conference voted to support the *Weekly Anglo-African* as its medium of communication. This newspaper was issued in New York City by Thomas and Robert Hamilton, sons of William Hamilton, one of the founders of the denomination. After the *Anglo-African* ceased publication in 1865, the church again attempted to issue a journal of its own.[10]

Following abortive efforts, a newspaper was permanently established with the founding of the *Star of Zion* in 1876. This paper was initiated by the North Carolina Conference and financed through a stock company. In 1880, the *Star of Zion* was presented to the General Conference, which designated it as the official journal of the denomination. The paper had started publication as a monthly, but it soon became a weekly and is still being published as the official weekly journal of the church.

The *A. M. E. Zion Quarterly Review*, like the *Star of Zion*, was initiated through local efforts and then transferred to the General Conference as an official publication. It was first issued in Pittsburgh. The site of publication was moved to Wilmington, North Carolina, in 1892, and beginning in 1896, the *Quarterly Review* was issued from the church's publishing house in Charlotte, North Carolina. The periodical began publication as the *A. M. E. Zion Church Quarterly*; the title was changed to the *A. M. E. Zion Quarterly Review* in 1895.

The founder and first editor was George Wylie Clinton (1859–1921), who was born a slave in Lancaster County, South Carolina. During the Reconstruction period, he attended the University of South Carolina at Columbia and later received theological training at Livingstone College in Salisbury, North Carolina. When he started the quarterly in 1890, Clinton was pastor of the John Wesley A. M. E. Zion Church in Pittsburgh and editor of a weekly newspaper issued in that city by a stock company. After publishing the quarterly for two years on his own resources, Clinton offered it to the church at the General Conference of 1892. The church accepted the quarterly and then elected Clinton as editor of the more prestigious *Star of Zion* newspaper. In 1896 he became a bishop in the church.[11]

John Campbell Dancy, Sr., succeeded Clinton and edited the *Quarterly Review* from 1892 to 1912. Dancy (1857–1920) was born in Tarboro, North Carolina, to slave parents. During the Reconstruction period, he attended Howard University, then returned home to become a schoolteacher. He also entered journalism and politics, editing a newspaper in Tarboro and winning election as recorder of deeds of Edgecombe County. His church elected him editor and business manager of the *Star of Zion* in 1885. He was in charge of this journal until 1892, when he became editor of the quarterly periodical. In politics, Dancy was active as convention delegate and campaign speaker for the Republican party at the state and national levels. He received presidential appointments as collector of customs at Wilmington, North Carolina, and recorder of deeds for the District of Columbia.[12]

Clinton founded the quarterly for the benefit of the A. M. E. Zion Church, but he projected a catholic scope for its contents. The periodical was "to represent the character, religious thought, development and general progress of the colored churches of America." Under Dancy's editorship, the periodical was broadened even more to include the general interests of "the Afro-American Race in America."[13] Clinton organized the *Review* into departments for feature articles, sermons, editorials, and biography. Dancy continued these and added a poetry section. The *A. M. E. Zion Quarterly Review* was primarily concerned with religious, political, and educational affairs. The individuals who wrote most frequently for the periodical were bishops and ministers of the Zion denomination, notably James W. Hood, Alexander Walters, and Joseph C. Price. However, lay people and other clergymen also contributed, among them Ida Wells Barnett, Walter H. Brooks, Blanche K. Bruce, James D. Corrothers, Alexander Crummell, Frederick Douglass, T. Thomas Fortune, Francis J. Grimké, Edward A. Johnson, William S. Scarborough, and Booker T. Washington.

The *National Baptist Magazine*, founded as a literary journal for the denomination,[14] began publication in Washington, D.C., in January, 1894, with William Bishop Johnson as editor. Among Negroes of the Baptist faith, independent local churches were organized as early as the 1770s and 1780s in southern communities and the first decade of the nineteenth century in the North. A national association of local churches, the American Baptist Missionary Convention, was formed in 1840; but after nearly forty years of operation, it went into decline. The Baptist Foreign Mission Convention was organized in 1880, the American National Baptist Convention (the sponsor of the magazine) in 1886, and the National Baptist Educational Convention in 1893. In 1895, these three groups met in Atlanta and consolidated into the National Baptist Convention of the United States, which was incorporated in 1915. This organization continued the magazine, and Johnson continued as editor throughout the magazine's existence.

Several changes occurred, however, in the business and publishing arrangements. At first, the periodical was managed by a publishing committee elected by the sponsoring convention. Later, a joint stock association, the National Baptist Magazine Publishing Company, was formed to finance and conduct the publishing operations. For a brief period in 1899, the magazine was issued by the National Baptist Publishing Board, which had been established in Nashville by the national convention to issue Sunday school literature. During this time, Richard Henry Boyd, who directed the publishing concern, was business manager of the journal. Ministers who served as associate editors to assist the editor included Charles Henry Clark of Tennessee, William Abraham Credit of Pennsylvania, A. W. Adams of Massachusetts, Samuel William Bacote of Missouri, Adam Clayton Powell of Connecticut, and George Edmund Morris of New Jersey. By November, 1900, the publishing board no longer was responsible for the periodical and the magazine had moved back to Washington.

William Bishop Johnson was pastor of the Second Baptist Church in Washington and also a teacher of mathematics and science at Wayland Seminary. (This seminary eventually moved to Richmond as the theological school of Virginia Union University.) Johnson (1858–1917) was a native of Toronto, Canada. He graduated from the normal school in that city, then earned a theological degree at Wayland. Prior to the founding of the *National Baptist Magazine*, he had edited an alumni journal for the seminary and a newspaper for the Virginia state Baptist convention.[15]

In the first issue of the *National Baptist Magazine*, the periodical was described as "the organ of Negro Baptists . . . in particular, and devoted to the interests of the Negro Race in general." The lead editorial in that issue gave this statement of policy: "In its publication we shall be conservative in the discussion of general subjects, inviting no useless controversy, and stirring no strife in the hearts of those with whom it may become our duty to occasionally cross swords; but we shall also be firm in placing the denominational tenets squarely before the world."[16]

The major contributors to this magazine were Baptist ministers. The most prolific was Elias Camp Morris, perennial president of the National Baptist Convention. Among the others were Edward M. Brawley, George W. Lee, Christopher H. Payne, Rufus L. Perry, Adam Clayton Powell, and Charles T. Walker. Although the Baptist church and its theology were the main subjects, feature articles discussed numerous other topics, such as the crime of lynching, the responsibility of teachers and parents in the education of children, the importance of manual training and industrial education, the British in the West Indies, the revolution in Cuba, and the Negro soldier in the Civil War. Among the lay contributors to the periodical were Judson W. Lyons, Kelly Miller, Robert H. Terrell, and Booker T. Washington.

Editorials likewise dealt with secular matters and contemporary issues—the segregated railroad coaches, racial discrimination in northern cities, emigration to Africa, the presidential elections, a Negro for the president's cabinet, disfranchisement, the National Afro-American Council, and the Negro and the Spanish-American War. In addition to feature articles and editorials, the magazine contained illustrated biographical sketches of ministers and laymen prominent in the denomination, book reviews, reprints of sermons, descriptions of Baptist churches and schools, and information on the meetings of the state Baptist conventions. Poetry was contributed by Charles Alexander, Walter H. Brooks, Solomon G. Brown, and Joseph S. Cotter, Sr.

Between 1880 and 1909, the publication of general periodicals through individual enterprise, without the sponsorship of established black institutions, occurred in fourteen states and the District of Columbia. Of the twenty-seven titles initiated, the largest number (fifteen) were in the Northeast—in Massachusetts, Pennsylvania, and New York. Periodicals also appeared in the southern, midwestern, and southwestern regions of the country.

In Massachusetts, five general periodicals were published, all in Boston. The first, entitled the *Negro*, appeared in July, 1886; the following year the *Negro-American* began publication. Neither of these two lasted for more than a few issues. Much more successful were the *Monthly Review*, founded in 1894 by Charles Alexander; *Alexander's Magazine*, established in 1905 by this same person; and the *Colored American Magazine*, launched by Walter W. Wallace in 1900. Detailed discussions of these three periodicals are presented at the end of the chapter.

The 1886 periodical, the *Negro*, did not name its publisher and editor; but according to John E. Bruce, a contemporary journalist, the editor was the black writer William Hannibal Thomas. Bruce was associated with Thomas for a few weeks in this publishing venture.[17] The periodical carried the subtitle *A Monthly Publication Devoted to Critical Discussions of Race Problems Involved in the Mental, Moral, Social, and Material Condition of the Negroes in the United States.* Lengthy feature articles by Thomas were printed in the July and August issues (the only ones that are currently available). Several years later, Thomas gained notoriety with his book *The American Negro: What He Was, What He Is, and What He May Become; A Critical and Practical Discussion* (1901). The opinions he expressed in this work were severely criticized by Bruce and other Negro writers, including W. E. B. Du Bois and Charles W. Chesnutt.[18]

After leaving the *Negro* periodical, Bruce joined with Thomas T. Symmons to publish the *Negro-American*. The first issue, which came out in January, 1887, included an article by T. Thomas Fortune on labor organizations and an essay by Henrietta Vinton Davis on the responsibilities of black women. By March, Bruce had severed his connection with that magazine. This was the pattern of his life: brief associations with innumerable newspapers and periodicals. Bruce made journalism his lifelong profession, although he had to supplement his income through jobs in government service. His career began in the early 1870s with a clerical job in the Washington office of the New York *Times*. When he died in 1924, he was a columnist for Marcus Garvey's newspaper, the *Negro World*.[19] Bruce was a prolific writer. Under the pen name "Bruce Grit" he contributed material to white and Negro publications. He also published and edited his own newspapers, and he was the author of several pamphlets on black history. With Arthur A. Schomburg, he established the Negro Society for Historical Research in Yonkers, New York, in 1911. Bruce was president and Schomburg the secretary of this society.

In 1898, while living in Albany, New York, Bruce was associated with *Prospect*, a magazine edited by Phil H. Brown. In a letter to Bruce in March of that year, the venerable scholar Alexander Crummell gave this advice: "I had a line the other day from Mr. Brown of the projected magazine—the 'Prospect.' I am glad you are in it; for it will serve to restrain that prodigal expenditure of genius and talent which, in your case seems to me should result in something large and permanent. Why can't you tie yourself down for a few months to a compact solid undertaking—a noble volume, which would tell [*illegible*] the interests of the race, and its reputation."[20] By 1900 Bruce was affiliated with *Howard's American Magazine* (published in Harrisburg, Pennsylvania) as associate editor; in 1903 he was editing a new monthly in New York City called *The Impending Conflict*; and in 1906 he was associated with the Philadelphia magazine *Ebony*. Bruce never achieved the stability that Crummell suggested would enhance his talents. Nevertheless he became one of the best-known journalists of his time, respected for his literary ability, his scholarship, and his forthright statements on the issues of the day.

In Pennsylvania, general periodicals were published in Philadelphia, Pittsburgh, and Harrisburg. The *Monthly Review* was transferred from Boston to Philadelphia in 1896. Also published in that city were *McGirt's Magazine*, founded in 1903, and *Ebony*, initiated in 1906. The *Colored Home Journal* and *Advance* were issued in Pittsburgh in the first decade of the 1900s. *Howard's*

Negro-American Magazine began publication in Harrisburg in 1889 and *Howard's American Magazine* in 1895.

McGirt's Magazine was published and edited by a southerner, James Ephraim McGirt (1874–1930), who was a native of North Carolina and a graduate of Bennett College in Greensboro. He lived in Philadelphia for a few years, from approximately 1903 to 1910, when he returned to Greensboro and engaged in business and real estate practice until his death.[21]

McGirt founded his periodical as a monthly in 1903; by 1909 he was issuing it as a quarterly. This publication promoted McGirt's own creative writing. His three volumes of poetry and a collection of short stories were publicized in the magazine, and poems and fiction by him were printed regularly. The early numbers of the periodical serialized a work of fiction by McGirt entitled "Black Hand," which had the following setting:

> This is the story of a young white newspaper reporter, who spent his time in writing articles for his paper against the Negro. The first chapter or part of the story told of how he was caught in an accident on the railroad cars, and his brain was affected to the extent that his color changed from white to that of the darkest Negro, and he was treated and taken for one everywhere he went. It told of the many hardships he experienced in this role—how he was refused by the woman that had promised him her hand—how his friends shunned him and the doors of the clubs closed in his face.[22]

McGirt's Magazine also carried material from many well-known authors: feature articles by Anna J. Cooper, W. E. B. Du Bois, Francis J. Grimké, Kelly Miller, Benjamin T. Tanner, Mary Church Terrell, and Richard R. Wright, Jr.; poems by Daniel Webster Davis, Paul Laurence Dunbar, Frances E. W. Harper, and Lucian B. Watkins; and fiction by John E. Bruce, Kelly Miller, and Watkins. McGirt tried, unsuccessfully, to secure short stories from Charles W. Chesnutt for his magazine.[23]

Much of the nonfiction writing in the periodical, including editorials and essays by McGirt, dealt with the participation of the Negro in politics. The magazine served as the official journal

80

James Ephraim McGirt, editor and publisher of
McGirt's Magazine. From J. E. McGirt, *For Your
Sweet Sake: Poems* (Philadelphia: J. C. Winston,
1906).

EBONY

The Journal of " The Three P's "

Vol 1   April 1906   No. 1

BONY——The Ebony's—mothers,
fathers, sisters, brothers, in short,
the whole blessed family,—here's
your chance to stand up and be
counted—at a dime a throw! We
come as your printed spokesman to tell YOUR
story. Needless to remark that we have passed
through the valley of great trials and tribula-
tions, that we may shed light into dark places.
The Society of "The Three P's" knows no
color-line. In its eyes all folks look alike; and
are alike. The mission of this little tid-bit is to
narrow the line which separates the sons and
daughters of Ebony from the blue-eyed darlings
of the nation, to help rather than hurt, to do
good instead of harm, and to keep tally with

1

Ebony

for the Constitutional Brotherhood of America, of which McGirt was secretary-treasurer. James E. Churchman of Orange, New Jersey, was the president; Solomon Porter Hood, also of Orange, was the national organizer. The objectives of the brotherhood were "to organize the Negro-American voters throughout the country, especially in doubtful States where they hold the balance of power; to exact a written statement from all candidates desiring the Negroes' vote, that if elected, their influence will be used to have the Constitution enforced to the letter, especially the Fourteenth and Fifteenth Amendments."[24]

McGirt's Magazine also supported other civil rights organizations, including the National Afro-American Council and the Niagara Movement. McGirt was convinced that the ballot was the only salvation of black people, and he urged them to exercise their right to vote. In an editorial, he sounded this warning to the Republican party: "We truly believe that unless the Republican party will be more mindful of the rights of the colored race it cannot hope to retain the Negro as a whole among its constituency. It is not a matter of the colored people tearing themselves away from the Republican party as is the party DRIVING the Negro away from it. . . . It is a fact that if the Republican party wishes to retain the Negro's allegiance it will have to at once adopt some kind of a policy that will show the Negroes that it is interested in them."[25]

Another periodical in Philadelphia during this time was the pocket-size *Ebony: The Journal of "The Three P's."* *Ebony* was edited and published by Thomas Wallace Swann and printed by the Society of "The Three P's." The first issue, April, 1906, did not identify this society, but it did promise that an article on "The Real 'P'" by John E. Bruce would appear in the May number. The April issue is the only one that can be located today. Swann was a journalist who associated with many newspapers and magazines around the country. For a brief period, he served as editor of *Howard's American Magazine.* He was also active in the movement to organize the National Afro-American party and to place Negro candidates in the 1900 presidential and state elections.[26]

The purpose of *Ebony* was "to keep tally with the progress Ebon-
ized Humanity is recording in the rapid ongoing of the world."[27]
Art, education, business, the stage, and politics were among the
areas to be covered. Contributors announced for future issues included Emmett J. Scott, who was Booker T. Washington's private
secretary; William Lloyd Garrison, Jr.; Meta Vaux Warrick Fuller,
the black Philadelphia sculptor studying in Paris; and two African newspaper editors, John P. Jackson of Lagos, West Africa,
and Alan Kirkland Soga of East London, South Africa.

The April issue included an article by Booker T. Washington
on the Negro in business and essays by editor Swann and Mary
Church Terrell eulogizing Paul Laurence Dunbar. An article by
S. Willie Layton described the Association for the Protection of
Colored Women, an organization that assisted young southern
girls who came North to work in domestic service. *Ebony* was
especially interested in the activities of Negroes in music, classical and popular. It gave a brief survey of the engagements of
Negro performers in Philadelphia, New York, Washington, and
London. An advertisement was carried for Keith's New Chest-
nut Street Theater, "the home of high-class vaudeville," and an
announcement was made of the forthcoming production of *Hiawatha* by the Samuel Coleridge-Taylor Choral Society of Washington. James Weldon Johnson contributed an article on the
Negro in music to this issue of *Ebony*.

The two periodicals published in Pittsburgh, *Advance* and the
Colored Home Journal, were edited by young men who were
subscription agents and writers for the Boston *Colored American
Magazine*. Oliver G. Waters founded the monthly *Advance*
around 1902. No copies of the magazine have been found, but a
contemporary Washington newspaper noted that in less than a
year Waters had placed his enterprise "on a safe financial basis."
This paper also stated: "It is possible that the Advance may be
moved here, as Mr. Waters believes the literary atmosphere of
Washington appeals more strongly to a high class magazine effort
than does the mechanical hum of Pittsburgh."[28] The *Colored*

Home Journal was issued by Thomas S. Ewell and Joseph Garner. Ewell had succeeded Waters as the Pittsburgh agent for the *Colored American Magazine*; he was also on the publishing board of that periodical. The initial number of the *Colored Home Journal* (the only issue that has been located) was dated February, 1903. It was devoted mainly to poetry and fiction and included a short story by Pauline E. Hopkins, editor of the *Colored American Magazine*.

The person responsible for the periodicals issued in Harrisburg was James H. W. Howard. Howard was born in Hamilton, Ontario, in 1859 and educated in the Buffalo, New York, public schools. He spent most of his life in Harrisburg, engaged in business, politics, and writing. Howard was a member of the city council during the 1880s, and later he held clerkships in offices of the state government.[29] He issued a weekly newspaper (the *State Journal*, 1882–85) and wrote a book (*Bond and Free: A True Tale of Slave Times*, 1886) before venturing into magazine publishing. His first periodical, *Howard's Negro-American Magazine*, was started in July, 1889. It was followed by *Howard's American Magazine*, which began publication in Harrisburg in 1895 and then moved to New York City around 1901. In 1912, Howard was editor of the *New Era Magazine*, published weekly in Washington by the National Colored Democratic League.

Howard was assisted in the editing of his first magazine by Reuben Hanson Armstrong, a Presbyterian minister in Harrisburg. For a few months in 1900, Thomas Wallace Swann served as editor and John E. Bruce served as associate editor of *Howard's American Magazine*. In New York City, George T. Knox and Thomas A. Church joined Howard as publishers of this magazine. Church, a lawyer and brother of Mary Church Terrell, also wrote extensively for the periodical, contributing essays, fiction, poetry, and book reviews. Both of Howard's periodicals were extensively illustrated and carried many advertisements. Articles in *Howard's Negro-American Magazine* concentrated on political and educational matters, but poetry and fiction were also included and a women's department was conducted by Sarah Greenfield. The January, 1890, issue reported on the National Afro-American League organized in Chicago that month.

When Howard began his periodical venture in 1889, he was commended for his initiative, but there was less praise for the magazine itself. The *A. M. E. Church Review*, speaking of the shortcomings of the publication, did note, however, that "great enterprises often have small beginnings, and this journal may grow with succeeding numbers."[30] Howard persisted in his effort, and at the close of the nineteenth century *Howard's American Magazine* was the outstanding general periodical issued through individual enterprise. In the September, 1900, issue Howard proudly announced that bound volumes of this magazine were included among the American exhibits at the Paris Exposition in a display of the progress of Negroes in the United States. He also announced that a western edition of the periodical was beginning publication in Chicago.

The subject scope projected for *Howard's American Magazine* was indicated by the subtitle: *Devoted to the Educational, Religious, Industrial, Social, and Political Progress of the Colored Race*. Only a few scattered issues of this periodical can be located today. A sampling of articles from these shows a wide range of subjects discussed by prominent individuals: "Abraham Lincoln," by Archibald H. Grimké; "What the Catholic Church Means to the Negro," by Frederick L. McGhee; "The Effect of Imperialism upon the Negro Race," by Kelly Miller; "The Negro Player," a survey of the Negro in the theater by Robert Cole; "The National Afro-American Council," by Ida Wells Barnett; "The Negro, West Point, and the Army," by William S. Scarborough; and " A Black Composer and His Song of Hiawatha," an essay on Samuel Coleridge-Taylor by Mary Church Terrell. The magazine published fiction by Frances E. W. Harper, reviews of current literature by Daniel A. P. Murray, and poetry by Paul Laurence Dunbar and James D. Corrothers.

The November, 1899, issue carried articles by Booker T. Washington and a symposium on his life and work with essays by

Washington's secretary Emmett J. Scott, Philadelphia merchant John Wanamaker, and journalist John E. Bruce. Bruce wrote frequently for this periodical, contributing fiction and nonfiction as well as editorials when he was on the staff. In one of his editorials, "Negro Aristocracy! A Myth," Bruce voiced this criticism: "The gulf between the educated and refined Negro so-called, and the illiterate and common Negro, is much wider than the former are willing to admit, or to have made public. . . . How can any class of people be called *superior* who neglect so plain a duty as the elevation of those around them, whose destiny is identical with their own?"[31]

The relocation of *Howard's American Magazine* in New York gave that city its first substantial black periodical of the twentieth century. No similar periodical had been published there since the *Anglo-African Magazine* of 1859–60. The transfer of the *Colored American Magazine* from Boston to New York in 1904 brought another significant publication to that city. These were the two most important post-Reconstruction periodicals in New York before the establishment of *Crisis* in 1910. Other general magazines were initiated but did not last for any length of time. *Brock's Magazine* was started in 1894, *Prospect* in 1898, the *Impending Conflict* in 1903, *Small's Illustrated Monthly* in 1905, and the *Freeman* in 1908.

The promoter of *Brock's Magazine*, Edward Elmore Brock, was a writer and newspaper correspondent whose columns, poetry, and short stories appeared in the Indianapolis *Freeman*, the *Colored American Magazine*, and other journals.[32] *Prospect* (one of the many periodicals with which John E. Bruce was associated) was a sixty-four-page monthly published "near Greater New York." Phil H. Brown was the editor; Charles H. Burrill and Will Marion Cook were on the editorial staff; Sol H. Johnson, Will A. Hall, and Will H. Dill were members of the managerial staff. The first issue (April, 1898) was well received by the black press and complimented for its typographical features and literary content. But soon after the periodical began, Brown left New York and the publication apparently folded.[33]

The Impending Conflict was published by Melvin Jack Chisum, a New York real estate entrepreneur, who engaged John E. Bruce as his editor. This monthly was also praised for its literary and typographical merits, but it too was short lived. Bruce moved on to other publications, and Chisum later became a prominent newspaper publisher in Oklahoma City.[34] *Small's Illustrated Monthly* was issued by Thomas Frederick Small, formerly a newspaper editor in Newport, Rhode Island.[35]

In May, 1908, Timothy Thomas Fortune was issuing a monthly magazine in New York called the *Freeman*. He had previously published the journal as a weekly, under the title *Fortune's Freeman*. In this periodical, Fortune proposed to discuss all race problems, not just those pertaining to Negroes. His lead article in the May issue was "Zionist Repatriationists and the Jewish Race." The *Freeman*, however, did not neglect national politics and the Negro people. This same issue carried a full-page display for the Negro-American Political League. The league had been organized in Philadelphia the previous month by William Monroe Trotter, Alexander Walters, J. Milton Waldron, J. Max Barber, and other militant leaders. One objective of the group was "to prevent the nomination of Secretary William H. Taft or Theodore Roosevelt as candidates for the Presidency by the Republican Party." President Roosevelt had fallen into disfavor with black people, especially because of the dishonorable discharge of Negro soldiers following the Brownsville, Texas, shooting disturbance. The league was promoting for president Joseph Benson Foraker, the U.S. senator from Ohio who spoke out in defense of those soldiers. The *Freeman* stated that its mission was "to deal on the square with the Right and to use the Big Stick on the Head of the Wrong."[36]

The *Freeman* was a short-lived publication and represented a futile attempt by Fortune, then fifty-two years old, to reestablish his journalistic career. This career had started in 1880, and before the end of the nineteenth century Fortune was recognized as the dean of black journalists. In 1907, however, he suffered a mental and physical breakdown, which forced him to give up the New

York *Age* newspaper that had established his reputation. From 1908 until his death in 1928 Fortune associated with a number of newspapers and periodicals in New York and other cities, but he never regained the position of leadership that he once held.

In Washington, D.C., the *National Afro-American* periodical was issued during 1890 and 1891. No copies have been located, but contemporary newspapers described it as an illustrated monthly with articles by such writers as Alexander Crummell, Francis J. Grimké, and John R. Lynch. The editor and publisher was John Willis Menard, who was employed as a clerk in the federal census bureau. Menard had formerly published newspapers in Florida and Louisiana. In 1868, as a resident of New Orleans, he had been elected to the United States House of Representatives from the Second Congressional District of Louisiana. This special election, held to fill a vacancy, was contested and Menard was not seated. The House resolved the issue by deciding against all the claimants. The seat remained vacant for the rest of the session, although the House did vote to give Menard one-half the salary of the office.[37]

Another, more auspicious general periodical issued in Washington was the *Horizon*, founded by W. E. B. Du Bois in 1907. For one year, it was issued from Alexandria, Virginia. Du Bois conducted the publication until 1910, when he discontinued it and established *Crisis* magazine. A discussion of the *Horizon* is presented at the end of the chapter. In the southern states, the outstanding general periodicals were the *Southland*, founded in Salisbury, North Carolina, in 1890; and the *Voice of the Negro*, established in Atlanta, Georgia, in 1904. Separate sketches for these two publications are also given at the close of the chapter. Other general magazines initiated in the South were *Lynk's Magazine* in Jackson, Tennessee, in 1898; the *New Citizen* in Columbia, South Carolina, in 1904; and *McConico's Monthly Magazine* in Birmingham, Alabama, in 1909.

Lynk's Magazine was an illustrated monthly issued by Miles Vandahurst Lynk, a physician who also conducted a publishing house. Although he advertised the magazine extensively, no copies can be found today. Earlier in the 1890s, Lynk had issued the *Medical and Surgical Observer*. (This periodical is discussed in chapter four.) The *New Citizen: A Magazine of Politics, Literature, and Current Events* was edited by I. Nathaniel Nesbitt. Other members of the staff were William N. Jones, literary editor; Samuel Louis Finley, editor of current events; J. Fred Fowler, business manager; and D. F. Thompson, field manager. The periodical pledged to stand by the Republican party, "the only political organization that looks upon the Negro as an American citizen." The editorial policy also declared that the magazine stood for "conservatism between the two races in the South, whenever such can be brought about without loss of manhood of either race."[38]

McConico's Monthly Magazine was more aggressive in philosophy and content. John F. A. McConico issued the periodical through a cooperative magazine company located in Chicago. By purchasing membership in this company, individual editors received thirty-two pages of standardized reading matter and advertising, to which their own front cover and pages of original material were added.[39] For his first issue (July, 1909), McConico added a front-cover photograph of Frederick Douglass, advertisements from Negro businesses and professional men in Alabama, and two articles: "The Negro a Man and Should Be Treated as a Man" and "Is the Negro Dead in Politics in the South, or Is He Asleep?" In the December number, the original material consisted of thirty or more short news items on reported lynchings and an essay entitled "Is Lynching To Be a Part of America's Civilization?"

In the midwestern region of the United States, the *Afro-American Budget* began publication in Evanston, Illinois, in 1889, and the *Afro-American Review* in the Illinois town of Mattoon ten years later. The Atlanta *Voice of the Negro* relocated in Chicago in 1906. The *Future State* was founded in Kansas City, Missouri, in 1891, and *Paul Jones Monthly Magazine* in Topeka, Kansas, in 1907. Periodicals were also published in the Southwest. In Texas the *Colored American Journal* was initiated in the town of Palestine in 1882 and the *Living Age* in Denison in 1891. The *Living Age* later moved to Langston, in the Oklahoma Territory. *Russell's Review* was also published in the Oklahoma Territory at the turn of the century.

The editor and publisher of the *Afro-American Budget* was an A. M. E. minister, Jesse S. Woods, who had come to Evanston as a young man to attend the Garrett Biblical Institute at Northwestern University. William Henry Twiggs, his roommate and also a student at Northwestern, became the corresponding editor. Twiggs later opened a printing shop in Evanston and remained in that city, engaged in the printing and real estate businesses, until his death in 1960 at the age of ninety-five. As a Methodist minister, Woods was more mobile. In the summer of 1890, he moved from Evanston to Decatur; by 1899 he was located in Mattoon. Woods continued to issue the *Afro-American Budget* in Decatur. In Mattoon he published the *Afro-American Review*, a periodical similar in content to the *Budget*.[40] The *Afro-American Budget: A Monthly Magazine Devoted to the Practical Problems of the African Race in All Parts of the World* had an encouraging beginning. Two bishops of the A. M. E. Church were among the contributors to the first issue of May, 1889: Henry McNeal Turner, writing on the "Civil Rights Decision"; and Benjamin Tucker Tanner, discussing "Youthful Infidels." The June number printed a letter of congratulation from Frederick Douglass.

As Douglass observed, the *Afro-American Budget* was concerned with "earthly as well as heavenly relations." One topic to which the *Budget* addressed itself was the question of whether or not Negroes should leave the South. Woods was convinced that "the only thing that will bring the desired relief to the 6,500,000 Negro population within the limits of the ex-slave states is to begin a stream of emigration from there into the northwest and the southwest." At the same time, he invited discussion of the question, and articles expressing various opinions were printed in the periodical.[41] Other essays in the *Budget* discussed temperance, the education of ministers, unity and organization among Negroes, and the status of Afro-American women. A column en-

titled "Our Afro-American Women and Children" was edited by
Adah M. Taylor. Woods was active in national black organizations and promoted them in the periodical. In January, 1890, he
attended the first convention of the National Afro-American
League in Chicago. The enterprising Woods took his publication
to the meeting and distributed "a few hundred copies gratis."[42]
The February issue of the magazine carried the constitution of
the league and the address given at the convention by T. Timothy Fortune, one of the organizers.

The *Future State* was published in Kansas City, Missouri, during the 1890s. This publication was initiated in 1891 as a weekly
newspaper, but after a few years it was changed to a magazine,
described by its promoters as "a monthly journal of Negro progress" and "the only periodical in the world presenting the opinions of the leading journals upon the Negro."[43] As a monthly, the
Future State was edited by Carrie A. Bannister and Ernest D.
Lynwood. In the March/April, 1895, issue, the excerpts from other
publications were mainly eulogies for Frederick Douglass. This
issue also included articles by John E. Bruce and Alice Ruth
Moore (who later married Paul Laurence Dunbar).

The *Paul Jones Monthly Magazine* began publication in October, 1907, in Topeka, Kansas. George S. Oliver was president of
the publishing company, and Paul Jones was the editor and general manager. The periodical welcomed contributions from white
and Negro authors, and a sampling of articles indicates the general tenor of the contents: "College Training a Business Handi-
cap," "Copy the Virtues and Not the Vices of Great Men," "Don't
Pretend To Be Richer than You Are," "Be Wise and You Will Be
Good," and "Get Up and Do Things Early; No Success Goes to
Lazy Man."

An editorial in the November, 1907, issue stated that the periodical was being received quite favorably by the public: "We are
sincerely and profoundly grateful to our white and colored friends
for their many expressions of good will and congratulations. . . .
Such universal expressions of appreciation by the learned and intelligent white people tend to prove indisputably that there is

nothing to the much discussed and so-called 'race problem.' The Negro who does something worthy and meritorious is seldom, if ever confronted with the 'race problem.'" This editorial ended, however, on an ambivalent note: "Of course, there can be no disputing of the fact that there is a great racial prejudice against the Negro in this country."[44] During the election year of 1908, the magazine supported William Jennings Bryan for president and also promoted candidates for state and local offices; Bryan's portrait was the frontispiece in both the September and October issues. The *Paul Jones Monthly Magazine* continued to be published, although irregularly, as late as 1936, and it continued to devote much of its space to the endorsement of political candidates.

The *Colored American Journal* began publication in 1882 at Palestine, Texas, with C. W. Porter as editor. This monthly was issued by a group of individuals who had formed a stock company. The corresponding editor was Hightower T. Kealing, president of Paul Quinn College in nearby Waco, who, fourteen years later, became editor of the *A. M. E. Church Review*. The *Colored American Journal* was devoted to "education, morality, and homesteading." The attitude of the periodical toward politics was indicated by a quotation printed on the front page: "Political Parties have their records; some dark transactions which the unnumbered ages of eternity will not blot out. Therefore, we eschew the evils thereof."[45]

During the late nineteenth and early twentieth centuries, S. Douglass Russell, an A. M. E. minister, issued a succession of newspapers and periodicals in the southwestern region of the country, first in Texas and then in Oklahoma. Russell was also active in civic and political affairs. After moving from Texas into the Oklahoma Territory in the early 1890s, he promoted the migration of Negroes into that area and encouraged them to take advantage of the federal homesteading opportunities. In 1906, when the territory was preparing for admission into the Union, Russell became head of an association organized by Negroes to protect their interests in the upcoming constitutional convention.[46]

The periodicals that Russell issued were the *Living Age* and *Russell's Review*. Copies of these magazines have not been located, and their history can be conjectured only from information in contemporary sources. The *Living Age* was initiated by Russell and E. H. Garland in Denison, Texas, in 1891. No record of its publication has been found for the years between 1893 and 1903; it is possible that during this period the *Living Age* was replaced by *Russell's Review*, which was established in 1898. Russell and his son issued the *Review* in the Oklahoma Territory, first in Kingfisher and later in Guthrie. In 1904 Russell revived the *Living Age*. At that time he was residing in Langston, an all-Negro community in the Oklahoma Territory. Within a year, the periodical was converted to a weekly newspaper, the *Western Age*.[47]

A. M. E. Church Review

In 1909 the *A. M. E. Church Review* celebrated its twenty-fifth year of publication. No other magazine published or edited by black persons in the United States had reached that milestone before. This periodical had been initiated by the 1884 General Conference of the African Methodist Episcopal Church, and only a few weeks after the conference ended the first issue of the *A. M. E. Church Review* appeared, dated July, 1884. From 1884 through 1909 the *Review* was published quarterly without interruption. During these twenty-five years, three men served as the editors: Benjamin Tucker Tanner (July, 1884–April, 1888), Levi Jenkins Coppin (July, 1888–April, 1896), and Hightower T. Kealing (July, 1896–April, 1912). The *Review* continued to be published regularly, and it is still issued today. The periodical began publication in Philadelphia, under the management of the A. M. E. Book Concern, and in 1908 was transferred to the Sunday School Union of the A. M. E. Church in Nashville, Tennessee.

In the anniversary issue of April, 1909, Tanner gave his recollections of the founding of the magazine. "For sixteen years we had edited the Recorder," he recalled, "and with others we had become thoroughly acquainted with the intellectual growth of our people, and were of the opinion that the time had fully come for the Church to have a Review or Magazine." In the first issue of the *Review*, Tanner had stated that the objective of the publication was to provide an outlet for Negro scholars "of the A. M. E. Church, . . . of the country, of the West Indies, of Africa and of the world."[48]

Tanner's successors reaffirmed this statement of purpose. In 1889 Coppin wrote: "While our Review is published under the auspices of the A. M. E. Church, it is nonsectarian in its purpose. The intent from the beginning was to produce a periodical that would give to the world the best thoughts of the race, irrespective of religious persuasion or political opinion. There has not been any departure from this rule." In 1908 Kealing wrote: "The *Review* was never started as a financial venture or investment, but because the A. M. E. Church realized that its mission to our race was one of mental, moral and religious uplift, and, in the opinion of our leaders and fathers, a magazine of the highest class . . . was the proper agency to do this work. . . . They had still another purpose. It was so to act and react upon the public opinion of the nation and the world that the real ability of a discredited race might be shown and its rights conceded."[49]

Although the *Review* remained constant in its objectives, the personalities and interests of the editors produced distinctive characteristics in the periodical during the years between 1884 and 1909. Benjamin Tucker Tanner (1835–1923), the first editor, was born in Pittsburgh. After receiving his education at Avery College and the Western Theological Seminary in Allegheny, Pennsylvania, he served as pastor of churches in Maryland and the District of Columbia. In 1868 Tanner became editor of the *Christian Recorder*, the weekly newspaper of the A. M. E. Church; he edited this publication until 1884, when he was elected editor of the new quarterly review. Four years later, Tanner was elected bishop. He retired as bishop in 1908 and lived in Philadelphia until his death.[50]

In the first issue of the *A. M. E. Church Review*, Tanner presented feature articles, biography, and poetry from a number of contributors, followed by the columns that he wrote himself. In his editorial section, Tanner dealt with secular matters affecting the Negro, as well as with ecclesiastical topics. In his literary section, he reviewed books on religion and theology, publications by and about black people in the United States and other countries, the current literary magazines, and the religious periodicals of all denominations. This pattern continued throughout Tanner's tenure: the magazine consisted of contributed articles on a variety of subjects; poetry (sometimes written by the editor himself); biography; and Tanner's comments on religious matters, current literature, and the events of the day. An article in the twenty-fifth anniversary number of the *Review* characterized Tanner in this manner: "As a writer his style is crisp, nervous and unadorned: his sentences are so sparing of words sometimes that they are not even skeletons, for a perfect skeleton has all of its bones; but many of Dr. Tanner's lack some of the bones, putting upon the reader the presumption often of knowing more than he does. This is always the fault of a bookish man. It makes him hard to read, but the more worth reading." This commentator pointed out that in the many books Tanner had written, he always showed "great reverence for authority," with "all his declarations backed up by liberal quotations from other authors."[51]

When the 1888 General Conference elected Tanner as bishop, Levi Jenkins Coppin was chosen to succeed him as editor of the *Review*. Coppin (1848–1924) was born of free parents in Fredericktown, Maryland. In 1887 he graduated from the Protestant Episcopal Divinity School in Philadelphia, then served as pastor of churches in Pennsylvania and Maryand, including the Mother Bethel Church in Philadelphia. Coppin was an unsuccessful candidate for bishop in 1896, but in 1900 he was elected to this office and became resident bishop of South Africa for four years. He later presided over several other districts.[52]

Coppin continued the same general pattern in the *Review* that Tanner had established, but he added a new feature by introducing short stories and serialized fiction. In presenting this type of literature, Coppin stated that it was his "constant aim to make the

Review a popular journal for the whole people." The article on Coppin in the anniversary issue observed that "his is a naturally philosophic cast of mind, and seeks always to give a reason for the faith that is in him. One therefore, might look often in vain for poetry in the editorial section of the magazine, but never in vain for thoughtful, suggestive, reliable, (unvarnished often) utterances of a man of strong convictions, and the courage necessary to express them 'in language understandable of the people.' "[53]

Hightower T. Kealing was the first lay person to edit the *A. M. E. Church Review*. He was elected to that position in 1896, when Coppin became a candidate for bishop. A native of Austin, Texas, Kealing graduated from Tabor College in Iowa in 1881. Returning to Texas, he worked in public schools and A. M. E.-sponsored institutions, serving as principal of Paul Quinn College in Waco, assistant principal of the state college at Prairie View, and supervisor of colored schools in Austin. In 1910 Kealing became president of Western University in Quindaro, Kansas. He relinquished the editorship of the *Review* in 1912 to devote full time to that institution.[54]

During Kealing's editorship, a number of changes took place in the *Review*. Kealing wrote many of the feature essays himself, and fewer contributed articles were published. The editorial section was expanded in length and in the variety of topics discussed; but less space was given to reviews of current literature. Poetry, fiction, and biography continued to be carried; but emphasis was placed on new sections designed primarily for information and assistance to the clergy. As an educator, Kealing was concerned with improving the preparation of ministers for their responsibilities. In the twenty-fifth anniversary number of the *Review*, this critique of him was given: "Prof. Kealing's style is effective, somewhat given to over-illustration; while his range of editorials covers all the subjects of general interest, from religion to the affairs that make up the every day life of the masses. He is conservative, but fixed in his opinions and never shows bitterness in the discussion of any question, feeling that right is never advanced by it and wrong intensified by it."[55]

In 1903 Kealing initiated a section on church architecture, which presented descriptive articles on specific churches accompanied by plans and illustrations. He pointed out that this series would include the "most costly cathedral-like buildings and the smaller ones as well, so that . . . others intending to build can be guided and, in large measure, save the expense of an architect's drawings."[56] That same year the *Review* began a series on the topic "What Is Good Preaching?" These essays were written by laymen and clergymen in order to give the viewpoint of both listeners and speakers. The most extensive feature established in the *Review* for the clergy was the "Disciplinary Course of Study," which was a correspondence course in the studies outlined by the church discipline for ministers entering the itinerant service of the denomination.

In the article that Coppin wrote for the anniversary number, he pointed out that the *Review* had given many beginning writers an outlet for their talent, an opportunity they otherwise might not have had. In addition, Coppin noted, "some of the ablest men and women of the race have availed themselves of the chance to speak for themselves and for their people."[57] A survey of the authors in the first twenty-five years of the *A. M. E. Church Review* confirms that this periodical did have an impressive roster of contributors. Among the most frequent writers (in addition to the editors) were Timothy Thomas Fortune, David Augustus Straker, James Theodore Holly, Frances Ellen Watkins Harper, Theophilus G. Steward, and Edward Wilmot Blyden. These persons appeared in volumes issued by all of the three editors. In the early years, William S. Scarborough and Frederick Douglass were also frequent contributors. During Kealing's tenure, the most prolific writers were Richard R. Wright, Jr., and Reverdy Cassius Ransom (who succeeded Kealing as editor). Both Tanner and Coppin continued to write for the *Review* after their editorship ended.

During the beginning years, many other well-known writers appeared in the *Review*: Blanche K. Bruce, Francis L. Cardoza, John W. Cromwell, Alexander Crummell, George T. Downing,

John Mercer Langston, John R. Lynch, John Willis Menard, P. B. S. Pinchback, George L. Ruffin, and William Still. Although many of these individuals were represented by only one article, their names enhanced the periodical and helped to establish its reputation. In later years, new names began to appear, people who were just coming into prominence: educators Fanny Jackson Coppin (wife of the editor), William Pickens, Booker T. Washington, Josephine Silone Yates, and Leslie Pinckney Hill; physicians Nathan F. Mossell, Charles V. Roman, and Daniel Hale Williams; women's leaders Ida Wells Barnett, Mary Church Terrell, and Fannie Barrier Williams; and lawyers Charles W. Chesnutt, John Stephens Durham, Archibald Grimké, Judson Whitlocke Lyons, George H. White, and S. Laing Williams. Throughout the first twenty-five years of publication, clergymen from other denominations contributed to the *A. M. E. Church Review*: Presbyterians Matthew W. Anderson and Francis J. Grimké; Baptists Edward M. Brawley, Walter H. Brooks, Elias Camp Morris, Rufus L. Perry, and William J. Simmons; Protestant Episcopal clergymen George F. Bragg, Jr., and James Theodore Holly; African Methodist Episcopal Zion bishops George L. Blackwell, George W. Clinton, James W. Hood, and Alexander Walters; and Colored Methodist Episcopal bishop Lucius H. Holsey.

The *A. M. E. Church Review* became a forum for the discussion of a wide range of subjects pertaining not only to religion but also to political, economic, and educational affairs. The *Review* presented essays on such topics as the attitude of organized labor toward the Negro worker, the disfranchisement of Negroes, and the growing pattern of racial segregation in American society. In the area of education, articles dealt with vocational versus higher education, separate versus racially mixed schools, Negro versus white teachers for black students, the advantages and disadvantages of coeducation, and federal aid to public education. Among religious matters of special concern was the question of whether or not women should be ordained for the ministry.[58]

Two special issues of the periodical under Tanner's editorship

presented symposia on the attitude of the black American toward
Africa and on the Democratic party's return to national power in
1884. Coppin issued memorial numbers for Bishop Daniel A.
Payne and Frederick Douglass. Among the special issues published by Kealing were the "Twentieth Century Number" of
January, 1901, in which the main contributors were women; and
the "National Number" of October, 1904, which focused on the
coming election. Kealing reminded his readers that "the management of this magazine has never forgotten that its mission is civic
and social as well as religious, and has never failed to point the
way of duty in temporal affairs while emphasizing spiritual."[59]

The *Review* was also interested in creative writing and artistic
endeavor among Negroes. It printed fiction by Victoria Earle
Matthews, Alice Ruth Moore, Frank J. Webb, Jr., and Katherine
Davis Tillman. Many writers contributed poetry, among them
Frances Ellen Watkins Harper, Albery Allson Whitman, Paul
Laurence Dunbar, James Edwin Campbell, Alice Ruth Moore,
John Willis Menard, T. Thomas Fortune, Benjamin T. Tanner,
Gertrude (Mrs. Nathan F.) Mossell, Molly E. Lambert, and Hen-
rietta Cordelia Ray. Music and art were represented by contri-
butions from Samuel Coleridge-Taylor, Madame E. Azalia Hack-
ley, Henry O. Tanner (the editor's son), and May Howard Jackson.

When the *A. M. E. Church Review* was launched in 1884,
Bishop Henry McNeal Turner wrote to editor Tanner, compli-
menting and encouraging him in this new journalistic enterprise.
In the letter, Turner expressed these thoughts: "The literature of
the world is the history of the world, call its different branches by
whatever name you please; and a people, race, country or Church
that has no history has no literature, and where there is no literature there is no development, progress or respectability. The
world knows nothing of their worth, because it knows nothing of
their history. . . . Our words and ideas must be carried, conveyed,
conducted."[60] The *A. M. E. Church Review* became the conveyor
of Negro thought, scholarship, and creative writing, and as a general periodical it performed this function for many years.

Southland

In 1890, two North Carolina educators combined their literary interests to bring forth the first general periodical published in the South by Afro-Americans. The two educators were Joseph Charles Price and Simon Green Atkins, president and teacher at Livingstone College in Salisbury. The periodical was the *Southland*, which they inaugurated in February of that year. In the magazine, Price was designated as the founder and Atkins as the editor.

Joseph Charles Price (1854–93), a native of Elizabeth City, became a schoolteacher when he was seventeen years old. A few years later, he decided to enter the ministry and went to Lincoln University in Pennsylvania for his training, graduating from the theological department in 1881. That summer Price attended the first Methodist Ecumenical Conference in London as a delegate from the African Methodist Episcopal Zion Church. He remained in England for one year to solicit funds for the Zion Wesley Institute, a newly established A. M. E. Zion school in Concord, North Carolina. When he returned home, Price was chosen president of the institute, which was moved to Salisbury and renamed Livingstone College. The school developed rapidly under Price's administration, and he became widely known and respected as a gifted orator and preacher, an outstanding educator, and a leader in the fight for civil rights. In 1890, he was elected head of two national Negro organizations formed that year: the National Afro-American League, organized in Chicago by a group of the younger leaders; and the American Citizens' Equal Rights Association, established in Washington by members of the "Old Guard." Price had before him a promising career, but he died at the age of thirty-nine, a victim of Bright's disease.[61]

Simon Green Atkins (1863–1934) was born in Haywood and grew up on a farm where his parents lived and worked. Like Price, he began to teach while still in his teens and then returned to school for further education. After Atkins graduated from the

Simon Green Atkins, editor of the *Southland*.
From Daniel W. Culp, *Twentieth-Century Negro Literature* (Naperville, Ill.: J. L. Nichols and Co., 1902).

Saint Augustine's Normal Collegiate Institute in Raleigh, Price employed him to take charge of the grammar school department at Livingstone. Atkins worked there for six years, serving the last two years as treasurer of the institution. He then accepted appointment as principal of the public school for Negroes in Winston (later Winston-Salem).[62]

While performing his duties at the public school, Atkins was also spearheading other activities. Realizing the importance of a good home and community environment in the education of young people, he started the Columbian Heights residential area and moved his own family into this new settlement. Atkins was founder and president of the Slater Industrial Academy that opened in the community in 1892; in 1895 he resigned from the city school system to devote full time to that institution. He developed it into a state normal school which, in 1925, was given a new charter under the name Winston-Salem Teachers College. Atkins continued as president of the school until the spring of 1934, when he resigned because of illness.

Atkins was one of the founders of the North Carolina State

Teachers' Association, organized in the early 1880s, and he was elected several times as president and as secretary. He was co-editor of the association's first periodical, the *Progressive Educator*, and also participated in the educational affairs of his church. When the A. M. E. Zion Church established an education department in 1892, he was chosen as the general secretary of education and served in this capacity for a number of years. He attended three of the Methodist Ecumenical Conferences (which were held every ten years)—in London in 1901, in Toronto in 1911, and in London again in 1921. In a speech delivered at the 1901 conference, Atkins expressed his views on education and the relationship of education to religion: "We want to educate the people for service rather than for success. We are not opposing industrial education; we believe in it. . . . But the tendency in the advocacy of purely industrial education for the Negro is to carry him into materialism. . . . We believe that whatever education is given him ought to comprehend his heart training, his intellectual training, and prepare him to be a brother among the people."[63]

The *Southland* was issued during 1890 and 1891. When Atkins changed jobs, the site of publication moved from Salisbury to Winston. Initiated as a monthly, the *Southland* became a quarterly publication in 1891. For a brief period Charles N. Grandison, president of Bennett College, was the business manager. The motto of the periodical was "Not the Old South nor the New South, but the Southland as it is and ought to be." The lead editorial in the first issue explained that the *Southland* was "not so much a combatant as a vindicator of truth and justice," concerned with every aspect of southern life, "whether educational, literary, social, political or otherwise." The philosophy of the *Southland* was that "the Negro must above all things have patience and hope" and that "the white people of the South must be led to see in the light of Christianity . . . that it is to the interest of all concerned to measure and regard all men according to the rules of justice and humanity." "This is no challenge," asserted the *Southland*. "It is only the voice of conciliation and an echo of the doctrine of the brotherhood of man."[64]

Other editorials in this first issue addressed a variety of topics, including the projected National Colored Chautauqua, debates in Congress relating to the migration of Negroes from the South, and the initial meeting of the National Afro-American League. The league's statement of principles was also printed in that issue. One of the regular sections of the *Southland* was the "Voice of the Press," which reprinted excerpts concerning race relations from white newspapers and periodicals. The *Southland* also had a book review section which presented critical discussion of current publications. All the content of the *Southland*, even the occasional poetry (such as Frances E. W. Harper's "A Rallying Cry"), was of serious import. Fiction was not included, and the feature articles dealt with the problems of the day.

Atkins called upon his former schoolteacher, Mrs. Anna Julia Cooper, to edit the woman's section. Mrs. Cooper (1859–1964), a native of Raleigh, earned a bachelor's degree and a master's degree from Oberlin College during the 1880s. Many years later, she studied abroad and earned the doctor of philosophy degree at the Sorbonne, University of Paris, in 1925. A teacher of classical and modern languages, she held positions at Wilberforce University, Saint Augustine's College, Lincoln University (Missouri), and in the District of Columbia school system. For twenty-five years Mrs. Cooper helped to build the reputation of the M Street High School (later Dunbar High School), first as principal and then as a teacher. Following retirement from the public school system, she conducted an adult education school in the spacious quarters of her Washington home. Her book on race relations, *A Voice from the South, by a Black Woman of the South*, was published in 1892.[65]

In accepting the editorship of the woman's section of the *Southland*, Mrs. Cooper noted that she was taking on a herculean task. In her initial column, she observed that fifty years earlier the area of women's activities had been "a pretty clearly defined 'sphere,' including, primarily, the kitchen and nursery and graced by the pre-eminently 'womanly' avocations of darning, knitting, sewing on buttons and painting on every discoverable bit of china and canvas, forlorn looking cranes balanced idiotically on one foot." She pointed out that the scope of a woman's section in a magazine had broadened and deepened: "No woman can afford to put herself or her sex outside any of the interests that affect humanity. *All* departments are hers, in the sense that her interests are in all and through all, and it is incumbent on her to keep intelligently informed of all the great movements of the times, that she may know on which side to throw the weight of her influence." In one column discussing the need for higher education for women, Mrs. Cooper made this appeal:

> We might as well expect to grow trees from leaves as hope to build up a civilization or a manhood without taking into consideration our women and the home life made by them, which must be the root and ground of the whole matter. Let us insist then on special encouragement for the education of our women and special care in their training. . . . To be plain, I mean let money be raised and scholarships be founded in our colleges and universities for self-supporting, worthy young women, to offset and balance the aid that can always be found for boys who will take theology. . . . Let us then, here and now, recognize this force and resolve to make the most of it—not the boys less, but the girls more.[66]

Education in general was a major concern of the *Southland*. Two issues were devoted to the American Association of Educators of Colored Youth. This interracial body was organized in 1890, following a call issued by a group of Howard University alumni. James Monroe Gregory, dean of the college department at Howard, was elected president, Atkins was the secretary, and Price served on the board of directors. The *Southland* printed the text of the organization's constitution, a listing of the officers, condensed proceedings of the annual meetings, and papers given at these sessions. Among the speeches included were those of President Horace Bumstead of Atlanta University; President Jeremiah E. Rankin of Howard University; and William S. Scarborough and Kelly Miller, who were teachers at Wilberforce and Howard.

The *Southland* was also interested in national politics and its impact upon developments in the South. In May, 1890, the peri-

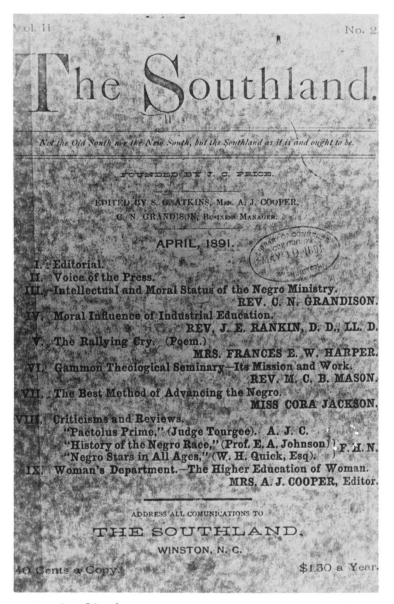

Vol. II   No. 2

The Southland.

Not the Old South nor the New South, but the Southland as it is and ought to be.

FOUNDED BY J. C. PRICE.

EDITED BY S. G. ATKINS, Mrs. A. J. COOPER.
C. N. GRANDISON, Business Manager.

APRIL, 1891.

I. Editorial.
II. Voice of the Press.
III. Intellectual and Moral Status of the Negro Ministry.
　　　　　　　　　　　　　　REV. C. N. GRANDISON.
IV. Moral Influence of Industrial Education.
　　　　　　　　　　　REV. J. E. RANKIN, D. D., LL. D.
V. The Rallying Cry. (Poem.)
　　　　　　　　　　　MRS. FRANCES E. W. HARPER.
VI. Gammon Theological Seminary—Its Mission and Work.
　　　　　　　　　　　　　　REV. M. C. B. MASON.
VII. The Best Method of Advancing the Negro.
　　　　　　　　　　　　　　MISS CORA JACKSON.
VIII. Criticisms and Reviews.
　　　"Pactolus Prime," (Judge Tourgee). A. J. C.
　　　"History of the Negro Race," (Prof. E. A. Johnson) } F. H. N.
　　　"Negro Stars in All Ages," (W. H. Quick, Esq).
IX. Woman's Department.—The Higher Education of Woman.
　　　　　　　　　　　MRS. A. J. COOPER, Editor.

ADDRESS ALL COMUNICATIONS TO

THE SOUTHLAND,

WINSTON, N. C.

40 Cents a Copy. $1.50 a Year.

Southland

Courtesy Library of Congress

odical presented a symposium on the question of dividing the Negro vote between the Republican and Democratic parties. Two of the persons contributing to this discussion were John R. Lynch, former U.S. Congressman from Mississippi and frequent delegate to the Republican national conventions; and John Mitchell, Jr., aggressive editor of the Richmond (Virginia) *Planet*. Both appealed for solid support of the Republican party. Lynch, speaking out of party loyalty, charged that "the Democratic party represents the sentiments and civilization, which insist that this is a white man's government, and that the colored people are here by sufferance and not by right." Therefore, Lynch argued, Negroes were obliged to remain in the Republican party "in self-defense . . . although thousands of them may not be in accord with that party on questions of policy and administration."

Mitchell, reasoning from nonpartisan logic, reminded Negroes that "history furnishes no record where any people who were contending for vital principles . . . ever succeeded in their endeavors by dividing before the object for which they were laboring had been accomplished." He pointed out that a trade union, for example, would look askance upon the person who, "when a great strike was pending, would advise one half of the organization to go over to the capitalists as the best means of accomplishing their purposes."[67] In this symposium, a different point of view was expressed by William Harvey Goler (who succeeded Price as president of Livingstone College). Goler advocated division of the Negro vote between Republican and Democratic parties; he believed that the Democratic South was not entirely prejudiced and that Negroes would benefit by giving some support to that party.

The *Southland* was established because its promoters believed that black and white people in the South could live and work together in mutual respect. The periodical appealed for the practice of a true Christian brotherhood: "It is to the interest of all concerned to measure and regard all men according to the rules of justice and humanity held sacred and inviolable among all enlightened Christian peoples from time immemorial. . . . The conscience of civilized and Christian mankind must not be permitted, if possible, to falter or dally."[68]

Colored American Magazine

In 1900, a group of young men in Boston founded the *Colored American Magazine* and organized a stock company, the Colored Co-operative Publishing Company, to issue it. Their venture soon met with financial difficulties. One year after the magazine began, the faltering enterprise was reorganized with support from some of the older established residents of Boston, but it was still unable to become a solvent publication. In 1904, Booker T. Washington took an active interest in the periodical, and, through his guidance and financial intervention, the publication moved to New York City under new management. In 1909, after Washington withdrew his subsidy, the *Colored American Magazine* ceased publication.[69]

The organizer and first president of the Colored Co-operative Publishing Company was Walter W. Wallace, who also served as managing editor. During the first year of operation, Walter A. Johnson was vice-president and advertising manager, Jesse W. Watkins the secretary, Harper S. Fortune the treasurer, and Peter B. Gibson the soliciting agent. Most of these young men had been born in Virginia in the 1870s and had migrated to Boston during the 1890s. Wallace was from Boydton, Virginia, had attended the Leonard Medical College of Shaw University, and was employed as a prescription clerk in a Boston drugstore. Fortune, a native of Richmond, moved North to study music. Johnson came from Norfolk and was working at a publishing house in Boston while attending the public evening schools. Watkins, from Chesterfield County, was also enrolled in the evening schools. He was investing in real estate and supported his family by doing electrical work. Another young man living in Boston, J. Alexandre Skeete, was appointed staff artist for the magazine. A native of British Guiana, Skeete had studied at the Cowles Art School

Pauline Elizabeth Hopkins, editor and writer for
the *Colored American Magazine*
Courtesy Trevor Arnett Library, Atlanta University

in Boston and after graduation had gone abroad for further training.[70]

Two other Boston residents also became associated with the *Colored American Magazine*: Pauline Elizabeth Hopkins and William Stanley Braithwaite. Pauline Hopkins (1859–1930) was born in Portland, Maine, but she was "raised a Boston girl, educated in the Boston public schools, and finally graduated from the famous Girls' High School of that city."[71] During the 1880s she appeared as a soprano vocalist in performances with her family, the Hopkins Colored Troubadours. The repertoire of the group included a musical drama that she had written.[72] Her early ambition was to be a playwright, but later she turned to nonfiction, short stories, and novels. Originally appointed to the staff of the *Colored American Magazine* to edit the woman's section, Pauline Hopkins immediately became the main writer in the periodical, contributing both fiction and nonfiction. In 1903 she was named literary editor, replacing Wallace as chief editor of the magazine.

William Stanley Braithwaite (1878–1962) was a native of Boston. He was self-educated, having acquired his literary background largely from the resources of the Boston Public Library, where he was a constant reader, and the Ginn and Company publishers, where he was employed as a typesetter. Braithwaite eventually achieved national recognition as a literary critic, lyric poet, and anthologist. When the *Colored American Magazine* started publication, his writings were just beginning to appear in the Boston newspapers, and the promoters of the magazine, recognizing his "inherent, critical ability as a talented young student of letters," engaged him as book review editor.[73]

Many years later, reminiscing about the history of the *Colored American Magazine*, Braithwaite wrote that young Wallace "dreamed of a general magazine that would publish the creative works of Negro writers together with informative articles which would record the Negro's progress in intellectual, social and political ideals. Wallace made no pretensions to either literary or journalistic ability. He was simply possessed of a burning aspiration and it drove him relentlessly into action."[74] Braithwaite recounted that Wallace and his associates, realizing that they lacked the technical skills to produce a magazine, secured the services of R. S. Elliott, a white man who resigned from the Lothrop, Lee and Shepard publishing firm to join them.

At Elliott's suggestion, the company also began to publish books, among them Pauline Hopkins' novel *Contending Forces*. This additional activity depleted the resources of the business, and in 1901 Wallace wrote to Booker T. Washington, requesting financial aid. In this confidential letter, Wallace stated: "We have dabbled in the publishing of books (an expensive luxury) from the surplus proceeds of the magazine to such an extent that we find the summer dullness upon us with no sinking fund to meet increased expense." Wallace also confided to Washington that the periodical was suffering from the slow sale of stock shares in the company and from delayed remittances from subscription agents around the country.[75] At this point, though, it was not Booker T. Washington but residents of Boston who came to the rescue of the magazine, chiefly William H. Dupree, John F. Ransom, and William O. West.

Dupree was a well-known citizen who held a high administrative office in the postal service in Boston and "possessed substantial means and an established credit."[76] Like Wallace, he was a Virginian by birth, but thirty-five years older. He was born in Petersburg in 1839 and grew up in Chillicothe, Ohio. During the Civil War, Dupree enlisted in a Massachusetts regiment of Negro volunteers. After the war, he settled in Boston and became a leader in civic organizations and a patron of musical activities.[77] John F. Ransom was also a Virginian by birth. He was educated at Oberlin College and participated in church and collegiate choral groups in Ohio. Moving to Boston in the 1870s, he continued his musical studies and became a music instructor in that city.[78] William O. West was born in Lynn, Massachusetts, in 1859. After attending public schools, he worked as a partner in his father's business, then moved to Boston in 1902.[79]

Braithwaite recalled the difficulties that Dupree encountered as president of the Colored Co-operative Publishing Company:

> Even though literature and journalism were beyond the scope of his personal interest and knowledge, he felt it his duty to back the ambitions of young Negroes who were blazing new trails to success. Between a temperamental editor in Miss Hopkins, the quiet but effective work of Elliott to shape the policies and purposes of the enterprise to insure the largest measure of personal benefits, and the insistent efforts of Wallace, the founder, Col. Dupree had on his hands a set of irreconcilable elements which his practical nature strove to fortify against the doubters and carpers who had been prophetic of its collapse.[80]

Dupree's efforts could not sustain the periodical. Eventually, with the purchase of shares in the publishing company by John C. Freund and Frederick Randolph Moore, the *Colored American Magazine* came under the controlling influence of Booker T. Washington.

By the early part of 1904, Freund, a white newspaper and music publisher in New York City, had obtained a financial interest in the periodical. By May of that year, Moore had purchased the stock held by Dupree and West. He relocated the magazine in New York City and organized the Moore Publishing and Printing Company. Pauline Hopkins and Jesse Watkins remained with the periodical when it first moved to New York, but only until that September.[81] Moore continued to publish and manage the *Colored American Magazine* until it went out of existence in 1909. Two persons who assisted him with the editing were Roscoe Conkling Simmons, associate editor from the fall of 1904 until 1906, and George W. Harris, editor of the last issues, from May to November, 1909.

Fred R. Moore was secretary and national organizer for the National Negro Business League, which Washington had founded in 1900. Moore, born in Virginia in 1857, spent most of his life in Washington, D.C., where he worked for many years as a messenger in the Treasury Department, and in New York, where he was involved in real estate, banking enterprises, journalism, and politics. He became editor and part owner of T. Thomas Fortune's New York *Age* newspaper when Washington gained control of the publication in 1907 and continued to edit and publish this paper until his death in 1943. During the 1920s he was elected twice to the New York City Board of Aldermen. He was also one of the founders of the organization that became the National Urban League.[82]

Roscoe Conkling Simmons (1875?–1951) was the nephew of Washington's wife, Margaret Murray Washington. He was Washington's protégé but worked only briefly with the *Colored American Magazine*, resigning after misunderstandings with Moore. Later he joined the staff of the Chicago *Defender* and also wrote for white newspapers in that city. A gifted orator, Simmons was active in the Republican presidential campaigns during the 1920s and 1930s.[83] George W. Harris (1884–1948), a native of Kansas, graduated from Harvard College in 1907. After attending Harvard Law School for a year or two, he became a newspaper editor and a politician in New York City, where he was a member of

Colored American Magazine
Courtesy Moorland-Spingarn Research Center, Howard University

the Board of Aldermen from 1920 to 1924. Harris also worked for Washington in the National Negro Business League.[84]

The differences in the talents and interests of the individuals who edited the *Colored American Magazine* in Boston and in New York resulted in a periodical of contrasts during these two phases of publication. The contrasts were evident in the philosophy and purpose of the magazine, in the contents and contributors, and in the organizations that the periodical supported. The scope projected for the *Colored American Magazine* when it began publication was indicated by the subtitle: *An Illustrated Monthly Devoted to Literature, Science, Music, Art, Religion, Facts, Fiction and Traditions of the Negro Race; A Co-operative Journal by Prominent Negro Statesmen, Scientists and Teachers, Together with Other Celebrated Authors.* During the first four years, under the editorial charge of Walter Wallace and Pauline Hopkins in Boston, the *Colored American Magazine* was primarily a literary periodical. It featured short stories, serialized novels, poetry, and book reviews; it also devoted much space to series of articles on history, biography, and travel.

During these years, a major portion of the contents was written by Pauline Hopkins. Three novels by her—*Hagar's Daughter, Winona*, and *Of One Blood; or, The Hidden Self*—were serialized in the magazine. *Hagar's Daughter* was written under the pen name "Sarah A. Allen," which was her mother's maiden name. Numerous short stories by Pauline Hopkins also appeared in the periodical. In addition, she was the author of four biographical series: "Famous Men of the Negro Race," "Famous Women of the Negro Race," "Heroes and Heroines in Black," and "Reminiscences of the Life and Times of Lydia Maria Child." William Stanley Braithwaite was also a prolific writer for the *Colored American Magazine* during the Boston period. His contributions included book reviews, lyric poetry, and short stories. Poems were contributed by Benjamin G. Brawley, Edward Elmore Brock, Olivia Ward Bush, James D. Corrothers, Daniel Webster Davis, Augustus M. Hodges, and Azalia Edmonia Martin. Among the nonfiction writers were Cyrus F. Adams, Charles Alexander, Theodora Holly, Alan Kirkland Soga, and David Augustus Straker. Adams, editor of the St. Paul *Appeal* and several times president of the National Afro-American Press Association, wrote a series on the editors of Negro newspapers. Alexander, a newspaper and magazine publisher, contributed book reviews and biographies. Miss Holly, whose father James Theodore Holly was the Protestant Episcopal bishop in Haiti, sent articles about life and customs in that country. The essays by Straker, a Detroit lawyer, dealt with sociological and political problems affecting the Negro. Soga, who edited a native newspaper in East London, South Africa, sent reports describing the oppressive living conditions of black people in that part of the world.

The Boston promoters of the *Colored American Magazine* supported the Constitutional Rights Association of the United States and the Loyal Legion of Labor. The Constitutional Rights Association was based in Richmond, Virginia, with the Reverend J. E. Jones as president and Giles B. Jackson as secretary. The association was campaigning against lynching and raising funds to bring cases that challenged segregation before the U.S. Supreme Court.[85] The Loyal Legion of Labor, with headquarters at Zanesville, Ohio, was a cooperative movement among existing organizations. It was concerned with the improvement of economic conditions as well as the protection of civil rights. Among the officers were Bishop Benjamin W. Arnett of the African Methodist Episcopal Church, the Reverend Lewis G. Jordan of the Baptist denomination, and George H. White, former U.S. Congressman from North Carolina. The Loyal Legion of Labor functioned through an education department, a legal advisory department, and an emigration and industrial department that dealt with problems precipitated by the migration of Negroes from the South into the North.[86]

When Fred R. Moore took over the management of the *Colored American Magazine*, he made this announcement: "It is our purpose to publish a magazine that shall record the doings of the race along material lines, and to demonstrate to mankind generally that we are worthy to have the door of opportunity kept

wide open for us as for other men. . . . The magazine will publish
the news items of the National Negro Business League throughout the country, devoting two pages each month to such work."[87]
Not only in a special news column, but also in Moore's editorials
and in feature articles, the *Colored American Magazine* promoted
the National Business League during the New York period of
publication. Moore denied that Washington owned or controlled
the periodical, but he acknowledged his admiration of Washington and his support of the philosophy that Negroes should try to
improve their status in America through self-help and economic
enterprise.

The Boston *Colored American Magazine* had opened its initial
issue (May, 1900) with a romantic short story. The first issue of
the New York *Colored American Magazine* (June, 1904) opened
with an essay by T. Thomas Fortune entitled: "What a Magazine
Should Be." This article affirmed the new editorial policy of the
periodical. Fortune wrote that in contemporary society "more
stress is laid upon what an individual or nation possesses mate-
rially than what it knows mentally." He admitted that "this is a
rank vulgarism, the exaltation of material values over mental and
moral values, but it has to be reckoned with all over the world."
He concluded that the materialism of the age dictates that a magazine must give priority to "what is being done . . . by individuals
as well as races."[88]

Although Fortune had appeared in the *Colored American Magazine* during the Boston period, he was a much more frequent
contributor of both nonfiction and poetry during Moore's management of the periodical. For a short time, he wrote a monthly
review of national and international affairs under the caption
"Way of the World." A similar feature, "The Month," was later
edited by Edward A. Johnson. Moore's own column, "In the Editor's Sanctum," also commented on political developments and
current events. Other regular departments instituted by Moore
were a column devoted to affairs in Washington, written by
Ralph W. Tyler and later by Edward H. Lawson; departments on
the activities of fraternal orders, edited by Samuel R. Scottron,

E. V. C. Eato, and William Preston Moore; and a section on education, conducted by Josephine Silone Yates. In addition to Mrs. Yates's column, the magazine regularly carried feature articles on educational institutions for Negroes in the South and in the North. Also described in the *Colored American Magazine* were business enterprises owned by Negroes throughout the country. In 1904 a series of essays by eleven well-known persons, white and black, presented views on the subject of industrial education.

Contributions by white persons became a significant part of the *Colored American Magazine* in the latter period of publication. Among these writers were Ray Stannard Baker, John E. Milholland, Mary White Ovington, Robert E. Parks, and William Lloyd Garrison, Jr. Articles reprinted from national magazines were also more numerous, especially in the last year of publication when the periodical was struggling to maintain its existence. The three essays by W. E. B. Du Bois that appeared in this magazine (one in the industrial education series in 1904 and two in 1909) were all reprints. During the New York period, many articles by Booker T. Washington were published. Other contributors included Roscoe Conkling Bruce, Carrie W. Clifford, Addie Waites Hunton, William H. Lewis, Daniel A. P. Murray, Wilford H. Smith, Robert H. Terrell, Ralph W. Tyler, Lester A. Walton, Josephine Turpin Washington (Mrs. S. H. H. Washington), and Fannie Barrier Williams.

After 1904, Pauline Hopkins and William Stanley Braithwaite no longer wrote for the magazine (although a poem read by Braithwaite before the National Medical Association convention in 1909 was printed in the periodical). When Pauline Hopkins left the *Colored American Magazine*, she began to write for the *Voice of the Negro*. Later, in 1916, she again collaborated with Walter Wallace to issue a periodical in Boston, the *New Era Magazine: An Illustrated Monthly Devoted to the World-Wide Interests of the Colored Race*. Between 1912 and 1917, Braithwaite was also active as a magazine editor in Boston. He edited the *Poetry Journal*, the *Poetry Review of America*, and the *Stratford Journal: A Forum of Contemporary International Thought*.

During the New York period, the *Colored American Magazine* frequently carried fiction by Gertrude Dorsey Browne and Ralph W. Tyler and poetry by Dunbar, Fortune, Tyler, and Charles Bertram Johnson. In general, though, belles lettres and book reviews were not as prominent in the periodical under Moore's management as they had been previously. Throughout its publication, however, from 1900 to 1909, the *Colored American Magazine* maintained an interest in musical and artistic endeavors among Negroes. Feature articles were written by and about artists, musicians, and performers who were becoming nationally and internationally known. Critical essays described the work of the painter Henry O. Tanner and the sculptors Edmonia Lewis and Meta Vaux Warrick Fuller. Articles told of the accomplishments of black composers and performers in classical music as well as in musical comedy and vaudeville.

In June, 1900, the *Colored American Magazine* reviewed the New York performance of *Carmen* by Theodore Drury's Grand Opera Company. Harper S. Fortune, the musical editor, reported that it was "the first affair of the kind executed successfully" and that "it was characterized by a high degree of suavity, with a total lack of friction or amateurism."[89] Three years later, the magazine also praised this company's production of *Aïda*. Theodore Drury himself contributed articles on classical music to the periodical. Pauline Hopkins wrote about the talents of vocalists Elizabeth Taylor Greenfield and Madame Marie Selika. An article by Margaret Murray Washington discussed slave songs and the rendition of these songs by the Fisk Jubilee Singers.

Reviews by Lester A. Walton acclaimed the successes of the comedian Ernest Hogan and the Williams and Walker vaudeville team. In 1908 Walton recorded that "Williams and Walker made history by remaining on Broadway, New York, for nearly three months, which was establishing a new record for colored shows." Walton also reported that "while illness prevented Ernest Hogan from working the entire season . . . he established a record of being the only single colored star to play the Grand Opera House, New York." The following year, when Hogan succumbed to tuberculosis, a full-page display in the *Colored American Magazine* announced that "Ernest Hogan, famous throughout America and European theatrical circles as the 'Unbleached American,' is dead."[90] A few years before, an essay of several pages had paid high tribute to this performer:

> Ernest Hogan, the comedian, is more than a comedian—he is an actor of ability, consummate ability.... The thousands who sit under his eyes and the roll of his tongue, feel always that before them is not only an actor, but also a man with a soul of power, a brain of thought, a heart full of love.... In future years, when the earlier history of the race shall be written, Ernest Hogan shall have a secure place as the last of the black-faced comedians and among the first of the Negro actors who made of their epidermis a badge of emotional power and originality.[91]

In an autobiographical article, George Walker traced the story of the Williams and Walker team. While still a young man, Walker left his native state of Kansas and migrated westward. He settled in San Francisco, where he met Egbert Williams. They formed a comedy team and appeared in the vaudeville theaters of that city during the 1890s. Ambitious to play in New York, they succeeded in getting eastern bookings and finally secured a New York City engagement. At that point, Walker related, they decided to break away from the traditional portrayal of the Negro in minstrel shows:

> Black-faced white comedians used to make themselves look as ridiculous as they could when portraying a "darky" character. In their "make-up" they always had tremendously big red lips, and their costumes were frightfully exaggerated. The one fatal result of this to the colored performers was that they imitated the white performers in their make-up as "darkies." Nothing seemed more absurd than to see a colored man making himself ridiculous in order to portray himself. My partner, Mr. Williams, is the first man that I know of our race to attempt to delineate a "darky" in a perfectly natural way, and I think much of his success is due to this fact.[92]

Other musicians and performers who contributed articles to

the *Colored American Magazine* were Bob Cole, Aida Overton Walker, Madame E. Azalia Hackley, and J. Rosamond Johnson. Johnson's essay was an explanation of the new phenomenon of ragtime music, as it was originating and developing among black people at that time:

> Since there is no record or definition in the dictionaries of music of "ragtime" we must then consider the appellation "ragtime" simply a slang name for that peculiarly, distinctive, syncopated rhythm originated by the American Negro. . . .
>
> The happy expressions of the Negro's emotions in music have been dubbed "ragtime," while his more serious musical expressions have been called "plantation" and "jubilee" songs, and these two styles of his expressions in music are all that I can see that is distinctively American music. . . .
>
> The popular ear both white and black likes the "ragtime" song, and just so soon as this peculiar American syncopation is developed into a classic form will the censors of music find a place for "ragtime" in the history of music. Perhaps they may call it con "Raggioso."[93]

The increased coverage that the *Colored American Magazine* gave to popular music during the New York period was one way in which Moore attempted to promote the circulation of the publication. It was his ambition to issue a periodical of interest to everyone rather than to just a select few, and he pointed out that "a magazine which devotes itself to difficult and complicated social problems or which addresses itself merely to those who are highly educated and cultured can not, of course, hope to reach the masses of the people."[94] With a reported circulation of 17,840, the *Colored American Magazine* was the most widely distributed Afro-American periodical before 1909.

Voice of the Negro

In the first decade of the twentieth century, the *Voice of the Negro* was the major Afro-American periodical issued in the South and a leading black periodical in the United States. This monthly magazine began publication in Atlanta, Georgia, in January, 1904. After the Atlanta riot of September, 1906, the periodical was transferred to Chicago, where it was published for one more year. The *Voice of the Negro* was initiated by a white publisher, Austin N. Jenkins, but the editorial and managerial staff and a majority of the contributors were black people. When Jenkins founded the periodical, he was managing the Atlanta office of J. L. Nichols, a subscription books publishing company with headquarters in Naperville, Illinois. This firm and its successor—Hertel, Jenkins and Company—had a Negro book department with a best-seller list that included Booker T. Washington's *Story of My Life and Work*. These publishers advertised that they had issued more books by Negro authors than any other company in America.

Jenkins engaged two persons as editors for the magazine. One of these individuals, John Wesley Edward Bowen, was already living in Atlanta, teaching at Gammon Theological Seminary. The other person, Jesse Max Barber, had just finished college at Virginia Union University in Richmond, where Jenkins had met him in the spring of 1903. Barber came to Atlanta that November. James A. Hopkins, Barber's classmate who had been working as a field agent for the publishing company, also joined the staff of the new publication. Hopkins was the business manager, but he remained with the periodical for only a few months. Later he edited the Atlanta *Age* and operated a bookstore on Auburn Avenue. Four associate editors were listed in the *Voice of the Negro* during the first two years of publication. Three of them were leading clergymen in Atlanta: Peter James Bryant, pastor of the Wheat Street Baptist Church; Henry Hugh Proctor, minister at the First Congregational Church; and Joseph Simeon Flipper, pastor of St. Paul's African Methodist Episcopal Church and, from 1904 to 1908, president of Morris Brown College. Listed as the fourth associate editor in the first eight issues of the periodical was Emmett J. Scott, who was Booker T. Washington's private secretary at Tuskegee Institute.[95]

Bowen and Barber were coeditors of the *Voice of the Negro*, but in the course of publication Barber became, in fact, the principal editor. These two men were a study in contrasts. Bowen (1855–1933) was the elder statesman, Barber (1878–1949) the young neophyte. Bowen, born a slave in New Orleans, eventually earned bachelor of divinity and doctor of philosophy degrees at Boston University. Before coming to Atlanta, he had been a minister and a teacher in Boston, Newark, Baltimore, Washington, and Nashville. He joined the faculty of Gammon Theological Seminary in 1893 and remained with that institution for forty years. During most of this time he was a professor of historical theology; from 1906 until 1910, he was president of Gammon. After the reorganization of Clark University and Gammon Theological Seminary placed the two institutions under a single president, he served for a period as vice-president. The organizations with which Bowen was affiliated included the American Historical Association, the American Negro Academy, and the National Negro Business League.[96] By 1903, when plans for the *Voice of the Negro* were being made, Bowen was widely known as an educator, minister, scholar, lecturer, and author.

In 1903 Barber was just graduating from college. A native of Blackstock, South Carolina, he took a teacher training course at Benedict College in Columbia and then enrolled in Virginia Union University. After receiving the bachelor's degree, he taught school for a few months before coming to Atlanta. At Virginia Union Barber had distinguished himself as a debater, student editor of the school newspaper, and valedictorian of his class,[97] but he was unknown outside his immediate circle when he became editor of the *Voice of the Negro*. After the *Voice* ceased publication in 1907, he was employed for a short while as editor of the Chicago *Conservator*. By 1909 Barber had moved to Philadelphia and enrolled in the dental school at Temple University. Following graduation he opened his office in Philadelphia and continued to practice dentistry in that city until his death. Barber was not actively engaged in journalism after leaving Chicago, although his name was listed in *Crisis* magazine as a contributing editor during the first three years of publication.[98]

Barber affiliated with the militant civil rights organizations of

Jesse Max Barber, editor of the *Voice of the Negro*

Courtesy Trevor Arnett Library, Atlanta University

his time. He was one of the twenty-nine black men who answered W. E. B. Du Bois's call to form the Niagara Movement in 1905, and he was also a member of the Constitutional League, an interracial group of which John E. Milholland was president. When the Georgia Equal Rights Convention met in Macon in 1906, he was one of fourteen persons who signed the convention's address to the public. In 1908 he participated in the organization of the National Negro American Political League, a group led by William Monroe Trotter and Alexander Walters. In 1909 Barber attended the meeting of the National Negro Conference in New York, which preceded the founding of the National Association for the Advancement of Colored People. During the early 1920s he was a member of the national board of directors of the NAACP. He was also an officer in the Philadelphia chapter for a number of years.

Bowen and Barber were able to attract many individuals as regular contributors to the *Voice of the Negro*. A few of these persons were, like Barber, at the beginning of their careers and found in this magazine an appropriate outlet for their developing talents. William Pickens' first article appeared while he was still a senior at Yale University. Benjamin Griffith Brawley was beginning a teaching career at Atlanta Baptist College (later Morehouse College), the school from which he had just graduated. William Stanley Braithwaite, a self-educated young man, was launching a literary career in his native city of Boston. However, most of the contributors were, like Bowen, in the prime of life and had already established their reputations by the turn of the century. John E. Bruce and T. Thomas Fortune had made their names in journalism. W. E. B. Du Bois, William S. Scarborough, and Kelly Miller had distinguished themselves in the academic world—Du Bois at Atlanta University, Scarborough at Wilberforce, and Miller at Howard. Mary Church Terrell and Fannie Barrier Williams were well known as lecturers, essayists, and promoters of the women's club movement. These and other contributors had achieved recognition in their chosen endeavors by 1900 and thus lent stature to the new periodical.

The *Voice of the Negro* was issued in Atlanta from January, 1904, through September, 1906. During the summer of 1906, certain circumstances brought about changes in its publication. The editors of the *Voice* were being criticized by other black journalists for working with a periodical owned and financed by white people. Prominent among the newspaper editors who censured Bowen and Barber were Benjamin Davis of the Atlanta *Independent* and T. Thomas Fortune of the New York *Age*. In June, Barber announced that these critics would be given an opportunity to own the publication themselves: "We have formed a corporation known as the Voice Publishing Company.... We have bonded the Magazine to the old company for $15,000. As soon as that is paid by the colored people, the Magazine is theirs."[99] This new company was organized when the white publishers decided to stop issuing the periodical. Barber, writing later about the fate of the *Voice*, said that Mr. Jenkins and Mr. Hertel indicated that the publication was costing more than they had anticipated. Barber stated that the loss of their support placed the periodical "on the verge of suspending."[100]

The future of the *Voice of the Negro* was finally decided when mounting racial tension in the city of Atlanta erupted into a riot on September 22, 1906. Barber was a key figure in the accusations that followed concerning the causes of the riot. An anonymous letter appeared in the New York *World* a few days after the disturbance started, written as a counterstatement to an earlier letter from John Temple Graves of the Atlanta *Georgian*. Barber was identified as the writer of this letter, which accused "sensational newspapers and unscrupulous politicians" of precipitating the riot. He charged that white Atlanta newspapers had fomented the riot with yellow journalism tactics in reporting assaults on white women by Negro men. When his identity was revealed, Barber left Atlanta to protect himself from threatened retaliation and "a legal lynching."[101] He transferred the periodical to Chicago and attempted to continue its publication in that city.

With the November, 1906, issue, John W. E. Bowen's name no longer appeared in the masthead, and Barber became the sole editor. Also with that number, the title of the periodical was shortened to the *Voice* in an effort to attract a wider range of advertisers. James W. Woodlee, who had been the circulation manager in Atlanta, came to Chicago with Barber and continued in that capacity until the end of the year. William P. Hamilton then became the new circulation manager. In 1907 the Voice Company was incorporated in the state of Illinois, with Barber as president-treasurer and Hamilton as secretary. One thousand shares of stock in the company were offered to the public at ten dollars each. However, the combined income from shareholders, subscribers, and advertisers was not sufficient to maintain the periodical. Publication became irregular, and the periodical dwindled to a few pages.

In October, 1907, journalist T. Thomas Fortune purchased enough shares in the Voice Company to become the majority stockholder. Fortune, who had sold his newspaper, the New York

Voice

Courtesy Trevor Arnett Library, Atlanta University

Age, came to Chicago to reestablish his journalistic career. In the months that followed, no issues of the *Voice* were published, and Barber, impatient with this inactivity, severed his relations with the magazine. He later reported that Fortune took the mailing list of the *Voice* and went back to New York to start another publication there.[102] Thus, the *Voice of the Negro,* in its fourth year of publication, ceased to exist.

During those four years, this magazine presented a variety of articles dealing with many subjects and geographical areas. An editorial in 1905 stated: "We are not local either in the range and scope of our editorials, our correspondence or subscriptions. We are not even national. We are international."[103] Viewing the world scene, the *Voice of the Negro* focused on two major aspects. First, editorials followed closely the foreign policies of the United States and the events of international affairs, such as the Russo-Japanese War and the building of the Panama Canal. Secondly, feature articles appeared regularly on nonwhite people in all parts of the world. A special issue was devoted to Haiti and the Dominican Republic. A series on living conditions in the Philippine Islands was written by T. Thomas Fortune, who had spent time there as a special commissioner for the federal government. Other series were those by W. E. B. Du Bois on slavery in the ancient world and by Pauline Hopkins on "The Dark Races of the Twentieth Century." The editors of the *Voice* kept constantly before their readers a concern for nonwhite people throughout the world, for they believed that the destinies of all these people were interrelated.

At the national level, the *Voice* kept a watchful eye on the presidential campaign, on party politics, and on the three branches of the federal government. After the 1904 election, President Theodore Roosevelt was hailed as "a man of clear vision," "in fact, . . . a statesman of the first magnitude."[104] Three times, between September, 1904, and October, 1905, his photograph appeared as the frontispiece in the periodical. By the end of 1906, this image had paled. Roosevelt was censured in the pages of the *Voice* be-

Political cartoon from the *Voice of the Negro*,
December, 1904

Courtesy Trevor Arnett Library, Atlanta University

cause of the dishonorable discharge of Negro soldiers following the Brownsville, Texas, shooting disturbance.

Although the *Voice* concentrated on political affairs, it also touched upon other areas, such as literature and the arts. In music, the Fisk Jubilee Singers and the composer Samuel Coleridge-Taylor were praised for their contributions. In art, the achievements of the painter Henry O. Tanner and the potential of the young sculptor Meta Vaux Warrick Fuller were recognized. In drama, the *Voice* followed the national tour of the *Clansman*, Thomas Dixon, Jr.'s play, which glorified the Ku Klux Klan. The adverse criticism that this play received in many parts of the country was reported with approbation in the columns of the periodical. Book reviews recommended literature that reflected the accomplishments of the Negro, or denounced works considered unfair in the portrayal of black people such as *The Negro: The Southerner's Problem* by Thomas Nelson Page and *The American Negro* by the Afro-American author William Hannibal Thomas.

National Negro organizations were given a prominent place in the *Voice*. The editor John W. E. Bowen was active in the National Negro Business League (which had been established by Booker T. Washington), and he publicized the league in his columns. The *Voice* gave much more coverage, however, to the Niagara Movement (which was founded by Du Bois). The editor J. Max Barber was a charter member, and he reported at length on the annual meetings and other activities of this organization. Du Bois contributed articles on the purpose and the progress of the movement. Women's organizations were also highlighted. Aware of the feminist liberation movement during this era, the editors welcomed female authors and printed many articles on the concerns of women. Early in its publication, the periodical had a special issue on women. In this July, 1904, number, the editors presented as contributors "the eloquent Miss Nannie Burroughs, Corresponding Secretary of The Woman's Auxiliary to the National Baptist Convention; the scholarly Mrs. Josephine Silone-Yates, President of The National Association of Colored Women; the versatile Mrs. Mary Church Terrell; the calm and

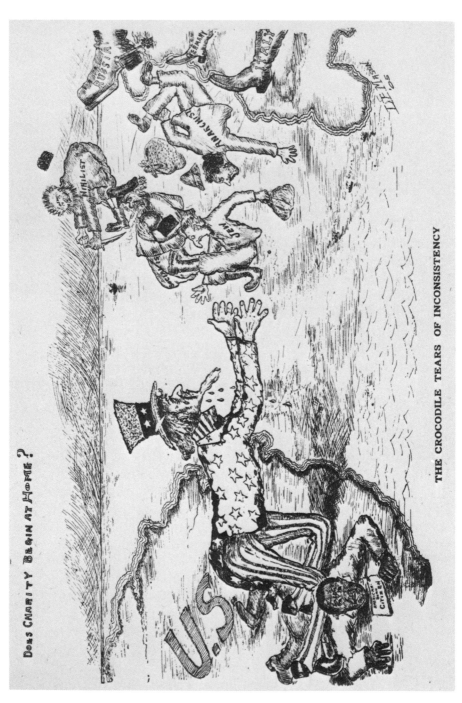

THE CROCODILE TEARS OF INCONSISTENCY

Political cartoon from the *Voice of the Negro*, September, 1905

equitably poised Mrs. Addie Hunton [president of the Atlanta Woman's Club and chairman of the Executive Committee of the Southern Federation of Colored Women]; the erudite Mrs. Fannie Barrier Williams and the wisely conservative Mrs. Booker T. Washington."[105] Other women contributing articles to subsequent issues of the periodical included Florence L. Bentley, Josephine B. Bruce (Mrs. Blanche K. Bruce), Emma Frances Grayson Merritt, Katherine Davis Tillman, and Josephine Turpin Washington (Mrs. S. H. H. Washington).

In appraising the southern scene, the *Voice* recognized the tremendous moral conflict in this region, the ancient and universal "conflict of good and evil transplanted to the Southern soil." Bowen observed: "With respect to the Negro the South is a seething pot of sympathy and antipathy, passion and compassion, benevolence and malevolence, love and hate, with the baser elements temporarily in the ascendency. As to the final outcome men of faith have no doubt." Bowen assured his readers that, although the *Voice* was "uncompromisingly opposed to narrow, bigoted politicians" such as Governor Vardaman of Mississippi and Senator Tillman of South Carolina, the periodical was not antisouthern. He was confident that there was "a large [white] constituency in the South who are tired of this race hatred and who want peace."[106]

A symposium in the January, 1905, issue presented "Messages to the Negro Race" by white and black leaders. The white contributors were Bishop Warren A. Candler, Reverend Henry S. Bradley, and Reverend W. W. Landrum of Atlanta; Judge Emory Speer of Macon; and William Hayes Ward, editor of the *Independent* magazine in New York City. The Negro spokesmen were W. E. B. Du Bois of the Atlanta University faculty and William H. Councill, founder and president of the state industrial school at Huntsville (Normal), Alabama. Among other white persons writing for the *Voice* were John D. Swain and Joseph C. Manning. Swain lived in Worcester, Massachusetts; Manning was a resident of Alexander City, Alabama, born and educated in that state, and a former member of the state legislature. Both criti-

cized the southern treatment of the Negro, and Manning called
for the organization of a league of southern white men dedicated
to the development of a truly democratic government.

The *Voice of the Negro* spoke out against lynching and the
peonage labor system. A series of articles exposing peonage practices was written by a young Atlanta lawyer, Thomas H. Malone.
The one contribution by the noted author Charles W. Chesnutt
to the periodical also discussed this subject. The *Voice* also carried news items reporting cases of lynching in the South and the
North, as well as editorials and feature articles speaking out
against this crime and calling for federal antilynching legislation.

Education for Negroes in the South was a frequent subject of
editorials and articles. In an editorial, Barber praised Anna T.
Jeanes of Philadelphia for her "far-sighted idea of statesmanship"
in donating one million dollars to the education of Negroes living in rural areas.[107] Considerable coverage was given to the colleges in Atlanta and to other institutions throughout the South,
particularly Tuskegee, Talladega, Hampton, and Virginia Union.
The sole article by Booker T. Washington, published in the initial
issue, emphasized his advocacy of technical and agricultural education. Tuskegee Institute was the subject of several complimentary articles and editorials, most of them written by editor Bowen.
Feature stories were carried on the Tuskegee conference that was
held annually to bring farmers and educators together. The *Voice*
also reported on the conferences sponsored by Atlanta University,
under the leadership of Du Bois, to further the sociological study
of the Negro.

The *Voice* sought to give equal coverage in the controversy
concerning industrial education versus liberal education for Negroes, and it supported both. An editorial in the April, 1905, issue
stated: "We shall advocate everything for the elevation of the race
from a pick-axe and plow to a telescope and spectroscope; from
a bank-book to a Bible-book; from a common school and an industrial education to a college training, a university course and a
professional degree. We are advocates of the incontrovertible

truth that whatever is good to elevate, dignify and make the white man great is good also for the black man."[108] The illustration for the front cover of the November, 1906, issue portrayed, in equal prominence, two young Negro men: one with hammer in hand, symbolizing the industrial worker; the other with books, symbolizing the intellectual and professional person. This cover was designed by the young Chicago artist William E. Scott.

At the state level, the primary focus of the *Voice of the Negro* was on political events. Uppermost in Georgia politics at that time was the long campaign that preceded the 1906 gubernatorial election. In the opening months of this contest, the *Voice* denounced Hoke Smith but reserved judgment on Clark Howell. By the spring of 1906, the editors were convinced that both of these candidates for governor were unfit for the office because of their appeals to race prejudice and their designs for disfranchising the Negro. An editorial in the March issue urged Negroes to adopt a "hands off" policy in the August election. Another editorial in that issue praised the Georgia Equal Rights Convention that had just met in Macon at the call of William J. White, with two hundred Negroes in attendance. Barber observed that "the absence of a sickening, ultra-conservatism on the floor of the convention" was "particularly gratifying." He reported that the conference, "with a boldness that was almost radical, put its finger on the glaring defects that operate to the detriment of our people in this state."[109]

Even though the *Voice* projected far beyond Atlanta, it did not neglect the local scene. The Atlanta riot of 1906 was reported and discussed in much detail, mainly by Barber. Editorials were written on Andrew Carnegie's offer of $10,000 to the city to build a library for Negro citizens, who were barred from the public library (a branch that was not constructed until 1921). The old folks' home at Friendship Baptist Church and the Carrie Steele Orphanage were singled out as effective social welfare institutions. An editorial noted that both Negro and white men loitered daily on Ivy and Decatur Streets in downtown Atlanta and urged that, when the police department dealt with this problem, "all cocaine fiends and vagrants ought to suffer and not the poor Negro only."[110]

A white lawyer was praised for defending Negroes in the local courts in cases involving loan shark businesses. The plans of a black New York firm to establish a bank in Atlanta were reported. Tribute was paid to Spelman Seminary on its twenty-fifth anniversary. A review of the football season at the black colleges was written by Samuel Howard Archer, teacher and coach at Atlanta Baptist College (later Morehouse College). Editorials criticized the crowded conditions and inferior education in the public elementary schools for Negro children. Another editorial commended the election of John Hope to the presidency of Atlanta Baptist College, the first appointment of a black person to head a major Baptist school. In this respect, the editorial observed, "the Methodist Episcopal Church has led the way and is still far in the lead."[111]

A feature article by John Hope in the first issue of the *Voice of the Negro* prophesied the future for the six black institutions of higher education located in Atlanta. Observing that no city in Georgia had a public high school for its black youth and that the elementary schools were generally inadequate, Hope pointed out that these Atlanta institutions were engaged mainly in elementary and secondary education. He recommended that when these schools eventually concentrated on higher education, they should have a planned division of responsibility. "Gammon Theological Seminary," he predicted, "may enlarge its sphere so as to absorb the theological work of other schools by having denominational departments." "Let Atlanta University become a graduate school," he proposed. (The highest degree offered at that time by this school was the bachelor's degree.) Hope also suggested areas of specialization for the other institutions. He warned that "without some such division, competition may result in an unseemingly struggle for existence, causing untold detriment to defenseless students."[112]

The contents of the *Voice of the Negro* during the Atlanta pe-

riod of publication followed a consistent pattern: many advertisements at the beginning of the issue; a frontispiece; Barber's
editorial and news columns of several pages; feature articles with
many illustrations; Bowen's editorial column; the "Wayside" section (mainly anecdotes and light verse) by Silas X. Floyd; and
more advertisements at the back of the issue. Throughout the
years of publication in Atlanta and Chicago, the periodical featured illustrations, political cartoons, and other work by young
Negro artists. The most frequent contributor was John Henry
Adams, Jr., a native of Georgetown, Georgia, who had studied art
briefly at Drexel Institute in Philadelphia. After returning to his
home state, he was appointed chairman of the newly established
fine arts department at Morris Brown College.[113]

Adams contributed a variety of work to the magazine, including designs for the front cover, illustrations for material in the
periodical, political cartoons, essays on art, and portrait drawings
of Negroes. Some of these portraits were sketches of individuals
drawn from life, such as those of W. E. B. Du Bois and John
Hope, accompanied by biographical text. Others represented
character types. In two sets of drawings in 1904, Adams portrayed "the new Negro woman" and "the new Negro man." The
Atlanta *Constitution* carried a feature story on Adams in 1902,
with a reproduction of one of his paintings. James Porter, historian and critic of Negro art, in describing portrait drawings
by Adams, has written that "this Boswell of the crayon had a real
understanding of the interpretation of physiognomic character
through line and delicate shading."[114]

In the pages of the *Voice of the Negro*, poetry was frequently
printed, but short stories and serialized novels appeared only
occasionally. Among the poets represented were James D. Corrothers, Daniel Webster Davis, Georgia Douglas Johnson, Benjamin Griffith Brawley, William Stanley Braithwaite, Olivia Ward
Bush, Carrie W. Clifford, and Azalia Edmonia Martin. Poems by
Paul Laurence Dunbar were published only after his death in
1906. Typical of the popular ten-cent magazines of that time, the
Voice of the Negro carried some creative literature and literary

criticism but gave much more space to current events. Barber solicited contributions from Charles W. Chesnutt, not for the short stories and fiction that had established his reputation, but for nonfiction in the muckraking style of the period. In a letter to Chesnutt in 1904, Barber made this request: "We would like to arrange with you to furnish us about eight articles this year. You might take up some line of thought and follow it out in a series of articles just as Miss Tarbell is doing in McLures [*McClure's*] Magazine. . . . We will pay you $100 for eight articles this year on some live subject."[115] The *Voice of the Negro* concentrated on reporting and interpreting developments that were taking place in the opening years of the twentieth century. For four years, in forty-two issues, this periodical reflected the black side of life in Atlanta, in Georgia, the South, the United States, and the world.

Monthly Review and *Alexander's Magazine*

Charles Alexander was convinced that the Negro journalist can "never grow rich in this world's goods." His career as a publisher of newspapers and magazines in the last decade of the nineteenth century and the first years of the twentieth century was testimony to this observation. Born in Natchez, Mississippi, in 1867, Alexander grew up in New London, Connecticut, and was educated in the public schools of that city. Eventually he moved to Boston and entered the merchant tailoring business. He also became active in journalism and worked with the *Reflector* newspaper. In early 1894, after this publication failed, Alexander initiated the *Monthly Review* magazine.[116]

The *Monthly Review* was issued in Boston during 1894 and 1895. Assisting Alexander with the magazine were James R. Ruiter and Ambrose A. Clark as managers and Peter Jefferson Smith, Jr., as associate editor. By January, 1896, Alexander had moved to Philadelphia and was publishing the *Review* in that city, with Edward C. Brown as manager.[117] Brown later established banking

Charles Alexander, publisher and editor of the
Monthly Review and *Alexander's Magazine.*
From G. F. Richings, *Evidences of Progress
Among Colored People* (Philadelphia: George
S. Ferguson, 1896).

and real estate businesses in Virginia and issued a quarterly periodical, the *Dollar Mark*, to publicize his enterprises.

Whatever may have prompted Alexander to relocate in Philadelphia in 1896, the move did not prove profitable for the magazine. In June of that year, in a letter to John E. Bruce, he spoke
of the difficulty he was having. Alexander asked Bruce if he would
give the *Review* "a good notice" in his columns (but only, Alexander added, if Bruce felt that the periodical really deserved
it).[118] The *Monthly Review* was praised as a first-class literary
magazine by many contemporary writers. One publication noted
that the periodical failed only because "the masses of the race
have not as yet acquired a taste for that sort of literature."[119] The
Review lasted only a few months in Philadelphia. With its demise,
Alexander's journalistic ambitions were temporarily deferred.

Having operated printing businesses in Boston and Philadelphia, Alexander became an instructor of printing, first at the
Alabama Agricultural and Mechanical College in Huntsville, then

at Tuskegee Institute, and finally at Wilberforce University in Ohio. After ten years of teaching, he returned to full-time journalism. He accepted Booker T. Washington's invitation to manage the *Colored Citizen* in Boston, which Washington was sponsoring as a competitor to the radical Boston *Guardian*, edited by William Monroe Trotter. Alexander went back to Boston, back to the editor's desk, and back to the frustrations of publishing a Negro journal. When the struggling *Colored Citizen* continued to be financially unsuccessful, Washington advised Alexander to suspend the weekly paper and start a monthly magazine.[120]

The first number of *Alexander's Magazine* appeared in May, 1905. The periodical was issued for four years, subsidized by Washington. For a few months in 1907 it was published under the title *Alexander's Magazine and the National Domestic*, having absorbed the *National Domestic* magazine issued in Indianapolis. In 1909, the periodical ceased publication, and once again Alexander's journalistic career was thwarted by inadequate financial resources. He migrated westward and settled in Los Angeles. Still the journalist, Alexander established the *Citizens Advocate* newspaper, which continued publication for several years. He also served as the western correspondent for the *New Era Magazine*, initiated in Boston in 1916 by Pauline E. Hopkins and Walter W. Wallace. Alexander died in Los Angeles in 1923.[121]

As an editor and publisher, he had met with the hardships that he described as the lot of the Negro journalist: "He must be prepared to labor under great difficulties and embarrassments for fully 18 hours out of every 24, make great sacrifices, meet with all sorts of discouragements, and sometimes suffer humiliation and deprivation in order to accomplish his purpose.... Indeed, the task of publishing a Negro newspaper or magazine is one that requires at the outset, great versatility and talent, remarkable executive ability and exceptional courage and tenacity." But Alexander had also experienced the rewards of this occupation. One of the opportunities offered the Negro editor, he said, was "the influence for good which he may exercise over the aspiring young men and women of his own race."[122] Although Alexander solicited contributions to his publications from well-known individuals, he also encouraged young writers by printing their beginning literary efforts.

One author whom the *Monthly Review* introduced to New England readers was Alice Ruth Moore. Alice Moore, born in New Orleans in 1875 and educated at Straight College (later Dillard University), was teaching in her hometown and was also developing her talents as a writer. In 1896 she moved North for further education. Even before Alice Moore left New Orleans, her writing had come to the attention of Alexander, and he published her essays and poems in the *Review* during 1894 and 1895. He also issued her first book, *Violets and Other Tales,* a collection of short stories and poems, from his Monthly Review Press in 1895.

The *Monthly Review* not only presented Alice Moore to a wider reading audience; it also introduced this young lady to her future husband. One person who noticed her contributions to the *Review* was another poet, also relatively unknown at that time, Paul Laurence Dunbar. He was impressed with her writing, but even more so with her photograph in the magazine. Dunbar introduced himself to Alice Moore by a letter sent to her in care of the *Monthly Review.* Thus began a romance by correspondence that led to their meeting two years later and culminated in their marriage in March, 1898. By that time Dunbar had published volumes that brought praise from outstanding white critics and established his literary reputation. But his fortunes soon changed. The marriage ended in divorce in 1902, and Dunbar died of tuberculosis in 1906. Several years later, Alice Moore Dunbar married Robert J. Nelson, a newspaper publisher from Harrisburg, Pennsylvania. She continued her teaching and literary careers and achieved recognition as an author in her own right.[123]

Alexander planned a broad scope for the *Monthly Review.* The periodical was to include "science, art, literature, biographies, history, politics, religion, Masonic orders, Odd Fellow news, great speeches, serial stories, short stories, poetry, sports, sociology." An editorial in the first issue (March, 1894) stated that the periodical "will listen to all conflicting opinions, no matter by whom expressed, so long as sincerity and dignity prevails. Radicals and conservatives alike will be given a fair hearing." The editorial further explained the policies of the periodical: "We are independent in politics because we are not inclined to believe that every man who professes to be a Republican is a saint, or that every individual who claims himself to be a Democrat is a sinner. We are independent in religion because we are not inclined to believe that Heaven is a celestial apartment house the choice suites of which are leased for eternity by any certain religious denomination."[124] Alexander's plans for the *Monthly Review* were extensive, but the periodical was of brief duration.

When Alexander reentered the magazine publishing field in 1905, he again projected a periodical of broad scope, one that would give "a reliable record of the distinguished achievements of the great men of the Negro Race in all parts of the world." Now, however, his outlook was from a somewhat different perspective. He advertised this periodical, *Alexander's Magazine*, as "the most conservative monthly publication issued at the present time in the interest of the Race." He defined this conservatism thusly: "*Alexander's Magazine* teaches the doctrine of optimism. It does not dramatize our misfortunes or paint in too glowing colors our limited acquisitions. It selects the best examples of Race development as a means of inspiration and helpfulness."[125] This same statement had been used in the advertisements for the *Colored Citizen* newspaper.

The masthead of *Alexander's Magazine* stated that the periodical was devoted to "the spreading of reliable information concerning the operation of educational institutions in the South; the moral, intellectual, commercial and industrial improvement of the Negro Race in the United States." The initial issue had a feature article on Hampton Institute, which was celebrating its thirty-fifth anniversary. A special number, one of the largest issues published, was devoted to the twenty-fifth anniversary of Tuskegee Institute. Richard R. Wright, Jr., reported on the agricultural and mechanical college in Savannah, Georgia, of which he was president. Smaller institutions were also described in the pages of *Alexander's Magazine*, such as the Berean Manual Training and Industrial School conducted in Philadelphia by the Presbyterian minister Matthew D. Anderson, and the Snow Hill Normal and Industrial Institute in Alabama, of which William J. Edwards was principal.

Another interest that *Alexander's Magazine* promoted, although only briefly, was migration to Africa and the settlement of a colony in Liberia. In 1907 the periodical initiated a column on Liberia and Africa edited by Walter F. Walker, Alexander's young assistant. The Liberian Development Association was organized that year, with newspaper editor Francis H. Warren of Detroit as president, Alexander as vice-president, and Walker as secretary-treasurer. Walker wrote enthusiastically about plans for one thousand Negro-Americans to establish a colony in the hinterland of Liberia. This development was to be called Turner City, in honor of Bishop Henry McNeal Turner, "the greatest and most insistent exponent of Negro emigration in Africa." On a tract of two thousand acres, the organization planned to erect an educational and business center, surrounded by the small individual farms of the colonists.[126]

After making a trip to Liberia in preparation for this venture, Walker was very disillusioned. He complained that prospective immigrants "have never been told the truth about Liberia and the difficulties confronting emigration to this republic." Walker described the country for the readers of *Alexander's Magazine*: "Almost impenetrable bush covers the back lands of Liberia. . . . There is not a single road leading out of Monrovia, the capital of the republic, into the interior. . . . There are no beasts of burden, except the natives be considered as such. . . . To maintain life even the healthiest foreigner must make of his body a miniature apothecary's shop." Walker felt that only after Liberia had been considerably developed should migration to that country be encouraged. He eventually moved to Liberia and became a schoolteacher there.[127]

Alexander's Magazine was also a medium for political campaigning. (Alexander himself had twice been an office seeker as a candidate for the Massachusetts House of Representatives.) The periodical displayed prominently the photographs of white persons endorsed for elective offices. A full-page advertisement from Negro citizens supported John F. Fitzgerald in his bid for reelection as mayor of Boston. This advertisement asserted that Mayor Fitzgerald had given the Negro race "more important appointments than it has ever before received in the New England States."[128] *Alexander's Magazine* also gave special support to Joseph Benson Foraker, the Republican senator from Ohio who had strenuously opposed the dishonorable discharge of the black soldiers in the Brownsville, Texas, shooting incident. Foraker sought, unsuccessfullly, to have these men reenlisted and restored to all their rights. (This restitution finally took place in 1972.) Foraker's speech in Congress on their behalf was printed in two successive issues of the magazine, April and May, 1908, and his address before the A. M. E. Church Conference in Baltimore that year was also carried in the April issue.

Many other areas of interest were covered by *Alexander's Magazine*. Special numbers of the periodical were devoted to Abraham Lincoln, William Lloyd Garrison, the Negro and the Catholic Church, and the Clifton Conference (an interracial meeting held in 1908 to discuss religious education for Negroes). Biographical accounts and photographs of contemporary Negro men and women in all fields of endeavor were a prominent feature, and some historical biography was included. Among the departments in the periodical were: "Notes and Comments," a column on current events by the Howard University professor Kelly Miller; "Practical Talks on Business" by William H. Davis, official stenographer for the National Negro Business League and head of a business school in Washington; "Bits of History Relating to Prince Hall Masonry" by Frederick S. Monroe; and "Book Notes and Comments," edited by Alexander, John Daniels, and Benjamin G. Brawley at various times. A section for women was conducted by Carrie W. Clifford of Ohio and later by the editor's wife, Fanny Alexander. This column carried news about women's clubs and their regional and national associations, as well as fashion forecasts, recipes, and household hints.

The range of Alexander's editorials is shown in the October, 1906, issue, in which he commented upon the Atlanta riot of the previous month, the forthcoming meetings of the National Afro-American Council and the National Baptist Convention, the "flourishing condition" of the four Negro banks in Richmond, the appointment of Roscoe Conkling Bruce as superintendent of Negro schools in Washington, the high rents charged for housing in urban areas, the campaign textbook just issued by the Republican party, the discovery of oil on land owned by Negroes in Oklahoma, the "frivolity of the Northern Negro" who squanders money on entertainment but does not contribute to civil rights organizations, and the need for cooperation among the national Negro associations working for civil rights instead of the "existing antagonistic feelings."[129]

Poetry, short stories, and serialized fiction were included in *Alexander's Magazine*. Among the contributors of poetry were William Stanley Braithwaite, Joseph S. Cotter, Sr., W. E. B. Du Bois, Paul Laurence Dunbar, Perry Marshall, Ralph W. Tyler, and Lucian B. Watkins. The only writing by Du Bois in this periodical was his poetry. On the other hand, articles by Booker T. Washington, often reprinted from other publications, appeared frequently. Contributions also came from other well-known individuals: a discussion of race prejudice by Charles W. Chesnutt, an essay on Abraham Lincoln by William Pickens, the reprint of a sermon by Adam Clayton Powell, a report on the Ohio Federation of Women's Clubs by Mary Church Terrell, an article on socialism and the Negro by Reverdy C. Ransom, and an essay on black organizations by Kelly Miller. Samuel Laing Williams, Chicago attorney and husband of Fannie Barrier Williams, contributed an essay entitled "The New Negro." In this article, published in the November, 1908, issue, he made these observations:

> We have in this country today what may be fittingly called a
> "new Negro," and the race problem may be defined as the failure
> of the American people to recognize this new Negro. . . . The race

problem of today, in spite of the people who think, feel and act as if it were the same as it was in 1860, is a new problem and may be defined: What shall be the status of this educated, high-spirited, ambitious and deserving man of the Negro race or this new Negro? He knocks and knocks persistently at the door of opportunity. Shall it be opened? Justice and fair play say, yes; race prejudice, in the spirit of 1860, says no.[130]

Other than Alexander himself, the most frequent contributor to this magazine was Archibald H. Grimké. In September, 1907, Alexander announced that Grimké would have full charge of the editorial department for the coming year. The *Horizon* periodical, edited by Du Bois, noted this appointment and commented that Grimké had "some vigorous matter in the September issue, which at once puts this magazine in a different class."[131] Grimké was listed as editor only in the September, October, and November issues. He continued to write for the periodical, though, just as he had done prior to his brief tenure as editor.

Grimké, born a slave in 1849 in Charleston, South Carolina, eventually earned degrees from Lincoln University (Pennsylvania) and Harvard Law School. He practiced law in Boston from 1874 to 1894, when President Grover Cleveland appointed him consul to Santo Domingo. After returning to the United States, he settled in Washington, D.C., where he lived until his death in 1930. Grimké pursued many journalistic and literary activities. During the 1880s he published and edited a weekly newspaper in Boston and wrote for white papers in that city. His biographies of William Lloyd Garrison and Charles Sumner were published in 1891 and 1892. During his residence in Washington, Grimké was president of the local chapter of the National Association for the Advancement of Colored People and held national offices in that organization. For several years, he was also president of the American Negro Academy, an organization of men of African descent that was devoted to research and publication on black history.[132]

Charles Alexander was the most prolific writer in his periodical. In addition to editorials, book reviews, and poetry, he was responsible for many of the feature articles. Alexander also contributed poetry and book reviews to other publications. Among the books that he wrote were *One Hundred Distinguished Leaders* (1897) and *The Battles and Victories of Allen Allensworth* (1914), both biographical works on Negroes. He assisted George F. Richings in compiling *Evidences of Progress Among Colored People* (1896) and collaborated with Herschel V. Cashin (his partner in the printing business in Huntsville) to issue *Under Fire with the Tenth United States Cavalry* (1898). In connection with his printing establishments in Huntsville, Boston, and Philadelphia, Alexander also operated bookstores.

At one time, Alexander expressed to John E. Bruce his desire to organize a society in the interest of Afro-American literature. During his residence in California, he gained a reputation as a lecturer, especially for his reading and interpretation of the poems of Paul Laurence Dunbar.[133] Charles Alexander was not only a publisher and editor of newspapers and magazines; at the turn of the century, he was a pioneering black literary critic, encouraging young writers and promoting the appreciation of Afro-American literature.

Horizon

The life of William Edward Burghardt Du Bois spanned a period of ninety-five years. He was born in Great Barrington, Massachusetts, on February 23, 1868, and died in Accra, Ghana, on August 27, 1963.[134] During many of these years he edited a succession of periodical publications. The *Horizon* is the only one within the scope of this book, but a brief review of Du Bois's editorial career shows that the *Horizon* was an integral part of this series of journals.

In an autobiographical work published in 1921, Du Bois recalled: "Away back in the little years of my boyhood I had sold the Springfield *Republican* and written for Mr. [T. Thomas] Fortune's *Globe*. I dreamed of being an editor myself some day."[135] His editorial career began in the 1880s when, during collegiate days at Fisk University, he was editor of the *Fisk Herald*, published monthly by the student literary societies. After graduating from this school, Du Bois continued his studies at Harvard University and the University of Berlin. He was awarded the doctor of philosophy degree by Harvard in 1895.

From 1897 until 1910 Du Bois was on the faculty of Atlanta University. During this period he was also active as an editor. In 1905, in association with Edward L. Simon and Harry H. Pace, he began "a small magazinelike weekly," published in Memphis, Tennessee, and called the *Moon Illustrated Weekly: A Record of the Darker Races*. Du Bois edited the *Moon* from December, 1905, until it ceased publication in the summer of 1906.[136] The following year, in cooperation with Lafayette McKeene Hershaw and Freeman Henry Morris Murray, he established the monthly *Horizon*. The *Horizon: A Journal of the Color Line* began publication in January, 1907, in Washington, D.C., where Hershaw and Murray were employed in the federal government.

Du Bois discontinued this periodical in 1910, when he resigned from Atlanta University and went to New York City to become director of publications and research for the newly organized National Association for the Advancement of Colored People. As a part of his activities in this position, Du Bois founded and edited *Crisis: A Record of the Darker Races*. He was editor of this monthly from November, 1910, through July, 1934, when he left the NAACP and again became a member of the Atlanta University faculty. During his residence in New York, Du Bois also founded and edited another periodical, the *Brownies' Book*, a monthly magazine for children. Associated with him in this venture were two *Crisis* staff members, Augustus G. Dill and Jessie Redmon Fauset. When Du Bois returned to Atlanta, he began making plans for a scholarly journal on world race problems. This periodical was inaugurated in 1940 as *Phylon: The Atlanta University Review of Race and Culture*. Du Bois was editor-in-chief of *Phylon* until 1944, the year of his retirement from the university.

From the *Moon* to *Phylon*, Du Bois sought to give substance to

The Impressionist School of Art in America.

Horizon
Courtesy Moorland-Spingarn Research Center, Howard University

an idea that he had nurtured constantly: the publication of a national Negro periodical. In 1899 he had written that "a strong, fearless, national newspaper or magazine which the Negroes could feel was their own, with sane views as to work, wealth and culture, could become, in years, a vast power among Negroes." Du Bois suggested that this was the opportunity for "a peculiar sort of philanthropic work, and one hitherto little tried—the endowed periodical." Six years later he wrote: "The Negro race in America is today in a critical condition. Only united concerted effort will save us from being crushed. . . . To this end there is needed a high class of journal to circulate among the intelligent Negroes, tell them of the deeds of themselves and their neighbors, interpret the news of the world to them, and inspire them toward definite ideals. . . . I want to establish, therefore, for the nine million American Negroes and eventually for the whole Negro world, a monthly journal."[137]

The *Horizon* was a part of this philosophy and plan. This periodical began publication in January, 1907, as a monthly pocket-size magazine of twenty-four pages, without illustrations. It continued in this format through December, 1908, published in Washington for the first year and then in Alexandria, Virginia. The masthead stated that the periodical was "owned by W. E. B. Du Bois, F. H. M. Murray, and L. M. Hershaw, who write it, type it, and print it."

Du Bois's two partners were long-time residents of the Washington area and held responsible clerkships in the federal government. Hershaw, a graduate of Atlanta University and Howard University Law School, was in the General Land Office of the Interior Department. He was active in community affairs and was one of the twenty-nine charter members of the Niagara Movement. Murray was employed in the War Department. He and members of his family established the Murray Brothers Press, a well-known printing business conducted in Washington for a number of years.

In 1908 plans were announced for an enlarged and reorganized journal, to begin publication in January, 1909. It was not until

November, however, that the magazine was resumed. The revised *Horizon* was issued in a larger format, with twelve pages per issue, and the front cover was usually illustrated. The periodical had the same title and subtitle, *The Horizon: A Journal of the Color Line*, and the same motto, "Seeking the Seldom Sort," as before. It now carried the by-line "edited by W. E. Burghardt Du Bois, assisted by L. M. Hershaw and F. H. M. Murray." The *Horizon* was printed by the Murray Brothers Press in Washington, with Murray as business manager of the periodical.

During 1907 and 1908, when the *Horizon* was in financial straits, the editors had paid the deficit "out of their shallow pockets." The financial arrangement announced for the enlarged *Horizon* was an attempt to place the magazine on a sounder basis and at the same time keep it "an unmuzzled monthly." Du Bois felt that Negroes were too poor at that time to establish a national journal financed by "a high subscription price or multitudinous advertisements." He pointed out that the only other methods were "to seek secret subsidy or openly to make up the annual deficit." Shunning subsidy because it could result in the "buying of a paper's policy," he appealed for open and regular support by those who believed in the principles for which the periodical stood. He called for one hundred persons to give twenty-five dollars to guarantee the publication of the *Horizon*. These guarantors were to become the proprietors, and the magazine was to be conducted by an executive committee appointed by them.[138] This proposal apparently did not materialize.

In the meantime, during the summer of 1910, Du Bois was planning a magazine that he wanted to publish in his new position with the NAACP. When the organization approved his plans, Du Bois notified *Horizon* subscribers that this periodical was being suspended and the balance of their subscriptions would be filled by the forthcoming *Crisis* magazine.[139] The *Horizon* ended with the July, 1910, issue.

Thirty-one issues of the *Horizon* were published from January, 1907, to July, 1910. A statement of causes that the periodical promoted appeared in the November, 1909, issue: "THIS IS A RADICAL

PAPER. It stands for progress and advance. It advocates Negro equality and human equality; it stands for Universal suffrage, including votes for Women; it believes in the abolition of War, the taxation of monopoly values, the gradual socialization of capital and the overthrow of persecution and dogmatism in the name of religion."[140] Very little of the content of the *Horizon* came from outside contributors. (Notable among them were William Stanley Braithwaite and James Weldon Johnson, whose poetry appeared in the magazine.)

Most of the material was presented in three sections written by the editors: "The Over-Look," by Du Bois, "The Out-Look" by Hershaw, and "The In-Look" by Murray. Included in these sections were editorials on national and international events; reviews of current literature and notices of new publications; digests and excerpts of racial news appearing in the daily newspapers and general magazines; extracts from Afro-American newspapers; and monthly listings of selected articles from black periodicals such as the *Voice, Alexander's Magazine, McGirt's Magazine,* and the *A. M. E. Church Review.* In "The Over-Look," during the latter part of 1908, Du Bois presented a series of "heart to heart talks with the Negro-American voter." He discussed the power of this minority vote and gave reasons for supporting the Democratic party in the national election that year. Poetry and other creative writing by Du Bois also appeared in his "Over-Look" section.

Two special sections of the *Horizon* were a monthly column, "Along the Color Line," devoted to topics of current interest; and the "Debit and Credit" page, an annual listing of developments that Du Bois considered significant indicators of progress or of retrogression for Negroes in the United States. Du Bois had formerly contributed this annual review to the *Voice of the Negro.* Another aspect of the *Horizon* that was familiar to those who had read the *Voice* was the art work of John Henry Adams. Cartoons by Adams appeared as front-cover illustrations for at least two issues of the *Horizon.* These features—"Along the Color Line,"

"Debit and Credit," and art work by Adams—were continued in the *Crisis* magazine.

Du Bois had been closely associated with the *Voice of the Negro*. The young editor of this publication, J. Max Barber, was among those who answered Du Bois's call in 1905 to form the Niagara Movement. Barber was active in the movement and publicized it through editorials and feature stories. Du Bois was welcomed as a contributor; he wrote articles on the philosophy and progress of the organization. In the first years of the twentieth century, the Niagara Movement was regarded as the most militant of the Negro associations working for civil rights. The *Voice of the Negro*, as long as it was published, was a major publicity channel for this movement. The *Horizon* succeeded the *Voice* in this function. In an editorial in the January, 1910, issue, Du Bois sent forth this proclamation:

> We are called agitators in the sense of irresponsible persons who get their chief amusement and their daily bread by making a noise; yet we must remember that some of the greatest movements in the world's history have been led by men who were also called agitators, and who were agitators in the sense that they tried to arouse the conscience of a nation or of a group to certain persistent wrongs. . . .
>
> The HORIZON, then is a demand for democracy—spiritual freedom for ten millions of people, and not for these only but for all men the world over. This is, we freely admit a large program, difficult to realize, but it is the ideal toward which we go.[141]

FOUR

After Reconstruction
Special Interest Periodicals

It being the first journal of its kind published
in America, will constitute a volume equally as
rare as it is interesting and instructive. Copies
of the first issue are now at a very great pre-
mium.

—*Medical and Surgical Observer*, July, 1893

❧

The publication of specialized periodicals was a major development in the Afro-American press during the post-Reconstruction
decades. Special interest magazines such as the *African Methodist Episcopal Church Magazine* and the *Students' Repository*
had been a part of the beginnings of this press in the antebellum
period. During the post-Reconstruction years, however, the special interest periodicals proliferated and exceeded in number the
general periodicals. They portrayed, perhaps even more vividly
than the general publications, the separate society that developed
among black people. They delineated the activities and the institutions to which members of this minority group turned in their
quest for basic livelihood, for economic and educational advancement, for spiritual strength, for racial solidarity, for entertainment
and diversion, and for equality and justice in American society.

The largest number of specialized publications were issued in
the southern states, but activity also occurred in the Northeast,
in the Midwest, and in the Middle Atlantic states, with a concentration of titles in New York City, Baltimore, and Washington.
By subject interest, these magazines can be classified as follows:

fifteen concerned with education (including the one periodical of the Reconstruction era), thirteen religious journals, seven women's magazines, four concentrating on music and the theater, three on medicine and health, five business periodicals, four magazines addressed to occupational groups, and two relating to agriculture and farming. Approximately half of the educational journals were sponsored by organizations, significant women's magazines were issued by women's clubs, and two of the periodicals in medicine and health were organizational journals. The majority of the special interest publications, however, were issued through individual enterprise, with the promoters sometimes forming stock companies to finance their publications.

The two specialized magazines issued over the longest period of time were sponsored by organizations. These periodicals—the *Journal* of the National Medical Association and the *National Association Notes* of the National Association of Colored Women —are still published today. Two periodicals issued by individuals maintained publication for more than forty years. Their longevity can be attributed to the durability of the editors, James Alexander Ross of the *Gazetteer and Guide* and the Reverend George Freeman Bragg, Jr., of the *Church Advocate*. Most of the specialized journals, though, like the general publications, lasted only a very few years.

In this chapter, the special interest periodicals are presented by subject groups, followed by individual sketches of the *Medical and Surgical Observer*, *Woman's Era*, the *Negro Music Journal*, *School Teacher*, and the *Negro Business League Herald*.

Within a few months after Emancipation a black organization in New York was issuing the *Freedman's Torchlight* to provide the rudiments of education for illiterate freedmen. In the post-Reconstruction years, the earliest educational periodicals were alumni publications established by the graduates of educational institutions. The *Alumni Journal* was issued by Hampton Institute graduates, and the *Alumni Magazine* was published by the alumni association of Lincoln University in Pennsylvania. These were followed by periodicals published by and for state teachers' associations: the *Progressive Educator* in North Carolina, the *Educational Era* in Maryland, the *Negro Educational Journal* in Georgia, the *Educator* in Alabama, the *Southern Teachers' Advocate* in Kentucky, and the *Colored Teacher* in Louisiana. In some cases, these journals were founded independently by their editors and then endorsed or officially adopted by the associations. These state publications, and the organizations that they served, agitated for "better teachers, better pay for better teachers, longer school terms for country schools, better schools with better equipment."[1] Periodicals with a broader geographical scope included the *Southern Educator*, published by a regional organization; the *Educator* (North Carolina), sponsored by the education department of the African Methodist Episcopal Church; and the *School Teacher*, issued by a group of administrators in the District of Columbia school system but widely circulated outside Washington. With two magazines, the *National Capital Searchlight* and the *Negro Educational Review*, the editors sought to represent the teaching profession at the national level.

The *Freedman's Torchlight* was a part of the literacy program of the African Civilization Society, originally established in 1858 as an interracial organization to sponsor emigration projects to Africa. By 1866 the association had been reorganized by blacks and was devoting its resources to education. The reconstituted African Civilization Society described itself as "an organization of pious and educated Colored people . . . who believe, and always have believed, that the black man of education can best instruct, direct, and elevate his race."[2] The society conducted schools in the South and published two journals, the weekly *People's Journal* and the monthly *Freedman's Torchlight*, which were issued from the printing establishment operated by the society at its headquarters in Brooklyn.

The *Torchlight*, a four-page periodical with a subscription price of fifty cents per year, was edited by Rufus Lewis Perry. The associate editors were Amos N. Freeman and Henry M. Wilson, president and corresponding secretary of the society. Perry, born of slave parents in Smith County, Tennessee, in 1834, had escaped to freedom when he was eighteen years old. After studying at the Kalamazoo Theological Seminary in Michigan, he served as pastor of churches in Ann Arbor, Michigan; St. Catharines, Ontario; and Buffalo, New York. Perry eventually went to Brooklyn, where he founded the Messiah Baptist Church and devoted much of his time to journalism. He edited both *Freedman's Torchlight* and the *People's Journal* for the African Civilization Society, and from 1870 until his death in 1895 he issued the *National Monitor* newspaper in Brooklyn.[3]

As a tool for teaching the rudiments of the English language, *Freedman's Torchlight* presented the alphabet in large block letters, followed by the basic combination of vowels and consonants. Spelling lessons for simple words were given; and short sentences were formed into reading lessons for arithmetic, grammar, history, and the Bible. An editorial in the first issue (December, 1866) explained that the periodical was "devoted to the temporal and spiritual interests of the Freedmen; and adapted to their present need of instruction."[4]

At Hampton Institute in Virginia, thirteen years after the school had been established by the American Missionary Association, a periodical was initiated by the graduates. The *Alumni Journal*, edited and managed by resident graduates and printed on the school press, was issued from 1881 until 1895. During these years the editors were William M. Reid, George W. Davis, and Frank D. Banks, who worked in offices on the campus. In 1904 the alumni association made plans to revive the publication, and William Taylor Burwell Williams, employed as a field director by his alma mater, was selected as the editor. The Hampton *Alumni Journal* had the "hearty approval and good will of the Principal and officers of the school."[5]

The *Alumni Magazine* published by the graduates of Lincoln University in Pennsylvania had a different orientation. The alumni association initiated the periodical in November, 1884, at a time when the organization was dominated by an aggressive leadership agitating for changes in the administration of the school.

This group was petitioning the board of trustees to place Negroes on the board and on the faculty of Lincoln, an institution that had been founded by the Presbyterian church in 1854 for the education of Negro men. The first black trustee was eventually elected in 1927, and the first black faculty member was appointed in 1932.[6]

One of the leaders of the association was Nathan Francis Mossell, who graduated from Lincoln in 1879 and from the University of Pennsylvania medical school three years later. As corresponding secretary, he also served as editor of the *Alumni Magazine*. Other alumni on the editorial staff were William W. Still, a lawyer (and son of William Still, who wrote the history of the underground railroad); J. P. Williams, an Episcopalian minister; and Joseph C. Price, president of Zion Wesley Institute (later Livingstone College) in North Carolina, who was the corresponding editor. Mossell, Still, and Williams were residents of Philadelphia, where the magazine was published. Mossell was engaged in private practice and later, in 1895, organized the Frederick Douglass Memorial Hospital and Training School. He was chief-of-staff and medical director of this institution until his retirement in 1933; he continued in private practice until his death in 1946.[7]

The *Alumni Magazine* was initiated as part of the campaign for black representation on the trustee board and faculty. It also reported events at the university and activities of the graduates, especially those working in the South. Beyond these functions, the *Alumni Magazine* served as a general periodical for Negroes. It included many feature articles by persons not connected with Lincoln University, information about other schools, book reviews, and poetry. Discussions were presented on such educational topics as classical versus industrial education and white versus black teachers for Negro students. A contribution from Alexander Crummell was entitled "Excellence, an End of the Trained Intellect." Frederick Douglass, writing for a symposium on "Caste in Colored Institutions," supported the alumni association and criticized the absence of Negro faculty and board members in institutions for black people. In addition to education, other areas of concern

were discussed in this magazine, such as the Democratic administration of President Grover Cleveland and the operation of the
convict lease system in southern states.

One of the books reviewed was George W. Williams' two-vol-
ume *History of the Negro Race in America, from 1619 to 1880*,
published in 1883. The reviewer considered this study the best
work available on the contribution of Negroes to American history. Poetry was contributed to the periodical by Frances Ellen
Watkins Harper and by the editor's wife, Gertrude Bustill Mossell. Although the only signed material from Mrs. Mossell was her
poetry, she may well have written the book reviews and generally
assisted her husband in editing the *Alumni Magazine*.[8]

Among the periodicals published in the interest of state teachers' associations, the *Progressive Educator* was probably the first.
It was established during the 1880s as the official journal for the
North Carolina State Teachers' Association and also for the North
Carolina schools of the African Methodist Episcopal Zion Church.
Charles N. Hunter and Simon Green Atkins were the editors of
this magazine, which was published in Raleigh. Hunter's teaching
career in North Carolina began in 1875 and extended over a period of more than fifty years. Atkins, a teacher at Livingstone
College, was one of the founders of the state teachers' association,
and for many years he was in charge of the educational work of
the A. M. E. Zion Church. After the *Progressive Educator* ceased
publication, he became editor of the *Southland* periodical.

Another early state journal was the *Educational Era*, issued in
Baltimore in 1892 by the Maryland State Teachers' Association.
The editor was William Ashbie Hawkins, who, while working as
a teacher, was also studying toward a law degree at Howard University. After graduating, he established his practice in Baltimore
and became a leading civil rights lawyer in that state.[9]

Serving as the official journal of the State Teachers' Association
of Georgia was the *Negro Educational Journal*. The Alabama
Teachers' Association also adopted the *Journal* as its medium of
communication.[10] This monthly publication was inaugurated in
November, 1894, at Cartersville, Georgia, under the editorship

of Floyd Grant Snelson, an A. M. E. minister and public school principal. William Baxter Matthews, a principal in the Atlanta public schools, was associated with him in editing the *Journal*. Both Snelson and Matthews had earned bachelor's degrees at Atlanta University. Beginning in January, 1895, Mrs. Waterloo B. Snelson was listed as editor of the periodical with her husband. She was also an Atlanta University graduate and a public school teacher. With the May, 1895, issue, the site of publication moved to Athens, where Snelson was appointed as a principal in the public school system. He did not remain in his native Georgia much longer. In 1896 the A. M. E. Church assigned him to the department of West African missions, with headquarters in Freetown, Sierra Leone.[11] The *Journal* possibly ceased publication when the Snelsons left the state.

In 1899 an educational journal was started in Huntsville, Alabama, by Robert D. Hunt. This monthly periodical, the *Educator*, became the official publication for the teachers' association of that state. Throughout its existence—from February, 1899, until December, 1909—the *Educator* was edited by Hunt, who was born and educated in Huntsville, graduating from the Normal and Industrial School in 1889. Alfred J. Hunt, his father and a teacher at the school, was business manager for the periodical.[12] The front page of the first issue of the *Educator* was devoted entirely to an article on industrial education by Booker T. Washington, accompanied by his photograph. During the first year of publication, one of the contributors was Charles Alexander, former publisher of the Boston *Monthly Review*, who was at that time a teacher at the normal school and one of the proprietors of the Cashin and Alexander printing establishment in Huntsville. Later he returned to Boston to edit *Alexander's Magazine*.

Lexington, Kentucky, was the site of publication of the *Southern Teachers' Advocate*, which was founded in 1905 in the interest of Negro education in Kentucky and throughout the South. It concentrated on state news and served as the medium of communication for the Kentucky State Colored Teachers' Association. The editors and publishers were Chapman C. Monroe and his wife, Mary B. Monroe. In addition to educational news and discussions, the *Advocate* frequently carried poems and short stories by Joseph Seamon Cotter, Sr., a well-known author and a principal in the Louisville public school system.

In New Orleans the *Colored Teacher* was published and edited from 1906 to 1908 by John F. Guillaume, who conducted a correspondence school in that city. This periodical was adopted by the Louisiana State Colored Teachers' Association as its official journal. In the editorial of the September, 1907, issue, Guillaume stated that the purpose of the *Colored Teacher* was to promote improvements in the educational system of Louisiana. He enumerated three specific goals: "a State Teachers' Association of one thousand members to give character and dignity to the colored teaching profession," "a normal school centrally located for the more efficient training of colored teachers," and "a general raise in the salaries of colored teachers in a majority of the parishes of the State."[13]

The concerns of other educational journals extended beyond state boundaries. The *Southern Educator* was advertised as the monthly publication of the Southern Colored Teachers' Association, located at Hawkinsville, Georgia. The Reverend S. Timothy Tice was corresponding secretary of the organization and managing editor of the periodical. This association operated a placement agency and promised that teachers of all grades could "be located on short notice on receipt of $1.00 and postage."[14]

The *Educator*, founded in 1898 at Kittrell, North Carolina, was the publication of the educational department of the African Methodist Episcopal Church and was edited by John Russell Hawkins, secretary of that department. Hawkins, an outstanding layman in his church, was president of Kittrell College from 1890 to 1896, secretary of the denomination's educational department from 1896 to 1912, and financial secretary of the church from 1912 until his death in 1939. The *Educator* was published to give historical and statistical information about the A. M. E. schools in the United States and Africa.

Other periodicals issued between 1900 and 1909 attempted to

function as national journals for Negro teachers. Although national teachers' organizations had been formed as early as the 1890s, apparently none of these associations issued a periodical before 1910, and certain individuals endeavored to fill this void. The *National Capital Searchlight* was published in Washington by M. Grant Lucas, a teacher and principal in the District of Columbia school system. In the initial issue (February, 1901), Lucas announced that he hoped "to build up a circulation of at least 10,000 subscribers among the 100,000 colored people in the District of Columbia, and as wide a circulation as possible throughout the country, especially among the 27,000 colored teachers." He outlined ambitious plans for the periodical, stating that it would give "a brief history of educational work among the colored people in each of the States." The *National Capital Searchlight* had a promising beginning. Letters of encouragement were received from the U.S. commissioner of education and from the superintendent of the District of Columbia schools. Among the members of the advisory board were Robert H. Terrell, then a high school principal in Washington, and Lewis B. Moore, dean of the teacher education division at Howard University.[15] Today, however, no issues beyond the second number (March, 1901) can be found.

David V. Bohannon, editor of the *Negro Educational Review*, also projected a national scope for his publication. He initiated the *Review* in Vincennes, Indiana, in November, 1904, as the "only national educational journal published in the interests of the teachers of the Negro youths and of universal education."[16] Expressing his concern about education in the United States in general, Bohannon contended that the inadequate education that all American children were receiving was a common nationwide problem that had to be solved through federal action. "The only way every American boy and girl can ever hope to have equal opportunities and equal facilities in our educational system," he proposed, "is for the national government to take hold and control the school affairs just as it does our postal system."[17]

Bohannon was assisted in the publication of this periodical by

R. L. Anthony and C. F. Gardner, business manager and treasurer of the Negro Educational Review Press. In 1905 Josephine Silone Yates and Roscoe Conkling Bruce were appointed to the editorial staff. Mrs. Yates, designated as the associate editor, was teaching at Lincoln Institute in Jefferson City, Missouri, and serving her second term as president of the National Association of Colored Women. Bruce, named the assistant editor, was a 1902 graduate of Harvard College and director of the academic department at Tuskegee Institute. Selections from the writings and speeches of Booker T. Washington appeared frequently in this periodical. An advertisement for the *Review* was carried until 1907 in the *Tuskegee Student*, a weekly newspaper from Tuskegee Institute, although the last issue of the periodical that has been located is that of November, 1905.

A periodical that achieved wide geographical circulation was the *School Teacher*, founded in Washington, D.C., in 1909. (A detailed discussion of this magazine is given at the end of the chapter.) The individuals responsible for the *School Teacher* were not named in the publication, but local newspapers identified them as Negro administrators in the District of Columbia school system, including Roscoe Conkling Bruce, who had been appointed assistant superintendent in charge of the colored schools in 1907.[18] In the *School Teacher*, feature articles were contributed by administrators and teachers from school systems located in the eastern, southeastern, and midwestern sections of the United States, and news items reported educational events and trends throughout the country. Emphasis, though, particularly in the editorials and news notes, was on developments in the Washington schools. In the initial number (September, 1909), the frontispiece was a photograph of the superintendent of the school system, and the lead article was written by the vice-president of the board of education. The quotation on the cover of all the issues, "The best is none too good for our children," was attributed to the president of the board. Clearly, harmony existed between the promoters of the *School Teacher* and the chief administrators of the District of Columbia school system.

Less cordial were the relations between Roscoe Conkling Bruce and many Negro parents and citizens who were critical of his administrative ability. A group called the Citizens' Committee was formed in opposition to Bruce and issued its own publication, a four-page periodical called the *Citizen*. The officers of this organization were Napoleon B. Marshall, president; James L. McNeill, secretary; and S. E. Lacey, manager of the *Citizen*. In the four issues of the periodical that appeared between December, 1909, and July, 1910, many accusations of mismanagement were leveled against Bruce, including the hiring of teachers who lacked the required formal education, the dismissal of highly qualified personnel without cause, the assignment of persons to subject areas in which they were not prepared to teach, and a lax system of examination for teachers that lent itself "too easily to the manipulation of those who believe in the policy of favoritism." The *Citizen* expressed concern that Bruce, "a young man of exceptional text book education and brilliant promise[,] should be forced as a pawn in the political game, to bear the burdens of an office for which he has not matured," and the journal called for Bruce's resignation. Prominent in the pages of this publication were statements by Daniel A. P. Murray, the scholar and bibliophile who was employed at the Library of Congress. Writing as a concerned parent, Murray contended that Bruce had "little real knowledge of the practical workings" of the school system.[19]

In the decades following Reconstruction, religious journals were the second largest group of specialized periodicals. Although the 1880s witnessed the sponsorship by religious denominations of general magazines with broad interests and subject coverage, there were other periodicals during the post-Reconstruction years that concentrated on religious subject matter. One of these, the *Theological Institute*, was issued under the auspices of established churches. Others were published through individual enterprise, without the official support of the church. Such journals were started in many parts of the country and issued by ministers of various faiths. Although these periodicals may not have had the sponsorship and the financial assistance of the church organization, they were generally concerned with the interests of the denominations to which the editors belonged. Sometimes they had a wider perspective and attempted to reach a larger audience. Whatever their scope, these religious periodicals reflected primarily the thinking of the individuals who edited them.

The church-sponsored *Theological Institute* was a unique publication. This journal, established in 1909, was an ecumenical venture among the Negro branches of Methodism. In February, 1908, a joint board of the bishops of three black Methodist denominations held its first convention at the Metropolitan A. M. E. Church in Washington. The meetings were conducted by the senior bishops: Henry McNeal Turner of the African Methodist Episcopal Church, James Walker Hood of the African Methodist Episcopal Zion Church, and Lucius Henry Holsey of the Colored Methodist Episcopal Church. An observer of the first day's proceedings recorded that "it was a magnificent sight to see twenty-three Bishops of different branches of colored Methodism arm in arm, marching up the aisle of the great church. It was a scene never to be forgotten."[20]

The following year, Turner, Hood, and Holsey initiated the *Theological Institute* as a monthly journal for the instruction of ministers and Sunday school teachers. The three bishops were listed as the editors, with Turner designated as editor-in-chief and publisher, and the journal was issued from Atlanta. The editors stated that the periodical would "teach every phase of Sacred Divinity, Ecclesiastical History in all ages, . . . forms of Prayer, Church government, and reserve a few pages for general correspondence." They suggested that "ministerial applicants for examination, will find The Institute indispensable," especially "young ministers who are not able to buy the necessary books." The *A. M. E. Zion Quarterly Review* heralded the *Theological Institute* as "a new idea in religious journalism" that "should be welcomed by the great mass of untrained preachers . . . as a messenger of helpfulness."[21]

The three individuals responsible for the *Theological Institute* had been active in their denominations for many years.[22] Henry McNeal Turner was elected a bishop in 1880 and became senior bishop of the A. M. E. Church fifteen years later. Previously he had served as manager of the publishing department, had compiled a hymnal, and had written other books for the church. He initiated three newspapers for the denomination: the *Southern Christian Recorder*, the *Voice of Missions*, and the *Voice of the People*. Turner had contributed to the *Repository of Religion and Literature* published by his church before the Civil War; he had urged the denomination to sponsor a magazine for women; and he had promoted the establishment of the *A. M. E. Church Review* in 1884.

Lucius Henry Holsey (1842–1920) began his ministry in the Methodist Episcopal Church, South. In 1870 he was a delegate to the conference at which the Colored Methodist Episcopal Church was organized as a denomination separate from the white church. At that meeting, he took the lead in planning a publishing house for the new denomination, and at the second conference, in 1873, he was elected bishop. Holsey also founded Paine College in Augusta, Georgia, and helped to establish Lane College in Jackson, Tennessee. He compiled a hymnal and a manual for the denomination and initiated one of the church newspapers, the *Gospel Trumpet*.

James Walker Hood was ordained a bishop in the African Methodist Episcopal Zion Church in 1872. He was one of the founders of Livingstone College and was chairman of the trustee board of the school from its beginning in 1879 until his death in 1918. Hood wrote an extensive history of the Zion denomination, which was published in 1895. Thus, *Theological Institute* was a continuation of the longtime concern of these three bishops for the education of the ministry and for the promotion of literary activities in their churches.

Between 1880 and 1909, religious periodicals published by individuals appeared in the Midwest, New England, the Middle Atlantic states, and the South. Three journals issued in the midwestern section of the country were the *Mouth-Piece*, the *Pulpit and Desk*, and the *Jewel*. The *Mouth-Piece* began publication in 1887 in Chicago under editor Thomas W. Henderson, a minister in the A. M. E. Church; the associate editors were Daniel P. Brown and John M. Henderson. In commenting on this periodical, the *A. M. E. Church Review* spoke of it as an interesting monthly, "designed to reflect the mind of the Bishop of the Fourth Episcopal Church [and] that of the preachers of the Northwest generally." Thomas W. Henderson was later elected business manager of the A. M. E. publishing house. The *Pulpit and Desk* also began publication in Chicago in 1887. It was a quarterly, edited by Baptist minister J. Bird Wilkins. In St. Paul, Minnesota, Lewis Charles Sheafe, also a Baptist minister, published the *Jewel*. He started this monthly in January, 1891, but discontinued it at midyear when the Chicago firm that printed it went out of business.[23]

In New England, Eli George Biddle issued the *Zion Trumpet and Homiletic Magazine*. Biddle, affiliated with the African Methodist Episcopal Zion denomination, was pastor of a church in New Haven, Connecticut, and a student at the Yale University divinity school. He was also presiding elder for the New England Conference of his church. One of the staff members of the *Zion Trumpet* was Simon Green Atkins of North Carolina, who served as assistant editor for educational work.[24]

Among the religious journals published in the Middle Atlantic states was *Thornton's Magazine*, issued in Wilmington, Delaware, by Montrose William Thornton, an A. M. E. minister. He was a native of Iowa and a graduate of the divinity school of Drake University. During his career of more than fifty years, Thornton was assigned to churches in a number of states, including the Mother Bethel Church in Philadelphia, and he was president of Campbell College, an A. M. E. school in Jackson, Mississippi. *Thornton's Magazine*, a monthly journal, began publication in 1907. By that time Thornton had become widely known as a speaker and writer. In 1903, when a Negro prisoner was taken from the Wilmington jail and burned to death, Thornton had spoken out against this crime, the first lynching of record in the state of Delaware.[25]

The *Colored Catholic* was issued in Baltimore by Charles Marcellus Dorsey. Dorsey, who operated a printing business and taught printing at an industrial school, founded this publication in 1909. As an active layman in the Roman Catholic Church, he had fought for the ordination of Negroes to the priesthood, a position that his brother John Henry Dorsey achieved in 1902.[26]

Baltimore was also the site of publication of a leading Protestant Episcopal periodical, the *Church Advocate*. This four-page journal was edited and published by George Freeman Bragg, Jr., rector of the St. James Episcopal Church. Bragg came to Baltimore in the fall of 1891 from Norfolk, Virginia, where he had founded the *Church Advocate* earlier that year. Previously he had also issued another periodical in Virginia, the *Afro-American Churchman*. The *Church Advocate*, like its predecessor, was initiated "in the interest of the colored race in general, and of the Episcopal Church in particular." In 1907 Bragg decided to limit the *Advocate* to local church activities because of "the lack of sufficient support, with no resources from advertisements." Bragg continued to issue this periodical until the 1930s. He also edited weekly newspapers in Virginia and in Baltimore, and he was the author of several books and pamphlets.[27] The newspaper that he issued during his early years in Baltimore was one of the publications from which John H. Murphy, Sr., developed the *Afro-American*, a nationally distributed paper that is still published in Baltimore today.

In addition to the periodicals that Bragg issued in Virginia, another religious journal in that state was the *National Pilot*. The *Pilot*, issued in Petersburg, began publication in the 1880s as a monthly and became a quarterly around 1890. By 1900 it was published as a weekly newspaper. The founder and editor throughout these years was Charles Benjamin William Gordon, a Baptist preacher trained at the Richmond Theological Seminary. The *National Pilot*, "devoted to the educational, moral, and religious improvement of mankind," also served as the medium of communication for the Virginia State Baptist Convention.[28]

Other southern periodicals were *Lowery's Religious Monthly* and the *Church and Society World*. *Lowery's Religious Monthly* (entitled the *Colored Preacher* when it began publication) was issued in Spartanburg, South Carolina, during the late 1890s and was edited by Irving E. Lowery, a Methodist minister, and his son Warren Scott Lowery.[29] The editor of *Church and Society World* was Thomas Hamilton Beb Walker, a Methodist minister in Florida, founder of a benevolent organization called the St. Joseph Aid Society, and author of novels and nonfiction. In 1900 he went to Atlanta to study at Gammon Theological Seminary, graduating from that school in 1903. While in Atlanta, Walker edited *Church and Society World*, a sixty-four-page illustrated monthly magazine.[30]

One of the best-known black preachers during the post-Reconstruction decades was the woman evangelist Amanda Berry Smith. In the early 1900s, during the last years of her life, she issued the *Helper* periodical. An autobiography published in 1893 told the story of her life up to that point: her birth in Maryland to slave parents in 1837; the purchase of the family's freedom by her father and their move to Pennsylvania; her three months of formal education; two ill-fated marriages and a poverty-stricken life as a domestic servant and washerwoman; her religious conversion in 1868; her tours as an evangelist and temperance lecturer, first in the United States and then in England and Africa; and finally her return to the United States after years of traveling and speaking abroad.[31] In 1899, at the age of sixty-three, Amanda Smith began a new phase of her life when she opened a home for "the care, education, and industrial training of orphan, destitute, needy children, especially those of colored parentage."[32] The Amanda Smith Industrial Home was located in Harvey, Illinois, a temperance community in the suburbs of Chicago. She published the *Helper* for several years to raise funds for the institution, and the contents of the publication reflected her interests in child care, evangelism, and temperance. Amanda Smith supervised the industrial home until 1912, when she accepted the invitation of a white millionaire friend to join the newly established retirement community of Sebring, Florida. She died in Florida in 1915 and was buried in Harvey.[33]

Other women editors were associated with the specialized women's magazines that developed during the post-Reconstruction years. Women and their interests had always been a significant part of the Afro-American periodical press: female writers had contributed to the very first periodicals, and the men who edited these journals had included the concerns of women within the scope of their publications. David Ruggles presented a "Ladies' Mirror" as one of the sections in the *Mirror of Liberty* in 1838, and his contemporary, William Whipper, spoke out for the equality of women in the *National Reformer*. The *Repository of Religion and Literature* of 1858 had a "Mothers' Department" and a "Young Ladies' Lecture Room." When Negro periodicals reappeared after Reconstruction, the editors of the general magazines again solicited contributions from women and again made the woman's department a feature of their publications. For example, *Howard's Negro-American Magazine* and the *Afro-American Budget* of the 1880s and the *Southland* of the 1890s had columns conducted by women. At the same time, a new type of periodical emerged during the post-Reconstruction years: the specialized magazine for women.

The African Methodist Episcopal denomination had considered the publication of a woman's periodical as early as 1880. One of the individuals promoting such a journal was Henry McNeal Turner, who, as business manager of the publication department, suggested to the General Conference of 1880 that the church should establish "a Quarterly Review and a Ladies' Magazine." The conference adopted this recommendation, with the provision that the periodicals were to be initiated "when the state of the treasury will admit." The quarterly, the *A. M. E. Church Review*, began publication in 1884. Although the *Ladies' Magazine* continued to be authorized, reports of the publication department during this period do not indicate that it was actually published.[34]

The 1880s did witness, however, the beginnings of the woman's magazine published through individual enterprise. *Our Women and Children* was established at Louisville, Kentucky, in 1888, and in 1891 *Ringwood's Afro-American Journal of Fashion* appeared in Cleveland, Ohio. During the first decade of the twentieth century, two women's periodicals were initiated in states west of the Mississippi: *Woman's World* in Fort Worth, Texas, in 1900; and the *Colored Woman's Magazine* in Topeka, Kansas, in 1907—both issued as monthly family magazines. Another type of woman's periodical was also inaugurated toward the end of the nineteenth century: the journal issued in the interest of women's clubs. The *Woman's Era* was started in Boston in 1894 as an activity of the Woman's Era Club in that city. The club's founder and president, Josephine St. Pierre Ruffin, published the *Era* for women's clubs throughout the country as well as for her local organization. *National Association Notes* was started in 1897 at Tuskegee, Alabama, by Margaret Murray Washington for the newly organized National Association of Colored Women.

No copies of the four family maganizes have been located, but information in contemporary publications indicates that they were substantial periodicals. The first issue of *Our Women and Children* appeared in Louisville in August, 1888.[35] The magazine was issued by the National Publishing Company, of which Charles H. Parrish was president; William J. Simmons was the editor and manager. Both of these men were Baptist ministers prominent in religious, journalistic, and educational activities. Simmons was president of the normal and theological school operated in Louisville by the state Baptist association and editor of the weekly *American Baptist* issued by that organization. He was a leader in the development of national associations among Negro Baptists and Negro journalists.[36] Parrish, in cooperation with Simmons, founded the Eckstein-Norton Institute at Cane Springs, Kentucky, and was president of that school for more than twenty years. He also served as pastor of Calvary Baptist Church in Louisville and as editor for the National Baptist Sunday School Publishing Board in Nashville.[37]

Simmons and Parrish gathered a corps of women writers as departmental editors for the magazine. Most of these women were living in Louisville and were closely associated with Simmons and the school of which he was president. Mary Virginia Cook, the education editor, was principal of the normal department of that institution. (She later married Charles Parrish.) Ione E. Wood, the temperance editor, was Simmons' niece and an instructor of Greek at the school. Lucy Wilmot Smith, editor of the department for women's work, was Simmons' private secretary. In addition to these local writers, Ida B. Wells (Mrs. Ferdinand L. Barnett), a teacher in Memphis, Tennessee, and editor of the *Free Speech* newspaper, was on the staff as editor of the home department.[38] Ida Wells eventually became nationally and internationally known as a leader in the fight against lynching and segregation. *Our Women and Children* was well received by the black press: the *A. M. E. Church Review* observed that the contributors were "chiefly persons of marked ability," and the Indianapolis *Freeman* commented on "the handsomely engraved title-cover."[39]

Ringwood's Afro-American Journal of Fashion was published and edited by Julia Ringwood Coston. Mrs. Coston was the wife of William H. Coston, an A. M. E. minister whose assignments took them to many cities. The periodical was published during their residence in Cleveland.[40] Departmental editors for the magazine included Adina E. White of Cincinnati for the art department, Sarah Mitchell of Cleveland for the home department, Earnestine Clark Nesbitt of Cincinnati for the "Mother's Corner," Susie I. Shorter of Wilberforce, who edited "Plain Talk to Our Girls," Molly E. Lambert of Detroit for the literary department, and Mary Church Terrell of Washington, who contributed biographical sketches.[41]

This magazine attracted much attention when it began publication in 1891 and was widely complimented, especially for the dress patterns and engravings of the latest Parisian styles. The *A. M. E. Church Review* stated that *Ringwood's Afro-American Journal of Fashion* was "neat and beautiful in its make-up." A white newspaper in an eastern city commented: "It is especially designed to be an Afro-American magazine, . . . but the pleasing fashion articles, instructive talks with girls and mothers; and witty all-around paragraphs and interesting love stories make Ringwood's *Magazine* a welcome addition to any home, whether its occupants be black or white."[42]

Woman's World, initiated in Fort Worth, Texas, in 1900, was edited by Jay W. Taylor, who also issued a weekly newspaper. An advertisement for *Woman's World* described the periodical as containing "good stories, with colored men and women as heroes and heroines; special articles that are informing as well as entertaining; special talks for girls; a page for children; a household page with timely articles for the economical, studious housewife; a fashion page with latest Paris and New York styles illustrated; a department of flower-culture; and many other good things for pleasure and instruction."[43] A few years later another magazine, also advertised as a national household journal, appeared in Topeka, Kansas. The initial number of this periodical, the *Colored Woman's Magazine*, was the Christmas issue of 1907. Mrs. C. M. Hughes was the editor, and Mrs. Minnie Thomas the business manager. Later, Mrs. M. A. Johnson edited the magazine. This periodical was probably published until at least 1920.[44]

The *Woman's Era*, founded in Boston in 1894 by Josephine St. Pierre Ruffin for the local Woman's Era Club, was an integral part of the women's club movement of the late nineteenth century. National organization among Negro women's clubs paralleled the formation of the General Federation of Women's Clubs by white women in 1890.[45] In 1892, an association of clubs, the Colored Women's League, was formed in Washington. Among the incorporators of this organization were Mary Church Terrell and Helen Cook, who was elected president. In 1895, under Mrs.

Ruffin's leadership, a conference of colored women held in Boston resulted in the National Federation of Afro-American Women, with Margaret Murray Washington as president. In the summer of 1896, these two groups, holding their annual conventions in Washington, joined together and established the National Association of Colored Women. Mary Church Terrell was elected as the first president. The *Woman's Era* served as the official journal for the National Federation of Afro-American Women; and when the National Association of Colored Women was established, the *Era* had a separate section for that organization, edited by Mrs. Washington. (A detailed discussion of the *Woman's Era* is given at the end of the chapter.)

In 1897 Mrs. Washington began a separate periodical for the organization, the *National Association Notes*, which was issued at Tuskegee as a four-page monthly newsletter. It had this format throughout the pre-1910 period of publication, although an enlarged illustrated issue was occasionally published. The association adopted the periodical as its official publication, and Mrs. Washington continued as editor until 1922. The journal, with the title shortened to *National Notes*, was issued until 1935, when the association suspended publication. In 1947 *National Notes* was reactivated, and it is published today as a quarterly journal.[46] Margaret Murray had joined the faculty of Tuskegee Institute in 1889, following her graduation from Fisk University. She married Booker T. Washington in 1892. At Tuskegee she was dean of women and director of industries for women, and she was president of the National Association of Colored Women for several years.[47]

As the official publication of this organization, *National Association Notes* included announcements and reports of the conventions, the text of the constitution, financial reports, news items on local clubs and clubwomen, and the names of the clubs affiliated with the national organization. The roster of clubs in the September, 1897, issue listed groups located in the District of Columbia and in twenty-six states of the Union. Feature articles in the periodical reflected the association's support of such causes as industrial education, the inauguration of kindergartens for pre-school-age children, the temperance movement, and the abolition of the separate railroad coach law in southern states.

The specialized journals in music were the *Musical Messenger*, initiated in 1886 by Amelia L. Tilghman in Montgomery, Alabama; the *Negro Music Journal*, founded in 1902 by J. Hillary Taylor in Washington, D.C.; and *Musical Advance*, edited in 1907 by J. H. Carter in Richmond, Virginia. The *Negro Music Journal* was the most substantial of these periodicals, and a separate discussion of this publication is given at the end of this chapter.

The *Musical Messenger* was advertised as "the first effort ever made towards musical journalism among the colored people in this country."[48] Amelia L. Tilghman, who was a native of Washington, D.C., graduated from the normal department of Howard University in 1871, and later studied at the Boston Conservatory of Music. During her career she taught music in Washington and in Montgomery, appeared as a soprano vocalist on the concert stage, and sang as a soloist with the Fifteenth Street Presbyterian Church choir in Washington. She began publishing the *Musical Messenger* while teaching in Montgomery. By 1888 Miss Tilghman had moved back to Washington, where she continued to issue the periodical.[49] The associate editor was Lucinda Bragg Adams of Baltimore, sister of the Reverend George F. Bragg, Jr., who published the *Afro-American Churchman* and *Church Advocate* periodicals.

The *Musical Messenger* was a slight publication of only four pages. An editorial in the July, 1889, number outlined plans for expanded issues in the future: "A short inventory will be kept of all our prominent singers. . . . We also intend to publish at different times, the names of all colored composers of music, what they have composed, and where their music can be found. It is also our intention to enlarge this paper soon and publish in each issue, some pieces of music by our colored composers."[50] No issues after the July, 1889, number have been located.

The *Musical Advance* in Virginia was advertised as a magazine containing "hints, talks, suggestions and articles on music in all times; also biographical sketches and photos of the noted colored musicians and musical organizations."[51] No issues at all of this periodical have been located.

The periodical *Sylvester Russell's Review* was devoted to the stage and theater. For forty years, Sylvester Russell was associated with the concert stage and vaudeville theater as a performer and critic. He started his musical career as soloist with church choirs in New Jersey and New York, then, in 1891, made his debut in vaudeville. After several years of tours and performances, Russell returned to his native city of Orange, New Jersey, and initiated the periodical. The *Review* began publication in January, 1906; it failed after six months. Following a brief return to the stage, Russell revived the magazine in 1907. This time, *Sylvester Russell's Review* was issued in Hazleton, Pennsylvania, with financial backing from a former resident of that town whom Russell had met on one of his tours. Again, he had problems publishing the periodical, and he eventually closed out the enterprise and moved to Chicago, where he started a book publishing business and a weekly paper. Russell wrote theater review columns for the *Chicago Defender* and the Indianapolis *Freeman* and also contributed to *Alexander's Magazine, McGirt's Magazine*, the *National Domestic*, and other periodicals. He continued as a critic of the stage and theater until his death in 1930.[52]

Periodicals in the field of medicine and health were the *Medical and Surgical Observer*, the *National Medical Association Journal*, and the *Hospital Herald*. The earliest of these was the *Medical and Surgical Observer*, issued in Jackson, Tennessee, from 1892 to 1894 by Miles Vandahurst Lynk. This magazine was a private venture that predated the formation of the National Medical Association and the subsequent establishment of the association's *Journal* in 1909. The *Medical and Surgical Observer* has been acknowledged as the first medical journal published by Negroes in the United States, and Lynk has been recognized as "a contributing force" in the founding of the national organization.[53] A separate discussion of this periodical is presented at the end of the chapter.

The National Medical Association was founded in Atlanta in 1895. Its purpose was expressed in this statement: "Conceived in no spirit of racial exclusiveness, fostering no ethnic antagonism, but born of the exigencies of American environment, the National Medical Association has for its object the banding together for mutual cooperation and helpfulness, the men and women of African descent who are legally and honorably engaged in the practice of the cognate professions of Medicine, Surgery, Pharmacy and Dentistry."[54] Charles Victor Roman and John Andrew Kenney were the members of the association largely responsible for the founding of the *Journal*, and Roman became the first editor-in-chief. The periodical was issued at Tuskegee, where Kenney, secretary of the organization and associate editor of the *Journal*, was located. Initiated as a quarterly in 1909, this periodical is still published today as a monthly journal. Roman was editor until 1918, when he was succeeded by Kenney. (Roman was also president of the association in 1903–1904.) The other members of the editorial staff in 1909 were W. G. Alexander, business manager; W. S. Lofton, dental editor; and Amanda V. Gray, pharmaceutical editor.

Charles V. Roman (1864–1934) was educated in Nashville at Fisk University and Meharry Medical College. Following postgraduate courses in Chicago and London and a period of private practice in Texas, he returned to Nashville, where he established a private practice and also taught at Meharry and Fisk. He organized the department of opthalmology at Meharry in 1904, which he directed until 1931. He was also the author of two books, *American Civilization and the Negro* (1916) and *Meharry Medical College: A History* (1934).[55] John A. Kenney (1874–1950) received his medical training at the Leonard Medical College of Shaw University. For more than twenty years he was personal physician to Booker T. Washington and medical director of the John A. Andrew Memorial Hospital at Tuskegee Institute. Later he moved to Newark, New Jersey, and established a hospital in that city. His book, *The Negro in Medicine*, was published in 1912, the same year he was elected president of the National Medical Association.[56]

In the first issue of the *Journal*, Roman stated that the periodical would serve as a channel of communication for members of the association and as a permanent record of papers read at meetings of the organization. "A means of communication and prospect of permanent record," he believed, "would quicken observation, stimulate research, and make original investigation a pleasure."[57] In addition to such papers, the *Journal* contained listings of the officers and members of the association, reports from the officers, summaries of meetings of the organization, information about state medical associations, and news about medical schools.

The *Hospital Herald* was a monthly journal issued in Charleston, South Carolina, and edited by Alonzo Clifton McClennan, a physician in that city. McClennan (1855–1912), a native of Columbia, graduated from the Howard University Medical School in 1880. Under his leadership, the Hospital and Training School for Nurses was established in Charleston in 1897, and McClennan became the surgeon-in-chief.[58] The following year, he began publishing the *Hospital Herald*, to solicit support for this institution.[59] Assisting with the periodical were: R. J. Macbeth, a dental surgeon, and Lucy H. Brown, a gynecologist—both members of the hospital staff—who were the associate editors; Anna DeCosta Banks, the head nurse on the hospital staff, who edited the department of nurse training; and two physicians in other cities, C. C. Johnson of Columbia and J. R. Levy of Florence, who served as corresponding editors.

The front-cover illustration for early issues of the *Herald* was a photograph of Mrs. Lavinia Baker receiving medical treatment at the hospital, following a mob attack in which she was injured and her husband, Frazier B. Baker, was murdered. Baker's appointment in 1898 as the postmaster at Lake City in Williamsburg County had aroused the ire of many whites. This racial hatred led to violence. One night in February of that year, a mob

The Hospital Herald.

A MONTHLY JOURNAL DEVOTED TO HOSPITAL WORK, NURSE TRAINING, DOMESTIC AND PUBLIC HYGIENE.

TERMS, 50 CENTS PER YEAR IN ADVANCE. SINGLE COPIES 5 CENTS.

VOL. 1.	APRIL, 1899.	No. 5.

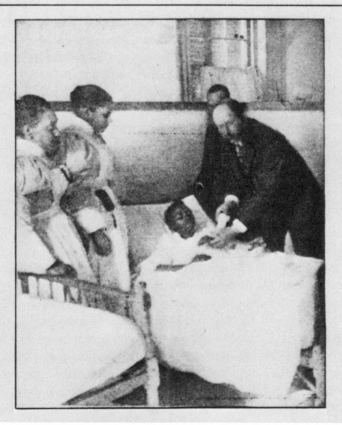

Hospital Herald

Courtesy Waring Historical Library, Medical University of South Carolina

set fire to the Baker home and shot down members of the family as they tried to escape. Baker and an infant child whom Mrs. Baker was carrying were killed, and she and the other children were wounded.

The contents of the *Hospital Herald* included reports from the auxiliary association that had been formed to support the hospital and training school, as well as other news about that institution. The journal also discussed topics relating to the health of Negroes in general, such as the treatment of tuberculosis, an adequate supply of pure drinking water in the cities, and the causes of high mortality among the poor. This periodical became the official journal for the Association of Colored Physicians of South Carolina (later renamed the Palmetto Association of Physicians, Pharmaceutists, and Dentists of South Carolina) and gave reports from the meetings of the organization and biographical sketches of its members.

Business journals issued in the first decade of the twentieth century were: the *American Magazine*, established in New York City in 1905 and superseded that same year by the *Union Magazine*; *Small's Negro Trade Journal*, published in New York in 1906; the *Dollar Mark*, issued in Newport News, Virginia, between 1906 and 1908; and the *Negro Business League Herald*, founded in Washington, D.C., in 1909.

The *American Magazine* solicited patronage for a realty company and other businesses operated by John E. Lewis, Junius C. Ayler, and Jesse W. Watkins. Watkins was one of the young men who had established the *Colored American Magazine* in Boston in 1900. He moved to New York City with this magazine in 1904 when Frederick R. Moore took over the management, but within a few months Watkins' connection with that periodical ended and he turned to other activities. Among the enterprises promoted by Watkins and his associates were the Afro-American News Company, to "handle everything published by the race at wholesale prices"; the Instant Relief Company, to "render aid and assistance" to the working people; and the United Workers' Realty Company, to "better their financial condition."[60]

Advertisements for the realty company stated that it had been established "to buy, rent, lease and build homes . . . , to operate stores of all kinds everywhere, to run laundries, express vans, employment bureaus, restaurants, news and stationery stores." In promoting the sale of shares in the business, Watkins made this appeal: "The time has come when we must take hold of enterprises, as a people, and do our best to maintain them, for we find that this is the only way to keep pace with the rapid strides of progress. . . . The Company will start stores in every city where they can get together 25 who will buy 5 shares each. In this way we will soon be able to employ many of our sons and daughters who are now idle."[61]

The *American Magazine* was a slight publication, taken up mainly with advertisements for these businesses and for the periodical itself. The initial number appeared in May, 1905, with the subtitle *A Monthly, Illustrated Magazine Devoted to the Interest of the Working People.* It was issued by the American Publishing Company, of which John E. Lewis was the superintendent. The editor's name was not given; but the front-page article, "Patience and Perseverance," was by Watkins. The second number, for June/July, 1905, was published by the Afro-American News Company, of which Lewis was also the superintendent. Junius C. Ayler, a Methodist minister, was listed as the editor. The *American Magazine* was superseded after the first few issues by the *Union Magazine*, also published by the Afro-American News Company. Advertisements for the *Union Magazine* described the publication as "the working people's friend" and promised that the realty company would find decent housing for persons moving to New York City; the advertisements appeared in the Richmond (Virginia) *Planet* from October, 1905, to January, 1906.

In the second issue of the *American Magazine*, in a feature article entitled "Will the Negro Race Unite?" Watkins made this observation: "If our people are to be any more than a tool in the hands of other races, no matter whatever we may be, we will have to unite ourselves in mind, in efforts, in politics and in wealth." The editor J. C. Ayler agreed with Watkins on the need for cooperation among Negroes and had been preaching the doctrine of unity to black people for a long time. In a lecture in 1887 on "The Solution of the Negro Problem," he urged "the attainment of education, and the acquisition of capital co-ordinately by the Negro race." Believing that this combination would eventually end racial prejudice, he pleaded with Negroes to "*educate, educate, make money, make money.*"[62]

Making money was also the theme of the *Dollar Mark*, a periodical issued in Newport News, Virginia, by Edward C. Brown to publicize his real estate and banking businesses. Brown had migrated South from his native city of Philadelphia around 1900. In Philadelphia he had been a journalist and had assisted Charles Alexander as business manager of the *Monthly Review*. In Newport News, he turned to more lucrative enterprises. Equipped with a business school education and a talent for advertising, he opened a small office and ventured into real estate, advertising in white and black newspapers that he "made a specialty of handling Colored tenement property." Brown soon had a prospering business and extended his real estate activities into other states, North and South. He incorporated his company and offered stock to the public, promoting this enterprise as the largest Negro real estate brokerage business in the South.[63]

The first issue of the *Dollar Mark* was for June, 1906. Readers were offered this quarterly free for six months, and Brown promised that articles in the magazine would tell how fortunes are made in real estate and how money could be invested to bring profits higher than the 4 percent interest paid by savings banks. He urged Negroes to take advantage of the money-making opportunities available in black enterprises. He explained, for example, how stock purchased in the Afro-American Amusement Company would bring large returns because this would be the only business providing entertainment for the thousands of Negroes expected to attend the 1907 Jamestown Exposition. Brown's reputation grew as he continued to expand his business operations. He was elected corresponding secretary and then president of the state Negro Business League, and he established banks in Newport News and Norfolk. Eventually returning to Philadelphia, he opened a bank there in partnership with Andrew F. Stevens, Jr. After this bank became a casualty of the depression in the 1930s, Brown moved to New York City.[64]

In the same year that Brown started the *Dollar Mark*, Thomas Frederick Small initiated a trade periodical in New York City to advertise Negro businesses in that area. Small, also a native of Philadelphia, came to New York from Newport, Rhode Island, where he had been a newspaper editor. In New York he issued *Small's Illustrated Monthly* (in 1905), which was succeeded by *Small's Negro Trade Journal* the following year.[65]

The most substantial of the business periodicals was the *Negro Business League Herald*, issued by William Sidney Pittman, an architect in Washington and president of the District of Columbia Negro Business League. A separate discussion of this publication is presented at the end of the chapter.

Special interest periodicals for various occupational groups developed in the first decade of the twentieth century. The *Gazetteer and Guide* was devoted to the activities of railroad porters and hotel waiters. A similar publication, the *Railroad Porters and Hotel Waiters Magazine*, was also issued during this time. The *National Domestic* was a magazine for coachmen, butlers, and other household employees. The periodical *"PI."* was published for the journalism and printing vocations.

Newspaper accounts identified George Waldo Chivis as the publisher of the *Railroad Porters and Hotel Waiters Magazine* and indicated that he issued this periodical between 1902 and 1904, first in Philadelphia and later in Chicago.[66] Chivis died in 1914, but apparently the periodical had ended before that time.

Its competitor, the *Gazetteer and Guide*, had a much longer life. James Alexander Ross initiated the *Gazetteer* as a monthly publication in Buffalo in November, 1901. As late as January,

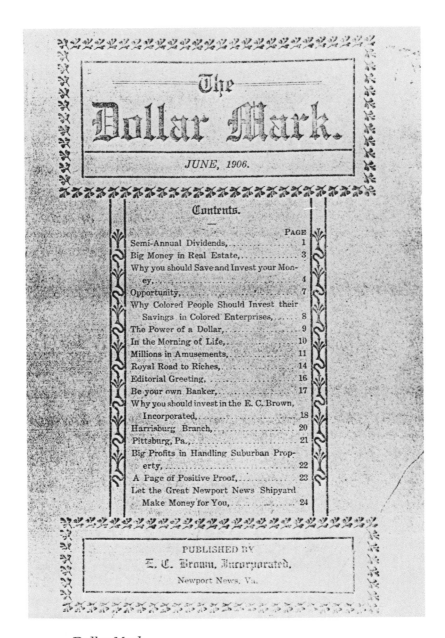

PUBLISHED BY
E. C. Brown, Incorporated,
Newport News, Va.

Dollar Mark

1948, Ross was still issuing this periodical in New York City as a quarterly entitled *For You Magazine and Gazetteer and Guide*. He called it "the oldest magazine published by the race with a new name." Between 1901 and 1948 the periodical changed titles more than once; it was sometimes called the *American Caterer and Gazetteer and Guide*, sometimes the *Caterer, Gazetteer and Guide*. Throughout all these years, however, the publication was edited by either James A. Ross or his wife Minna K. Ross. A native of Missouri, Ross spent most of his adult life in New York State, engaged in law practice, real estate, and politics.[67]

The *Gazetteer and Guide* was initiated in the interests of the National Colored Men's Railroad Association of America, the Head and Side Waiters National Association, and the Masonic orders and auxiliaries. Directories of the officials for these organizations, as well as pictures and personal notes of individual waiters and porters, were included in the periodical. During the early years of publication, when the *Gazetteer* was in competition with the *Railroad Porters and Hotel Waiters Magazine*, Ross advertised that his journal had "larger circulation among Railroad Porters and Hotel Waiters than all similar publications combined." In 1905, the circulation was reported as 7,500.[68] Branch offices were listed for cities in the eastern and midwestern sections of the United States and in Canada.

From its beginning, the *Gazetteer and Guide* was a vehicle for political campaigning and frequently carried photographs of white politicians endorsed for elective office at the state and national levels. In 1907 the *Gazetteer* was promoting Vice-President Charles W. Fairbanks for nomination as the Republican candidate for president. Ross later joined the Democratic party, and in 1941 he boasted that his periodical had supported Franklin D. Roosevelt for vice-president in 1920, for New York governor in 1928 and 1930, and for the presidency in 1932, 1936, and 1940. He claimed that "no other Negro publication has this record." Ross himself at one time aspired to political office, running in 1946 as an independent candidate for the New York state senate from the nineteenth district.[69]

The subtitle of the *Gazetteer* indicated the broad interests of the periodical: *An Illustrated Colored American Publication, Devoted to Literature, Facts, Fiction and Industrialism of the Race Throughout the United States and Canada.* Many photographs of persons in political, business, social, and entertainment circles appeared in the magazine. The first two issues of the *Gazetteer* carried articles by Booker T. Washington on "Industrial Training for the Negro" and a listing of the officials of the National Negro Business League (which Washington had founded the previous year). In each of these issues, approximately half the space was given to advertisements for hotels and other businesses in Canada and the United States. Poetry, fiction, and women's columns were regular features of the periodical, and news about the theater and vaudeville stage was also included.

The *National Domestic* magazine covered theatrical events even more extensively than the *Gazetteer and Guide*, presenting reviews of performances and news notes about the performers. The *National Domestic* also attempted to be a literary magazine and was one of the few Negro periodicals of its time that reprinted the fiction of Charles W. Chesnutt, serializing the novel that had brought him national recognition, *The House Behind the Cedars.* The *National Domestic* was published for coachmen, butlers, and other domestic employees. A special column for women was written by Martha A. Sissle (Mrs. Noble Sissle, Sr.). This periodical began publication in Indianapolis in 1905; Archibald Greathouse was president of the publishing company, and John Dalphin Howard was secretary and responsible for editing the magazine. Howard had formerly been on the staff of the Indianapolis *Freeman*, and when the *National Domestic* was absorbed by *Alexander's Magazine* in 1907, he returned to the newspaper field.[70]

"*PI.*", the journalism periodical, was initiated at Tuskegee in April, 1895. The individuals issuing it were not identified in the magazine; the only information given was that it was published by "Mann & Thornton." At that time, Thomas L. Mann was teaching in the printing department at Tuskegee Institute;[71] and he was probably one of the publishers. *"PI."* presented articles on printing techniques as well as portraits and biographical sketches of outstanding black newspapermen. The editorial page urged that "there should be more instruction given in the different branches of the printing trade," observing that "the theory is lost sight of in most printing offices."[72] No issues of this periodical beyond the first number have been found.

Special periodicals in the first decade of the twentieth century relating to farming were the *Negro Agriculturist* and the *Western Lever.* The *Negro Agriculturist* was published at Sandy Spring, Maryland, a community in Montgomery County that had been settled during the mid-eighteenth century by the Society of Friends. Shortly before the Revolutionary War, members of this society made provisions for emancipating their slaves, and, as a result, by the end of the nineteenth century there were Negro families living in the community who had been free for four and five generations. Many other blacks had migrated there before and after the Civil War, attracted by the relatively better wages and living conditions. In September, 1908, the county board of education opened an agricultural and industrial school for Negroes at Sandy Spring.[73]

The following February, the school sponsored its first farmers' institute. At this meeting, concern was expressed about "the great influx of youth to the cities," and money was donated to start a journal that would promote techniques of more productive farming and thus, the founders hoped, stem the tide of migration from rural areas. The first issue of this monthly publication was dated February, 1909. The masthead described the *Negro Agriculturist* as a "journal for the farm . . . edited and published by the Faculty of Maryland Normal and Agricultural Institute, George H. C. Williams, Principal." A slight publication of four pages per issue, it carried some news about the school; but the main purpose was "to put within the possession of the Negro farmer the known scientific facts and principles of farm practice which he can apply successfully in his operations."[74] The periodical presented questions and answers on practical problems in agriculture and also reported on activities sponsored by the school for the benefit of the local community and the state, such as the farmers' institutes, free correspondence courses in agriculture, and the Maryland Negro State Fair.

The *Western Lever* was established at Des Moines, Iowa, in September, 1908. In this monthly journal, the editor, Julius Dean Pettigrew, expressed concern about two trends that he saw developing in America: the increasing plight of poor people in the cities and the rising tide of racial prejudice against Negroes throughout the country. Two articles that he printed, and reprinted, in the periodical were addressed to these problems. In the article entitled "Western Opportunities in Free, Cheap and Valuable Lands," he spoke to Americans in general: "We have come to that stage, in the development of our country, when the problems of life and the struggle for existence, all demand that the poor people of every race, should leave the cities and go 'back to the farm.' . . . The great western part of our country, with her teeming millions of acres of free and cheap land, invite[s] the poor and the needy of all races to come to her and find a home and independence and a fortune."[75] The *Western Lever* described the lands available for settlement in South Dakota, Washington, and other western states and in western Canada and told success stories of homesteaders, including black persons, who had taken advantage of these opportunities.

In the article on "The Colored Co-operative League Movement," Pettigrew gave a special warning to Negroes: "In the development of our race in this country, we have come to the point where we are destined to become an ostracised race in the midst of this national body politic. . . . If our race is destined to be largely left alone to develop its own future, then in order to have a happy future it must organize, for the purpose of developing itself along the necessary lines that make for self-preservation." Pettigrew observed that "there is already wealth enough and intelligence enough, and moral character and force enough, to make a splendid beginning in this direction, if it were only concentrated and used as a single racial force along these lines." For this purpose, Pettigrew said, he had organized the Colored Cooperative League and established the *Western Lever* as its official publication. His objective was to encourage business enterprise, home and land ownership, and improved methods of farming among Negroes.[76]

Julius Dean Pettigrew, a minister, had been living and farming in the West at least nine years before he initiated the periodical. He had spent much of that time traveling and lecturing in the interest of his organization, and black newspapers in that region had expressed mixed reactions to his program. At first, the Helena (Montana) *Plaindealer* thought it was a good move that "should mark a new epoch" in the progress of Negroes. But after having kept a weather eye on the organization for a few months, the paper concluded that it could not see any benefits to be derived from this movement, since the National Negro Business League had already been established by Booker T. Washington. The Seattle *Republican* also felt that blacks should affiliate with Washington's league, charging that "there are too many different movements and organizations purporting to be for the betterment of the Race." On the other hand, the Butte (Montana) *New Age* reported that many black people were favorably impressed with Pettigrew's program.[77]

In the winter of 1908–1909, Pettigrew decided to move from his farm in Klickitat County, Washington, to Des Moines, Iowa, where he had already set up the publication office for the *Western Lever*. Mrs. Bess Stuart Hughes was in charge of that office.[78] Pettigrew's wife assisted him in editing the journal, and their young son, Julius D. Pettigrew, Jr., wrote about life on the farm for the children's column. The *Western Lever* apparently had a brief existence, for the March, 1909, issue is the last one that has been found.

Medical and Surgical Observer

In an autobiography published in 1951, Miles Vandahurst Lynk recalled his sixty years in medicine, telling how he earned a medical degree and became a licensed physician at the age of nineteen, initiated a medical journal—the *Medical and Surgical Observer*—at twenty-one, participated in the founding of a national medical association at twenty-four, and helped establish a medical school at twenty-seven. Miles V. Lynk was born in Brownsville, Tennessee, in 1871. At an early age, he decided to become a physician, and after finishing the limited education offered by the county school he was tutored by John Robert Gloster, a teacher in his hometown. He then enrolled in the Meharry Medical College at Nashville. Following graduation, he opened his office in Jackson, Tennessee.[79]

In cooperation with other leaders in that town, he established an institution named the University of West Tennessee. Lynk, as president of the school, publicized it as a unique type of Negro professional university. Courses of study were offered in medicine, dentistry, pharmacy, nursing, and law, and a hospital unit afforded practice for students in the medical and nursing programs while providing free medical services for poor people in the community and surrounding area. When Lynk moved to Memphis, the school was transferred to that city. It was closed in 1923 after twenty years of operation; but Lynk continued to practice medicine in Memphis for a number of years.[80]

A physician by profession, Lynk pursued many avocations, especially in the literary field. In Jackson he established the M. V. Lynk Publishing House, which he advertised as "the only Negro publishing plant equipped and run exclusively in the interest of subscription books, of Negro make up."[81] At least two of the publications were compiled by Lynk himself: *The Afro-American School Speaker and Gems of Literature* (1896) and *The Black Troopers; Or, the Daring Heroism of the Negro Soldiers in the Spanish-American War* (1899).

The *Afro-American School Speaker* was an anthology of poetry and prose by black authors, including Phillis Wheatley, Paul Laurence Dunbar, Frances E. W. Harper, Frederick Douglass, Booker T. Washington, and Mary Church Terrell. Lynk was critical of what he called a "faulty system of education," in which the schools were exposing Afro-American youth to the writings and ideas of Anglo-Saxons only. Believing that a "knowledge of the literature (which must necessarily reflect the thoughts and inner life) of a people is one of the most powerful and potent factors in its development," he presented this anthology as an inspiration for Negro children. He issued *The Black Troopers* because he felt that the general public should know more about the accomplishments of Negroes in the military service of the United States. Twenty years later, he compiled a similar publication relating to World War I, *The Negro Pictorial Review of the Great War* (1919). In 1900, the Lynk Publishing House advertised the forthcoming *Afro-American Newspaper Directory*, but no evidence of its actual publication has been found.[82]

Lynk also edited and published periodicals. The first of these was the *Medical and Surgical Observer*, founded in 1892. Between 1898 and 1900 he issued a general illustrated monthly, *Lynk's Magazine*. Both of these were published in Jackson. Several years later, after moving to Memphis, Lynk edited the *Negro Outlook: A National Journal of Opinion and Current Events*, a monthly that began publication in January, 1921. The journalist T. Thomas Fortune, also a Memphis resident at that time, was associated with the magazine. Lynk's main contribution to the black periodical press, however, was the *Medical and Surgical Observer*.

In recounting the establishment of this periodical, Lynk wrote in his autobiography: "I always felt that having entered the profession, I should do something to elevate the standard as well as to add something to the sum total of medical knowledge. . . . Without precedent, and not being backed by an organized group, I decided to found a medical journal." In the initial number of the *Observer* (December, 1892), Lynk presented this statement of objectives: "We recognize the necessity for thorough organization among the increasing numbers of educated Negro physicians of the U.S., that there may be inculcated and fostered among them a more decided ardor for original research and investigation. With this end in view has the OBSERVER come. It recognizes the necessity of a higher standard of medical education in this country."[83]

Fourteen monthly numbers of the *Medical and Surgical Observer* were published from December, 1892, to January, 1894. The *Observer* was devoted to the interests of physicians, dentists, and pharmacists and contained articles and clinical reports, medical formulae reprinted from other journals, book reviews, personal news notes, and information about medical schools and state associations. Typical of the feature articles in the *Observer* were two communications printed in the August, 1893, number. One was written by Doctor S. C. Snelson of Savannah, Georgia, on the subject of surgical practices. The other, "Consumption Among the Colored Race," was by Lincoln Laconia Burwell, a physician in Selma, Alabama. Concerned about the increasing incidence of tuberculosis among Negroes, Burwell presented his theories on the reasons for this trend and then suggested preventive measures for controlling the disease. Miles V. Lynk stated that in publishing the *Observer* he was supplying the colored medical profession with "a very necessary weapon in combating disease, ignorance and quackery." His periodical, he asserted, contained "all the progressive ideas of the profession—minus the chaff."[84]

The *Medical and Surgical Observer* carried advertisements for medicinal preparations, for the four black medical schools (Howard, Meharry, Leonard Medical School at Shaw University, and the medical department of New Orleans University—later Dillard University), and for other medical journals in the United States. Lynk pointed out to potential advertisers the advantages offered by his periodical as the only medical journal published in that region of the Mississippi Valley. Through the *Observer*, Lynk campaigned for national organization among Negroes in the medical professions, and in his autobiography he recalled that the editorials "fairly bristled with pleas for the unification of the profession."[85] In 1895 Lynk participated in the founding of such an organization when a group of physicians, dentists, and pharmacists met in Atlanta and established the National Medical Association.

Woman's Era

Josephine St. Pierre Ruffin, editor and publisher of the *Woman's Era*, was born in Boston and lived practically all her life in that city.[86] In 1858, at the age of sixteen, she married George Lewis Ruffin. He graduated from Harvard Law School in 1869, and his career included election to the Massachusetts state legislature, election to the Boston city council, and appointment as a municipal judge in Boston—the office he held at the time of his death in 1886. Five children were born to this couple, but rearing a family did not prevent Josephine Ruffin from leading an active public life. During the Civil War she recruited for the Union army and participated in relief work for the soldiers. In the post-Reconstruction period, she organized an association that sent clothing and money to black people who had joined the 1879 exodus to Kansas and found themselves in destitute condition in that state.

During the early 1890s, Josephine Ruffin became active as a journalist and clubwoman. She was on the staff of a black weekly newspaper; and she was a member of the New England Women's Press Association and the New England Woman's Club, associating with Julia Ward Howe, Lucy Stone, and other feminist leaders. With the cooperation of her friend Maria Louise Baldwin and her daughter Florida Ruffin Ridley, Mrs. Ruffin organized the Woman's Era Club in Boston. Florida Ridley was a schoolteacher; Maria L. Baldwin, acknowledged as the first Negro woman principal in Massachusetts, was principal of the Agassiz Grammar School in Cambridge.[87]

The Woman's Era Club was an active civic organization engaged in the study of current issues and the support of educational and charitable causes. The club was "not necessarily a colored woman's club, but a club started and led by colored women," organized "not for race-work alone, but for work along

The Woman's Era.

VOL. II. NO. 1.   BOSTON, MASS., APRIL, 1895   PRICE 10 CENTS.

JOSEPHINE ST. P. RUFFIN.
(By permission of Boston Journal.)

FLORIDA RUFFIN RIDLEY.

NOTES AND COMMENTS.

Mrs. Abby Morton Diaz gave the first in her series of talks on the "Science of Human Beings" before the Era Club Tuesday evening, March 28, at the Charles St. Church vestry. At a time and in a community where people are talked to, and at, and about until they are more inclined to run from rather than to lectures, it is gratifying to note that, so novel in scheme and so inspiring in result was this talk, that the enthusiasm created by it is likely to run and spread and create a wide interest to hear the remainder of the course. These lectures are given at the Club's expense and are free to the public. The next one will be given April 11.

Mrs. Fannie Barrier Williams, editor of the Illinois department of the WOMAN'S ERA and secretary of the Illinois Woman's Alliance, is expected to deliver a series of lectures in New England in April.

The March literary meeting of the Woman's Era Club was in charge of the Committee on Manners and Morals, Miss Eliza Gardner, chairman.

Two well prepared papers were read, one by Mrs. Agnes Adams on "Our Needs," and the other by Mrs. Alice Casneau on "Morals and Manners." As a result of suggestions made by Mrs. Casneau, the following resolution was adopted by the Club:

WHEREAS, The Woman's Era Club having had their attention called to the very common practice of putting tickets in the hands of children to be sold for the benefit of different objects, do herewith

RESOLVE, That inasmuch as the custom of permitting young girls to solicit men to buy tickets from them is damaging to modesty and a menace to morality, we do set the seal of our condemnation upon it, and call upon the church people especially to help us abolish the custom.

The Club then listened to an interesting narration by its president, who went as a delegate to the Triennial Council of Women at Washington, and then farther south on a visit to Women clubs in that section. The president reported that she had returned with health and enthusiasm in and for our women but more brightly than ever. Her stay was short, long enough to show her that the women of the south-land are as active in trying to "help make the world bet-

Woman's Era, with editor and publisher Josephine St. Pierre Ruffin

all the lines that make for women's progress."[88] Mrs. Ruffin tried to build cooperation between Negro and white clubwomen, as well as among Negro women throughout the United States, and she affiliated the Woman's Era Club with the Massachusetts State Federation of Women's Clubs and with the national organization, the General Federation of Women's Clubs. In 1900, however, when she went to the federation's convention in Milwaukee, she was denied recognition as a delegate from the Women's Era Club because of racial prejudice. When the National Association of Colored Women was organized in 1896 with Mary Church Terrell as president, Mrs. Ruffin was elected one of the vice-presidents. She remained active in club work until her death in 1924.

Although the *Woman's Era* periodical developed from the Boston club, Mrs. Ruffin published this journal in the interest of women's clubs throughout the country. The first issue (March, 1894) reported on the activities and the history of the Woman's Era Club, but it also gave news of clubs in Providence, Rhode Island; New York City; Washington, D.C.; and Kansas City, Missouri. Later issues included news items from clubs in Chicago and in Norfolk and Hampton. When the National Federation of Afro-American Women was formed, the *Era* became its official publication. Then, when the National Association of Colored Women was established, this group also chose the *Woman's Era* as a medium of communication, and a special department in the *Era*, edited by Margaret Murray Washington and others, was devoted to the organization. This arrangement continued until Mrs. Washington initiated *National Association Notes* as a monthly newsletter for the association in 1897.

In a statement issued in November of that year, Mrs. Ruffin announced that the *Woman's Era* had "accomplished the work it was started to do, that of organizing the colored women of the country to do systematic work for the uplifting of their race." She indicated that, although the *Era* would continue to keep the women's clubs in touch with one another, it would now "devote itself especially to advocating the cause of Prison Reform in the South." The convict lease system and the imprisonment of young boys and girls for minor offenses became concerns of the *Woman's Era*.[89]

This periodical, though, was devoted primarily to the interests of women, especially the black educated woman who was hemmed in by "the limitation of her surroundings and the circumscribed sphere in which she must move." Josephine Ruffin established the Woman's Era Club and the periodical to broaden the horizons of these women and to provide outlets for their talents. She cooperated with other women who were working toward this same objective. Mrs. Fannie Barrier Williams, active in clubs and social service in Chicago, expressed support of Mrs. Ruffin in a statement prepared for the *Woman's Era*: "To thousands of our women your paper will come as the first intimation of the wideness of the world about them and the stretch of human interest and sympathy. Thousands of them will discover their own strength and a certain sense of importance in this gradual coming together of our women all over the land in clubs and leagues organized for high purposes."[90]

As a journal for women's clubs and national organizations, the *Woman's Era* reported the activities of these groups, including minutes and proceedings of the national conventions and news about clubs sent in by departmental editors. Among these editors were Victoria Earle Matthews, New York; Mary Church Terrell, Washington, D.C.; Fannie Barrier Williams, Chicago; Josephine Silone Yates, Kansas City, Missouri; Elizabeth Piper Ensley, Denver; Alice Ruth Moore, New Orleans; S. Willie Layton, California; Dora J. Cole, Pennsylvania; Sada J. Anderson, Ohio; Sylvia Mann Maples, Tennessee; Rosa D. Bowser, Virginia; Alice W. McKane, Georgia; and Cora L. Smith, Texas.

As a journal devoted to the interests of women, the *Woman's Era* carried columns on a variety of topics: "Literature," by Medora Gould; "Women at Home," by Elizabeth Johnson; "Chats with Girls," by Leslie Wilmot; "Social News," by Irene DeMortie and Marion Ridley; and "The Open Court," a public opinion column conducted by Gertrude Bustill Mossell. A music and drama section was also included. Feature articles were carried on subjects such as "Domestic Science," "Nursing of Sick Children," and "Health and Beauty from Exercise." These were usually papers prepared in the study committees of the Woman's Era Club and read at the meetings. Biographical sketches of eminent women were presented—Lucy Stone, Harriet Beecher Stowe, Harriet Tubman, and others. The periodical promoted the establishment of kindergartens and supported southern educational institutions; editorials expressed opinions on current issues such as unemployment, temperance, and lynching. Occasionally a poem or short story appeared, but belles lettres were not a significant part of the contents.

The *Woman's Era* carried a number of advertisements, many of them from black business and professional men in Boston. The editors pointed out that "the *Woman's Era* is a woman's paper, but it is such a true woman's paper that it is intensely interested in man and all that he does."[91] One of these advertisements was for the Monthly Review Press, where the *Era* was printed. This press was operated by Charles Alexander, who also published the *Monthly Review* periodical. An advertisement for Atlanta University appeared regularly in the *Era*. The president of the institution, Horace Bumstead, had spoken to the Woman's Era Club during one of his fund-raising tours in the North. The club gave a benefit entertainment and raised a scholarship for the school.[92] A free souvenir number of the *Era* was distributed at the Washington conventions in the summer of 1896. For this issue, advertisements had been solicited from businesses in the many cities represented by the delegates. The *Woman's Era* placed much emphasis on advertising. Readers were urged to patronize the advertisers, and advertisers were reminded of the national circulation of the periodical, "particularly among women of the refined and educated classes."[93]

The motivation that led Josephine St. Pierre Ruffin to publish a journal in the interest of these women was articulated in the editorial of the first issue:

The stumbling block in the way of even the most cultured colored woman is the narrowness of her environment. But let the fact be emphasized that in the work for the betterment of the world the claims for recognition of this class cannot be overlooked, it is a large and growing factor in the intellectual as well as industrial life of the country; and the strength of the chain of woman's advancement will be determined by the strength of this weak link. It is to help strengthen this link by hastening on the day when a keener appreciation of the hindrances of this class and a better understanding between all classes shall exist that this little venture is sent out on its mission.[94]

Negro Music Journal

The *Negro Music Journal* was published in Washington, D.C., during 1902 and 1903, with J. Hillary Taylor as editor and Agnes Carroll as the assistant editor. Taylor, a private piano teacher and founder-director of the Burleigh Choral Society, was also associated with the Washington Conservatory of Music; and the *Journal* served as its official publication. This school was founded by Harriet A. Gibbs (later Mrs. Napoleon B. Marshall), graduate of the Oberlin Conservatory and assistant director of music in the Washington public schools. Taylor taught pianoforte, the history of music, and musical biography, and he was the librarian and secretary of the school's managing board. Among his colleagues on the faculty were Madame E. Azalia Hackley, voice instructor; and Clarence Cameron White, a recent Oberlin graduate who taught violin and was registrar of the school.[95]

The mission of the *Journal* was to encourage Negroes to develop knowledge and appreciation of the best in music. The editors stated that the *Journal* would treat "not only the technical, but the historical, biographical and theoretical sides of the art in a way that students, parents and music lovers can understand and appreciate them as well as the experienced musician."[96] The magazine also emphasized music as "an educator and moral builder." Agnes Carroll believed that the study of music has "the power to elevate mankind morally," and Taylor asserted that the diligent pursuit of music would teach individuals "how to be industrious, studious, systematic, patient, benevolent, loving, unselfish and refined in manner." He was especially concerned about the musical education of children, pointing out that "if music be an art whose influence is toward the moral and intellectual upbuilding of those who study and seriously reflect upon it, then certainly, it is an art that should enlist parents' sympathy and goodwill."[97] One column in the *Journal*, "The Child's Musical Life," featured fables and short stories designed to teach moral values through the study of music.

Articles in the *Journal* were sometimes reprinted from *Étude* and other musical journals, but much original material was also presented. The column on violin teaching and study was written by Clarence Cameron White, Taylor was responsible for the section on piano, and Agnes Carroll conducted a department on the organization of music clubs. Essays by Taylor and White traced the development of the Negro in music, noting especially the slave songs and their rendition by the Fisk Jubilee Singers. Other articles emphasized the achievements of Negroes who were vocalists, instrumentalists, and composers in classical music, such as the baritone soloist Harry T. Burleigh, violinists Joseph H. Douglass and Will Marion Cook, soprano vocalist Elizabeth Taylor Greenfield (the "Black Swan"), and the British composer Samuel Coleridge-Taylor (best known for his opera *Hiawatha*). The *Journal* frequently carried biographical sketches of classical composers—Bach, Beethoven, and others—and news items were given about local musicians and music teachers in Washington and other eastern cities.[98]

The *Negro Music Journal* featured the major classical performances that were being presented by Negro groups. Full-page displays advertised the forthcoming productions of *Hiawatha* by the Samuel Coleridge-Taylor Choral Society in Washington and of Verdi's *Aïda* by the Theodore Drury Opera Company in New York. Reviews of *Aïda* were reprinted from other publications, and the performance was discussed at length in the editorial column of the *Journal*. The periodical observed that, according to the press reviews, this was the most outstanding of Drury's grand opera productions of the past four years. The *Journal*, however, expressed disappointment that a white orchestra and chorus had to be engaged for the production. "In this connection," commented the *Journal*, "it behooves our colored singers and musicians to give this beautiful form of the art more attention. A manager must be able to find suitable colored material that will give satisfaction in every respect before he can venture to bring such large productions before the public with an entire colored cast."[99] The *Journal* noted with much interest Theodore Drury's announcement that he had acquired land in New York City and was organizing a stock company to build an opera house. The periodical urged its readers to buy the stock (which was selling at one hundred dollars a share) and support this enterprise.[100]

In the pages of the *Negro Music Journal* black musicians were constantly urged to organize choral activities, orchestras, and opera companies and to develop their proficiencies in these areas. For one type of music, however, this periodical gave no praise or encouragement. When the editors announced that the purpose of the *Journal* was to promote an interest in good music, they were not including ragtime and other popular music. Taylor contended that "the lower type of 'rag-time'—and the bulk of it—has done much to lower the musical taste and standard of the whole musical public, irrespective of color or nationality." "It is an evil music," he asserted, "that has crept into the homes and hearts of our American people regardless of race, and must be wiped out as other bad and dangerous epidemics have been exterminated." Taylor found some solace in his belief that "the country is awakening to the real harm these 'coon songs' and 'rag-time' music are doing, and measures are being taken to lessen their influence."[101] Whatever those measures might have been, they did not succeed. Ragtime music, created in the 1890s by Scott Joplin, Eubie Blake, and others, continued to flourish in the 1900s until the period of World War I and was revived in the 1970s. Notwithstanding its attitude toward this type of music, the *Negro Music Journal* must be recognized as the most substantial Afro-American music periodical published before 1910.

School Teacher

In 1907 Roscoe Conkling Bruce was appointed Assistant Superintendent of Public Schools in Washington, D.C., the city in which he had been born twenty-eight years earlier, when his father, Blanche K. Bruce, was serving as a U.S. senator from Mississippi. Bruce graduated from Harvard College in 1902 and was immediately employed by Booker T. Washington to head the academic department at Tuskegee Institute. He came to the District of Columbia system from Tuskegee in 1906. As the administrator in charge of the Negro schools, Bruce soon encountered severe criticism from many black people in Washington who disagreed with his personnel policies and curricular programs. Groups were organized in opposition to his administration, demanding his removal from office; but Bruce continued as assistant superintendent until 1921, when he resigned and became principal of a high school in Virginia. Shortly afterward he ended his career as an educator and entered the real estate business.[102]

Bruce expressed his views on education and answered his critics through the *School Teacher*, which began publication in Washington in September, 1909. In the periodical itself, the individuals responsible for the publication were not named, but in the New York *Age* of September 2 the Washington correspondent indicated that Miss Marion P. Shadd was chairman of the board for the periodical and Garnet C. Wilkinson the managing editor. Marion Shadd, who had been employed in the Washington public schools since 1877, was supervising principal for one of the divisions of the system, and in 1924 she was appointed an assistant superintendent in charge of elementary education.[103] Wilkinson was a teacher at the M Street High School (later renamed Dunbar High School), from which he had graduated in 1898. After earning a bachelor's degree at Oberlin College, Wilkinson returned to Washington and to a fifty-year career in the school system. Beginning as a teacher, he became a principal, and from 1924 until his retirement in 1951 Wilkinson was the first assistant superintendent in charge of the Negro schools.[104]

The Washington correspondent of the New York *Age* heralded the *School Teacher* as "the finest magazine as far as make-up is concerned ever attempted by local colored management" and as a periodical representing "the best element" of the teaching profession. After the first two or three issues had appeared, the *Age* reported that the *School Teacher* "has been thriving on the attacks of various critics and has sold well in Washington, Baltimore, Philadelphia and Indianapolis." The Washington *Bee* was one of those critics. This newspaper was apprehensive of the periodical's orientation: "The School Teacher is on the catering order. The first issue doesn't demonstrate a manly front. . . . The title of its leading editorial is: 'Promotional Examination for Teachers,' when it should have stated the aim and mission of the publication. . . . If the *Bee* is to judge by the editorial, it would say that the editor is connected with the schools and he is making a defense of himself."[105]

This editorial in the *School Teacher* had stated that "the promotion of the teacher should be no mere reward for length of life; it should be a potent instrumentality for securing better and ever better service to the children." The writer maintained that experience in other large school systems "has abundantly shown that the introduction of a system of promotional examinations greatly stimulates the teaching corps to vigorous professional growth."[106] During this time, the Washington school administration was being criticized for failing to give promotions to certain Negro teachers who had been with the system for a number of years. Although the *School Teacher* did not identify Bruce as the writer of this editorial, several other editorial statements were signed by him.

Bruce also contributed feature articles to the periodical. One of these was the Memorial Day address that he had delivered at Harvard University in 1906, outlining the educational needs of the American Negro. Speaking of the Negro farming population in the fertile black belt of the southern states, Bruce expressed concern that education in the public schools "does not vitally connect itself with the actual life and need of these people." "If the school arts be ill-taught," he observed, "agriculture and the household arts are hardly taught at all." Turning to the cities, he stated that "the urban Negro dwells in sullen poverty; his death rate is alarming; he commits excess of crime." Bruce believed that this situation existed because "little or no provision is made to train him in the arts and industries by which he might sustain himself." Bruce maintained that "it is certainly to the interest of the cities to place within reach of their Negro populations not only the usual facilities of good grammar schools and good high schools, but also adequate training directly for economic independence. It is rather more farseeing to train than to imprison— it costs less in moral liability and in dollars."[107]

The *School Teacher* emphasized the value of manual training, not only in the high schools and vocational schools but at the elementary level as well, and recommended courses of study in manual training from kindergarten through eighth grade. Such a program for the elementary school pupil, it contended, would "give him an understanding sympathy with his fellow-men in their various kinds of work and aid him to discover and define such aptitude as he personally may have for a given occupation."[108] In general, the articles in the *School Teacher* dealt with all grade levels from kindergarten to normal school and with a variety of subjects. Among the topics discussed were the training of slow learners, the medical inspection of schools, oral hygiene, the teaching methods in elementary schools, foreign language instruction in high schools, the place of dancing in physical training, and the retirement of teachers.

The contributors to the periodical included persons in key positions in the District of Columbia schools, as well as educators in other systems. Edward C. Williams, principal of the M Street High School, wrote a series on "The Value of the Study of Biography." Williams had just moved to Washington from Cleveland after serving fifteen years at Western Reserve University, first as the head librarian and then as a professor in the newly organized library school at that institution.[109] Articles came from Kelly Miller, dean of the liberal arts school at Howard University, and from Lewis B. Moore, dean of the teachers' college at that institution. Leslie Pinckney Hill, principal of an industrial school in Manassas, Virginia, wrote a poem on the teacher and a three-part treatise on "The Application of Herbart's Theory of Apperception." Also among the contributors were Mary Church Terrell and Booker T. Washington.

Although well-known individuals appeared in the *School Teacher*, the promoters of the publication indicated that contributions were sought and valued not for the names of the writers, but for their ideas. Hallie E. Queen, a recent college graduate, sent an article from Puerto Rico. This young teacher, describing her class in American history for teenage students, presented these observations and theories:

> During the entire class you will notice a spirit of restless activity; a lack of repose we would call it in American students. Hands go up, and students squirm and frown as they are not called upon. . . .
>
> And all of this restlessness—what is it? May it not be the outward evidence of the temperament of the race, combined with the eager, almost frantic desire of the students to learn those things which are going to fit them for American citizenship? . . . The men who to many American children are tiresome paper bores, become to them the living, pulsing souls who made and held the mecca of their ambition—American citizenship.[110]

An editorial in the September, 1910, *School Teacher* reviewed the policies and contents of the periodical and gave this assessment: "The articles, while serious and substantial, are short and, in the main, pithy. Wisdom as well as wit, we are persuaded, may be sprightly! . . . Editorially, the magazine has proved not insurgent, but progressive; if not invariably wise, at least thoroughly honest and independent—its face toward the light."[111]

Negro Business League Herald

When William Sidney Pittman was a student at Tuskegee Institute, he was often reprimanded for "talking in the dining room," and his name was frequently called out in chapel for this misdemeanor. After one such occasion, he wrote a letter to his principal, Booker T. Washington, stating that the monitors were being unfair to him: "I must say Mr. Washington that it is a mistake. . . . Since my name was read out last week 4 time[s] I have been trying to do better in the way of quietness in the dining room. As to my knowledge I know that I havn't talked at least once since I heard my name so many times last week. . . . It seems to me that the monitor[s] just get the same names every time if they cant get any new ones." He closed the letter by assuring Washington that he was enrolled at Tuskegee "for the right thing and not for the wrong."[112] This young student eventually became one of Tuskegee's best-known graduates in his time and one of the pioneering black architects in the United States. He also became an active supporter of the National Negro Business League that Washington founded. And he became Washington's son-in-law.

William Pittman, whose home was in the nearby city of Montgomery, enrolled at Tuskegee in 1892 to study mechanical and architectural drawing. After finishing this course, he received a scholarship to Drexel Institute in Philadelphia, where he earned a degree in architecture in 1900. Returning to Tuskegee as a faculty member, Pittman helped to plan many of the buildings on the campus. While renovating Washington's home, he met the principal's daughter Portia, whom he eventually married in 1907. Pittman left Tuskegee in 1905 to establish an architectural practice in Washington, D.C. He designed buildings in the capital city and also won the federal contract to design the Negro building at the Jamestown, Virginia, Tercentennial Exposition. Pittman was active in several business ventures in the District of Columbia area, but he was dissatisfied and impatient with the limited progress of his architectural firm. Seeking greater opportunities, Pittman relocated his family and practice in Dallas, Texas, in 1913. He lived there until his death in 1958.[113]

The *Negro Business League Herald* was one of Pittman's many enterprises during his residence in Washington. This periodical was issued by the Negro Business League of the District of Columbia. Pittman was president of the group, which was affiliated with the national organization, and also president of the publishing company formed to issue the *Herald*. Associated with him on the staff of the journal were Robert L. Pendleton, a printer, and George F. Collins, an attorney. The editor was not identified in the periodical; but a local newspaper indicated that Pittman was the editor and Collins the business manager.[114]

The *Negro Business League Herald* was issued monthly from April through at least November, 1909. It predated a publication with the same title that was founded at Tuskegee in 1912 as the official journal of the National Negro Business League. Thus the Washington *Herald* served as a reporter for both the local league and the national organization. The first issue carried a letter of endorsement from Booker T. Washington, who pointed out that "such a journal can render a distinct service not only in Washington but throughout the country."[115] His photograph was the front-cover illustration for this number, and portraits of other officials of the national league appeared on subsequent covers.

The editorial policy announced by the *Herald* concurred with Washington's suggestion that the publication should "leave aside politics and kindred subjects and devote itself to the economic and business development" of the Negro people. The periodical was concerned, however, with the operation of the local government, and one matter that received much attention was the District of Columbia school system. From the first issue, editorials appeared in the *Herald* on this subject. One editorial questioned a bill before Congress that would appropriate $993,000 for the white schools in the District and only $32,000 for the colored schools, even though the Negro pupils constituted one-third of the total enrollment.[116]

The *Herald* was critical of the Citizens Committee, a group of Negro Washington residents who had gone to the education board with charges of incompetence against Roscoe Conkling Bruce, the assistant superintendent for the colored schools. These individuals issued the *Citizen* to publicize their opposition to Bruce.

The *Herald* accused them of taking an abnormal interest in the administration of the schools by demanding explanations whenever black teachers were transferred, demoted, or discharged, and it admonished them to "cease grinding away their lives trying to manage the schools and direct their interest and their energy more toward helping their business men, and their mechanics, and their professional men."[117]

The *Negro Business League Herald* devoted regular columns to reports on the monthly meetings of the local league; notes about businessmen in Washington, Anacostia, and Alexandria; and news items received from the national league on business enterprises around the country. A special series of articles described the black businesses along 14th, U, and 7th streets in Washington. Feature stories gave accounts of the Negro banks in Mississippi and businesses in Louisville, Kentucky (site of the 1909 convention of the national league). The *Herald* carried the membership directory of the local organization, and numerous advertisements from members and from other business and professional people appeared in the magazine.

The *Herald* publicized extensively two major ventures over which Pittman presided, the Fairmount Heights Community and the Lincoln Memorial Building Company project. Fairmount Heights was a residential suburb of Washington, started in 1903 as a new town inhabited entirely by black homeowners. When Pittman moved to Washington, he built his home in this community and became a leader in its development; by 1909 he was president of both the Citizens' Association and the Mutual Improvement Company. Geographically, Fairmount Heights lay two-thirds in Maryland and the remainder in the District of Columbia, and in the absence of a local government, the Citizens' Association was formed. It worked with District and Maryland officials on matters such as school facilities and the extension of public roads into the area. Through entertainments and contributions, the association itself raised money for street lamps, sidewalks, and other improvements. The Mutual Improvement

Company was organized to build a public meeting hall for the community, which was completed in 1909.[118]

The Lincoln Memorial Building Company was incorporated in 1907 by Pittman and other black business and professional men to develop a multipurpose structure in the central business district of Washington. Advertisements and articles in the *Herald* described the project as a theater and office building complex that would include several stores, a roof garden, a lecture hall for educational programs and social gatherings, meeting rooms for fraternal organizations, a restaurant, billiard rooms, and bowling alleys. Capital of a quarter million dollars to finance the complex was to be raised through the public offering of shares in the company.[119] This project apparently failed.

In Washington, Pittman was increasingly frustrated by the racial prejudice that hemmed in his architectural practice. He also became critical of black associates who did not support his business enterprises. Pittman moved to Dallas in search of a more receptive environment, but there the pattern soon repeated itself. These problems intensified his bitterness and brought tension into his family life. In 1928 Portia Washington Pittman left her husband and returned to Tuskegee Institute, where she worked in the music department for several years. Eventually she moved to Washington, D.C., and lived there until her death in 1978. Pittman remained in Dallas. During the last several years of his life, he engaged in very little architectural practice, and he died in 1958 after a long illness.[120] Pittman did not fully realize his ambitions and his potential as an architect. However, in journalism the *Negro Business League Herald* stands out as the most substantial black business periodical before 1910.

FIVE

In Retrospect

> We would call attention distinctly to the
> *permanent* and *reference* value of the contents
> of each number. Lapse of years will not dimin-
> ish the value of these papers; on the contrary,
> they will increase in value.
> —*A. M. E. Church Review*, July, 1896

The ninety-seven Afro-American periodicals presented in this
survey were initiated or proposed between 1838 and 1909. During these seven decades, magazine publishing in general was
undergoing significant growth in the United States, and, in many
respects, the development of the Afro-American periodical press
followed the same pattern as that of the general press. Magazine
publishing began in the United States in 1741 with Andrew Brad-
ford's *American Magazine* and Benjamin Franklin's *General
Magazine*, both issued in Philadelphia. The definitive history of
American magazines by Frank L. Mott shows that the periodical
press did not begin to flourish until the nineteenth century; during the early years, American periodicals experienced the hardships of an emerging press in a developing nation.[1]

The editors and publishers of the first American magazines
were usually men prominent in other professions who wanted to
communicate information and ideas to the public and were not
attempting to establish profit-making enterprises. These individuals saw their mission as one of service to their contemporaries
and to posterity, and they issued the periodicals, in a format suit-

able for binding, as repositories of material that they thought had both current interest and historical value. In some instances, the publishers reissued individual numbers in bound volumes. Their primary financial concern was simply to secure enough revenue to sustain publication. For this income they depended on subscribers, who were numbered more often in the hundreds than in the thousands and who were habitually delinquent in the payment of their subscriptions. Advertising was not a significant source of income; only a few local advertisements, if any at all, appeared in the early magazines.

For the contributors as well as for the editors, this activity was a labor of love. The few individuals who wrote for periodicals seldom received remuneration. Much of the content of the early journals consisted of material reprinted from other publications, supplemented by the writing of the editors themselves. In addition, publishers were constantly faced with problems of distribution. The population of the country was relatively small, predominantly rural, and widely dispersed, and the distribution of periodicals beyond the localities of their publication was hindered by inadequate means of transportation. Furthermore, the postal regulations at that time put magazines at a disadvantage and placed an additional financial burden on the subscribers.

As valiant an effort as the editors and publishers made to maintain their journals, and as optimistic and self-sacrificing as these persons may have been, the early periodicals were inevitably doomed to a precarious existence and, in most cases, a short life. In describing the magazines published in the latter half of the eighteenth century, Mott has written: "Surely a faith born of enthusiasm, rather than a prospect of success derived from calm calculation, presided over these early ventures."[2] This observation applies equally to the first Afro-American periodicals, published between 1838 and 1865.

Toward the middle of the nineteenth century, the fortunes of the general American periodical began to improve. By the end of the century, magazine publishing had moved from an age of personal journalism into an era of corporate business enterprise.

The general magazine, which had been a regional activity, now became a national product. Several factors contributed to this development. Although the boundaries of the United States were being extended, the total population was rapidly increasing. Between 1850 and 1900 the population more than tripled, from twenty-three million to seventy-six million. The steady trend of the country toward urbanization was stimulated by the rise of industrialism, and the urban population increased from 15.3 percent in 1850 to 39.7 percent in 1900.[3] The development of public school systems throughout the country served to reduce illiteracy among the American people.

With the joining of the eastern and western railroad lines in 1869, transcontinental transportation was assured. In addition, postal regulations more favorable to periodicals were enacted. Magazines were given second-class mailing privileges, and the rate on second-class mail was greatly reduced; at the turn of the century rural free delivery was instituted. Advances in printing machinery, in the manufacture of paper, and in techniques of illustration made possible the mass production of attractive periodicals that could be sold at low prices. Magazine contributors were achieving the status of a professional class, and some were well paid by the general periodicals. Circulation figures for the major magazines were recorded in the hundreds of thousands. By the beginning of the twentieth century, the *Ladies' Home Journal* reached the one-million mark. The publisher, Cyrus Hermann K. Curtis, solicited national advertising as the main source of revenue for the *Journal* and for the *Saturday Evening Post*. From that time on, advertisements, rather than subscriptions, became the financial base of the national magazine.

The years between 1885 and 1905 also witnessed the introduction and the tremendous success of the quality ten-cent magazine, such as *Cosmopolitan* and *McClure's Magazine*. These general monthlies were characterized by "copious and well-printed illustration, liveliness and freshness in presentation of nonfiction articles, variety in subject matter, a serious treatment of contemporary problems, and a keen interest in new invention and progress

in general."[4] They concentrated on history, biography, and economic and social affairs, rather than on fiction and poetry, and
they competed with newspapers in their coverage of current
events. Leading writers such as Ida Tarbell and Lincoln Steffens,
who were concerned with social reform and with the exposure
of corruption in high places, introduced a type of writing that
came to be known as "muckraking."

Afro-American periodicals in the last quarter of the nineteenth
century benefited to some degree from the same circumstances
that led to the stability and the expansion of American magazines
in general. As the total American population was becoming ur-
banized and industrialized, Negroes also tended to migrate to the
cities and to seek jobs in the factories. Illiteracy among Negroes
also decreased as educational opportunities became available.
Afro-American magazines likewise gained from the more favorable postal regulations, improved transportation, cheaper and better production methods, and, eventually, the financial support of
advertising. It was not until the mid-twentieth century, however,
that the black periodical press achieved the stature of a financially successful business institution. Throughout the nineteenth
century and the first decades of the twentieth century, it remained basically a press with a cause and little or no capital.

Yet there were those Negro journalists at the turn of the century who saw the direction in which the business of periodical
publishing was moving and realized the part that advertising and
efficient management would have to play in a financially profitable enterprise. In 1896, the New York columnist Augustus M.
Hodges outlined a plan for the publication of a national Negro
magazine. Hodges was a frequent contributor to newspapers and
periodicals, often writing under the pen name "B. Square," and
had once edited his own newspaper in Brooklyn. In an essay appearing in the Indianapolis *Freeman* on June 27, 1896, he analyzed the past failures in Negro periodical publishing and then
made suggestions for a more successful course in the future. A
national Negro magazine, he said, must be conducted upon
strictly business principles and must have enough funds for the

first year of publication "regardless of subscribers, readers, or advertisers." Money should be available to pay for all contributions, from both established authors and beginning writers. The staff should include an experienced agent to solicit advertisements from national firms. The magazine ought to be distributed through newsstands and bookstores across the country. The contents of the periodical, freely illustrated with original photographs, must be of interest not only to Negroes but also to "literary and progressive whites." Hodges suggested that the magazine should be published in Washington, Philadelphia, or New York City. He called Washington "the Negro Athens of the United States" and Philadelphia "a city of progressive colored people," but he believed that "the colored people of New York are far behind the average city North or South, from the literary point of view." "Still," he observed, "New York is the best place for publication from the fact it is the great business mart of the country, teeming with printers, engravers, and advertisers."

Afro-American periodicals remained in an unstable financial position as long as their revenues came primarily from subscriptions, local advertising, and the sale of shares in stock companies —sources that were not able to sustain the publications. This was the situation throughout the nineteenth century. Also, in both the pre-Civil War years and the post-Reconstruction era, the principal method of distribution (individuals engaged as agents by the publishers) proved to be unsatisfactory.

Sometimes additional techniques were utilized to promote circulation, such as combination subscriptions with other publications at special rates, the organization of clubs to support the periodicals, and premiums for subscribers or for persons bringing in new subscriptions. There were numerous examples of such efforts. *Alexander's Magazine* was offered in combination with *Woman's Home Companion* and *Farm and Fireside*. The *Colored American Magazine* was promoted through the Colored American League, organized in Boston in 1904. The *A. M. E. Church Review* gave new subscribers an engraved photograph of Frederick Douglass. The *Woman's Era* awarded premiums to individuals who secured subscriptions for the periodical: one year's tuition at the Emerson School of Oratory in Boston for fifty subscriptions, a typewriter for twenty subscriptions, and a biography of Douglass for five subscriptions. The *Voice of the Negro* gave a Liberty pocket watch, "gold plate finish, guaranteed for one year," to young men who brought in at least four subscriptions.[5]

These techniques may have increased circulation to a small extent, but eventually in the twentieth century a new source of revenue—national advertising—became the major base of the commercially published black periodical. As J. Max Barber observed in 1907, "no magazine that is living to-day is living on its subscriptions. It must live by advertising." One reason Barber gave for changing the name of the *Voice of the Negro* to the *Voice* was to attract a wider spectrum of advertisers.[6]

Although the Afro-American periodical press was influenced ultimately by the same factors that stimulated magazine publishing in general, this press was affected more immediately by the status of the Negro in American society. Black journals published in the 1830s and the 1840s were concerned with the emancipation of the slave from bondage and with the liberation of the free Negro from inequities and restrictions. As the position of free Negroes tended to deteriorate rather than improve, they became increasingly alarmed about their situation. The editor of the *Anglo-African Magazine* wrote: "the wealth, the intellect, the Legislation, (State and Federal,) the pulpit, and the science of America, have concentrated on no one point so heartily as in the endeavor to write down the Negro as something less than a man." This magazine and others were issued "to uphold and encourage the now depressed hopes of thinking black men, in the United States" and during the 1850s and early 1860s more black periodicals were published than previously.[7]

When the Union military victory in the Civil War ensured the emancipation of the slaves and when the federal government established citizenship for all Negroes, Afro-Americans seemed to be on the threshold of integration. Thus, between 1865 and 1879, with this expectation of full participation in American society, the Afro-American press was dormant. But with the end of political reconstruction in the South, the fortunes of Negroes were reversed. Legal and extralegal measures against the Negro population were instituted in the South and generally condoned by the North. Throughout the United States, black people encountered barriers and inequities, imposed openly or subtly by racial prejudice. As a result, during the post-Reconstruction period, they again concentrated their activities in their own institutions; they again utilized the periodical press to serve their needs in segregated communities and to agitate for acceptance into an integrated society.

Another development during the post-Reconstruction years that had considerable impact upon Afro-American magazines was the leadership position that Booker T. Washington maintained from 1895 until his death in 1915. Washington did not publish a general periodical from the Tuskegee campus, and the newsletters that he issued were mainly promotional publications for the Institute. During the 1880s and 1890s, journalist T. Thomas Fortune occasionally talked with him about issuing a magazine of wider scope, but such a publication did not materialize.[8] Yet Washington had a great influence upon black newspapers and periodicals, directly and indirectly. He secretly subsidized some of these journals; and his prestige prompted many magazines to feature him in their initial issue and frequently to reprint selections from his writings.

The genesis and growth of the Afro-American periodical was an integral phase of the evolution of literary traditions among black people. In the period of fifty or more years before the first journals were issued, a small group of individuals were creating a body of written literature that became the forerunner of the periodical. And before there was recorded literature, black people were transmitting their history and culture orally from generation to generation.

In the 1770s and the 1780s, the development of recorded literature was exemplified in the petitions for freedom and equality that blacks were presenting to northern state legislatures. In the

1790s, individuals were sending letters to government officials beseeching them to use their influence to redress grievances, as did Benjamin Banneker to Thomas Jefferson and William Hamilton to John Jay. In the latter part of the eighteenth century and in the early nineteenth century, sermons and orations delivered by black preachers and leaders began to be preserved in printed form. Other pamphlets and broadsides were also issued, and a few fugitive slaves were writing authentic accounts of their experiences. Free people in northern and southern cities were establishing literary societies for both men and women, and these associations, through the libraries and programs that they sponsored, were nurturing the speaking and writing capabilities of their members.

In the 1830s black persons were writing for the first Afro-American newspapers and also for white abolitionist journals. They were engaged as lecturers by the antislavery societies, and they were drafting documents and addresses for their own national conventions and other organizations. These activities served as training experiences for a small vanguard of individuals who, by 1840, could initiate their own periodicals and, by 1860, could produce such magazines as the *Anglo-African Magazine* and the *Repository of Religion and Literature and of Science and Art*. In the years following Reconstruction, magazines continued to be closely related to other forms of literary activity and publication. Just as in the pre-Civil War period, the lines of demarcation between periodicals and newspapers were often indistinct.

In a survey of Negro newspapers that were initiated between 1827 and 1950, Armistead S. Pride observes that these publications "have usually taken on the fads and fashions of the moment in journalism."[9] Afro-American periodicals likewise turned to contemporary American magazines for prototypes. The *Anglo-African Magazine*, founded in 1859, was modeled after the *Atlantic Monthly*, which had started publication two years earlier. The *A. M. E. Church Review* was similar to *Harper's Magazine* in format. The *Southland*, founded in 1890, bore strong physical resemblance to the *Forum*, which had been established in 1886.

Also in the manner of the *Forum*, the *Southland* made the symposium an important feature of its contents. During the 1890s *Future State*, published as "the only periodical in the world presenting the opinions of the leading journals upon the Negro," was patterned after *Public Opinion*. Two black journals of the first decade of the twentieth century—*Ebony* and *Horizon*—were among the innumerable American magazines that imitated the format of Elbert Hubbard's pocket-size *Philistine*. Even that periodical's by-line, "printed . . . for the Society of the Philistines," was copied by *Ebony*, which was "printed by the Society of 'the Three P's.'" A contemporary writer noted that *Alexander's Magazine* "represented to the colored people what *The Forum, The North American Review,* and *The Arena* represent to the white people."[10] The *Colored American Magazine* and the *Voice of the Negro* imitated the format that made *McClure's Magazine* an outstanding monthly in the mid-nineties and the early 1900s.

In the main thrust of its contents, however, the black periodical was in sharp contrast to the general American magazine. In this respect, it was similar to the "little magazine" that began to develop in the early twentieth century. Both the Negro periodicals and the "little magazines" published material that was unacceptable to the general press because of nonconformist points of view or limited interest. The general magazines, as corporate business enterprises dependent upon national advertising for their financing, concentrated on material of wide popular appeal and acceptance. Writers who espoused causes that had not gained public support had to initiate their own publications; thus Negro periodicals and "little magazines" were founded. As journals with limited appeal, they frequently suffered from insufficient support and inadequate financing.

The Afro-American periodicals discussed in this book have been classified as either general magazines or special interest publications; however, the contents of these periodicals were not always so distinct. For example, editorials in the Washington *Negro Business League Herald* were constantly concerned with the District of Columbia school system. The *National Domestic,* published for persons employed in household services, carried extensive news of the stage and theater. Among the general periodicals, *Alexander's Magazine* had a large number of features on educational institutions. The *Colored American Magazine* was a regular source of information on business enterprises among Negroes; it also included many articles by and about Negro musicians. In fact, the *Colored American Magazine* gave a much broader view of musical activities among Negroes than its contemporary, the *Negro Music Journal*. The *Journal* concentrated on classical music and dismissed popular music, especially the ragtime that was created by black composers at the turn of the century. The *Colored American Magazine* carried articles on all types—the grand opera productions of Theodory Drury as well as the vaudeville performances of George Walker and Bert Williams.

Many recurring themes appeared in the black periodicals issued between 1838 and 1909. One major theme was that of education. In 1838, at the opening of the school year for the Pennsylvania public schools, William Whipper, in the *National Reformer*, urged parents to send their children to school for as much education as possible. In 1862, in California, John J. Moore also appealed to parents, through the pages of the *Lunar Visitor*, to be concerned about the education of their children. Through the *Students' Repository*, published in Indiana in the early 1860s, Samuel H. Smothers tried to awaken an interest in education among black people in that region of the country. The *Freedman's Torchlight* was initiated shortly after Emancipation to teach reading and writing to Negroes in the South. Throughout the post-Reconstruction decades, the Afro-American periodicals continued to promote educational institutions and to encourage black people to take advantage of educational opportunities. During both the antebellum and the postbellum periods, attention was given especially to the education of ministers and of women.

Another frequent theme was the appeal for unity and cooperation among Negroes. In 1841, in the *Mirror of Liberty*, David Ruggles pleaded with his black brethren to "unite and energize in securing . . . immediate relief and enfranchisement." In 1862, in the *Lunar Visitor*, John J. Moore advised that "unity is the source of strength, of power, operative or resistant." In 1895, in the *Woman's Era*, Josephine St. Pierre Ruffin wrote: "So long as we all suffer together, just so long must we all work together to bring about a different state of affairs"; and in 1905, in the *American Magazine*, Jesse W. Watkins urged Negroes to unite "in mind, in efforts, in politics and in wealth." In 1909, in the *Negro Business League Herald*, William Sidney Pittman stated that one of the purposes of the periodical was to promote cooperation among Negroes in developing financial and commercial enterprises. Also in 1909, in the *Western Lever*, Julius Dean Pettigrew called for the organization of resources among black people into "a single racial force" as a means of self-preservation in a country in which they were becoming an ostracised race.[11]

Despite the lack of unity and cooperation that editors observed among black people, the periodicals supported numerous organizations that Negroes formed or joined for the advancement of their civil rights. The first two Afro-American periodicals, the *Mirror of Liberty* and the *National Reformer*, grew out of their editors' participation in such organizations. The *Mirror of Liberty* was initiated by David Ruggles to publicize the New York Committee of Vigilance, an interracial group of which he was secretary and also a founder. This periodical also promoted the American Reform Board of Disfranchised Commissioners, with which Ruggles was associated. The *National Reformer* was the official publication of the American Moral Reform Society, and its editor, William Whipper, was one of the founders of this organization.

At the turn of the century, three major secular organizations among Negroes were the Afro-American League (later reactivated as the National Afro-American Council), the National Negro Business League, and the Niagara Movement. The Afro-American League, founded in 1890 under the leadership of T. Thomas Fortune and Alexander Walters, was publicized in the *Afro-American Budget* and in *Southland*. The National Negro Business League, established in 1900 by Booker T. Washington (and still in existence today as the National Business League), was supported by the *Negro Business League Herald* in Washington and by the

Colored American Magazine when it was published in New York City. Coverage was also given the League in the *Voice of the Negro* as long as John W. E. Bowen was one of the editors. This periodical, however, gave much more publicity to the Niagara Movement, organized in 1905 by W. E. B. Du Bois, for the editor, J. Max Barber, was a charter member of the movement. Du Bois's own journal, the *Horizon*, succeeded the *Voice of the Negro* as the major medium of communication for the Niagara Movement.

Other organizations, less extensive in membership and influence, were also supported by various periodicals during the first decade of the 1900s: the Constitutional Brotherhood of America by *McGirt's Magazine*, the Liberian Development Association by *Alexander's Magazine*, the Constitutional Rights Association of the United States and the Loyal Legion of Labor by the *Colored American Magazine*, the Colored Co-operative League by the *Western Lever*, and the National Negro American Political League by the *Freeman*. Women's organizations were publicized in the *Woman's Era*, and beginning in 1897 the National Association of Colored Women had its own journal, *National Association Notes*.

Throughout the post-Reconstruction decades, black periodicals urged Negroes to become active politically. *Howard's Negro-American Magazine, Paul Jones Monthly Magazine*, the *Gazetteer and Guide*, and the *Voice of the Negro* campaigned for, or against, candidates in state and national elections. *McGirt's Magazine* and the *Horizon* urged Negroes to exercise their right to vote. The *A. M. E. Church Review*, the *A. M. E. Zion Quarterly Review, Southland*, and the *Alumni Magazine* presented symposia on the effect of the Democratic administration of President Grover Cleveland upon the Negro. The magazines also took an interest in the foreign policies of the United States, especially as related to countries inhabited by colored peoples. Feature articles described living conditions in Haiti, the Philippines, Uganda, and the Belgian Congo, and biographies were presented of black leaders, contemporary and historical, from many lands. Emigration to Africa and the establishment of black nations in other countries were promoted. Concern for the destinies of nonwhite people throughout the world was prevalent in the Afro-American periodicals during both the antebellum and the post-Reconstruction years.

With regard to domestic policy, the periodicals criticized the collusion of the North and the South in their treatment of the Negro. In 1859, Martin R. Delany's novel *Blake*, serialized in the *Anglo-African Magazine*, depicted the political and economic interests that united these two sections of the country to the detriment of the black population. In 1904, an article by Mary Church Terrell in *McGirt's Magazine* spoke out against northern acquiescence in the brutal treatment of Negroes by southerners. "For years Negroes have been shot, flayed alive and burned to death in the South with the full knowledge of the North," Mrs. Terrell wrote. "Ask the North why she does not cry out against such barbarities and she bids you be silent, lest the question offend the South. The crime of all crimes to-day in the opinion of the once liberty-loving North is arousing sectional feeling."[12]

Certain periodicals supported the boycott as a technique to be utilized by Negroes in seeking equality and justice. In the 1830s, the *National Reformer* urged the patronage of grocery stores that boycotted the products of slave labor and sold only goods produced by free people. In the first decade of the twentieth century, the *Colored American Magazine*, the *A. M. E. Church Review*, and other periodicals supported the boycotting of segregated street cars. An editorial in the *Colored American Magazine* in 1905 stated: "The Negroes of Texas are true blue. For four years they have successfully carried on the boycott against the street railway system in both Houston and San Antonio. . . . Nashville has now a separate car law. . . . The leaders in Nashville, if they have no horses, should walk; and the mass of Negroes will walk with them."[13] In an article in the *Voice of the Negro* in 1904, Daniel A. P. Murray suggested that a boycott by the black labor force in the South could "lessen if not wholly stop the evil of lynching." He believed that "if every man, woman and child in the country would resolve to go on half rations for ten days, giving up every form of labor and devote the time to prayer until the perpetrators were punished, there would not be a second lynching in any county in the South." An editorial in the *Voice* reacted to this article by saying "Our advice to the race is, DO IT."[14]

The periodicals constantly sought to instill race pride in Negroes and sometimes proposed specific ideas for developing self-esteem in black children. The educator and historian Edward A. Johnson, writing in the *Colored American Magazine* in 1908, suggested that "one of the best ways to teach Negro children to respect their own color would be to see to it that the children be given colored dolls to play with." In 1906, the *Voice of the Negro* offered for sale reprints of the portraits of Negroes that John Henry Adams had sketched for the magazine. The editor J. Max Barber noted that "beauty in ebony has not been exploited to any considerable extent." He believed that if black youth are to develop self-respect, "pictures of their own race must hang on the walls of their own parlors and dining rooms."[15]

The Afro-American periodical press also addressed itself to white people in an effort to make them more aware of the achievements of Negroes. A significant portion of the readership and support of the black antebellum periodicals was among white abolitionists. William Lloyd Garrison publicized the *Mirror of Liberty* extensively in the *Liberator*, and many, if not all, of the individuals who contributed to the fund for placing the *Anglo-African Magazine* in public libraries were white people. The editors of the *Repository of Religion and Literature* spoke of the interest of the white subscribers in that periodical. In the post-Reconstruction period, the *Southland* was issued to promote brotherhood in the South. The publishers of the *Colored American Magazine* reported that within two years after its founding, "fully one-third" of the regular readers were white and that interest in the magazine was constantly on the increase among both white and black people.[16]

In an attempt to make the periodicals more appealing to all readers, some editors sought to enhance their publications with illustrations. During the antebellum period, the *Repository of Religion and Literature* and the *Anglo-African Magazine* occasionally had frontispiece portraits of black leaders engraved by John Sartain, a leading illustrator of American magazines. Such engravings, however, were the exception rather than the rule; in general, the antebellum periodicals were sparsely illustrated. During the post-Reconstruction decades, however, the majority of the periodicals were illustrated, and many of them extensively so. In addition to illustrations for feature articles and short stories, the magazines carried political cartoons; reproductions of the works of the black artists Henry O. Tanner, Meta Vaux Warrick Fuller, Edmonia Lewis, and William A. Harper; pictures of Negro churches, schools, and businesses; and photographs of men and women in all fields of endeavor. The black photographer Addison N. Scurlock, whose career extended from 1904 to 1964, was represented in some of the magazines. A master craftsman, his sensitive and aesthetic portraits brought him national reputation soon after he opened a studio in Washington, D.C.[17] (This studio is still conducted by members of his family.)

Throughout the first seventy years of the Afro-American periodical press, institutions and organizations established by Negroes played important roles in the development of this press. The church especially sponsored significant publications, during both the antebellum and the post-Reconstruction years. At the same time, these seven decades were largely an age of personal journalism. Many of the periodicals were issued as private enterprises by persons who were both the editors and publishers; and these publications usually ceased to exist when their founders were no longer active. Even those periodicals published under the auspices of institutions and organizations were shaped by the personalities and the philosophies of the individuals who edited them.

A large number of the people associated with the Afro-American periodicals were ministers and educators, but other vocations were also represented. There were, for example, William Whipper, the businessman who founded the *National Reformer*; Nathan F. Mossell, the physician who edited the *Alumni Magazine*; and William Sidney Pittman, the architect who promoted the

Negro Business League Herald. Although many of the editors had earned degrees in higher education, others had gone no further than high school, if that far; and others—like Frederick Douglass and William Whipper—had no formal schooling at all. Some of the editors were nationally recognized leaders among the black people—Daniel Alexander Payne, Frederick Douglass, and W. E. B. Du Bois. But there were also individuals who were relatively unknown: Thomas S. Ewell, who dreamed of making the *Colored Home Journal* a national magazine; Walter W. Wallace and J. Max Barber, whose visions of nationally circulated periodicals came closer to realization with the *Colored American Magazine* and the *Voice of the Negro*; and John F. A. McConico, who spoke out against lynching in a magazine published in the Deep South.

Most of the editors and publishers were journalists by avocation only; but a few—Thomas Hamilton, Charles Alexander, and T. Thomas Fortune, for example—were engaged full-time in journalism and publishing. The great majority of the editors were men, but there were also women editors: Josephine St. Pierre Ruffin and Margaret Murray Washington, national leaders in the women's club movement, who published the *Woman's Era* and *National Association Notes*; Amelia L. Tilghman, who initiated the *Musical Messenger* as the first Afro-American music periodical; Pauline E. Hopkins, who guided the *Colored American Magazine* in its early years; Amanda Berry Smith, the evangelist who issued the *Helper*; Carrie A. Bannister, who coedited the *Future State*; and Julia Ringwood Coston, who published *Ringwood's Afro-American Journal of Fashion*, a magazine praised by both the white and black press.

The first black periodicals, just as the early American magazines in general, were published to serve future generations as well as contemporary readers. In presenting the *Mirror of Liberty* to the public, David Ruggles announced that it would be published "on a super royal sheet of fine paper, in an octavo form, and shall contain 16 pages neatly covered; at the end of the volume the subscriber may possess 64 pages of valuable and interesting mat-

ter in a style for binding, which can be preserved." Frederick
Douglass, in promoting *Douglass' Monthly*, stated that "its size is
that most convenient for binding" and promised that "its matter
shall be such as will be permanently useful and interesting to its
readers." For some of the periodicals, the publishers reissued the
current numbers in bound volumes. Volume one of the *African
Methodist Episcopal Church Magazine*, priced at $1.50, was ad-
vertised as "a progressive History of the Church." Thomas Hamilton offered the 1859 *Anglo-African Magazine* in a choice of bind-
ings, muslin at $1.38 and half-morocco at $1.62. The editors of the
Repository of Religion and Literature and of Science and Art
emphasized the permanent value of the bound volumes of this
periodical: "Being in book form, it is better adapted to preserve
the current literature of our Church, and of sister denominations
for the use of posterity."[18]

The desire to preserve information for future generations was
expressed by editors during the pre-Civil War period more frequently than during the post-Reconstruction decades. Yet this
motivation was articulated by a few of the editors of the later
periodicals. When Hightower T. Kealing became editor of the
A. M. E. Church Review in 1896, he called attention to the permanent and reference value of the periodical. He urged readers
to have the *Review* bound and to place it in their libraries.[19] In
1904, this same thought was uppermost in the mind of J. Max
Barber. Barber's editorial in the first issue of the *Voice of the
Negro* revealed him to be a person with a sense of history and a
feeling of commitment to the future. Although other editors may
not have been so consciously aware of this mission or so dedicated to fulfilling it, all of the Afro-American periodicals published between 1838 and 1909 did, in fact, perform this function.
Thus Barber spoke prophetically for all of these periodicals when
he said of the *Voice of the Negro*:

> We want it to be more than a mere magazine. We expect to
> make of it current and sociological history so accurately given
> and so vividly portrayed that it will become a kind of documen-
> tation for the coming generations.[20]

Publication Data
and Selected Finding-List
for the Periodicals

This appendix gives the following information, to the extent available, for each of the ninety-seven periodicals included in the study:

Title and subtitle
Motto
Date of first issue
Frequency of publication
Place of publication
Editor
Publisher
Price
Circulation
Format: average number of pages per issue, page size, columns
    per page, inclusion of illustrations and advertisements
Number of extant issues
Publication history for the extant issues (volume, issue number,
    and date)
Notes
Availability:
    Selected library locations of extant issues
    Listing of the periodical in the *Union List of Serials in Libraries
      of the United States and Canada*, 3rd. ed., 1965 (cited as
      ULS), and in the *National Union Catalog, Pre-1956 Imprints*
      (cited as *NUC, Pre-1956*)

Listing of the periodical in *Guide to Reprints, 1980* (cited as
Reprints, 1980) and in *Guide to Microforms in Print, 1980*
(cited as *Microforms in Print, 1980*)

The names of editors and publishers are given in full, even
though they may not have appeared in that form in the magazines. In general, information relative to the post-1909 publication
of a periodical is not included, other than the date of the last
known issue. Exceptions have been made for three titles: *Citizen,
Horizon,* and the *School Teacher.* For these, the last issues located were published in 1910; therefore, the complete files have
been documented.

The selected finding-list shows the extent to which the periodicals have been preserved in a single library or in a combination of
libraries. The inclusion of a library in this listing does not mean
that its holdings for all the titles in the survey have been given.
In some cases, fragmentary files of periodicals held by libraries
have not been listed if they are duplicated in more extensive
holdings of other libraries. Extant issues were located for sixty-
three of the ninety-seven periodicals. For those magazines for
which no issues were found, secondary sources of information are
given under "Notes."

The author would appreciate receiving information about additional issues, or other periodicals within the scope of this book,
that have not been recorded here. Such information is solicited
from libraries, other institutions and organizations, and from individuals who own these periodicals or know where copies are
located. Communications may be addressed to: Penelope L. Bullock, 631 Hightower Road, N.W., Atlanta, Georgia 30318.

SYMBOLS FOR LIBRARIES

ATT	Tuskegee Institute, Tuskegee, Alabama
CL	Los Angeles Public Library, Los Angeles, California
CU-B	University of California, Bancroft Library, Berkeley, Cal-
	ifornia

CtHT-W	Trinity College, Watkinson Library, Hartford, Connecticut
CtY-Be	Yale University, Beinecke Library, New Haven, Connecticut
CtY-D	Yale University, Divinity School, New Haven, Connecticut
DA	U.S. National Agricultural Library, Beltsville, Maryland
DHEW	U.S. Department of Health, Education, and Welfare, National Institute of Education, Washington, D.C.
DHU-Mo	Howard University, Moorland-Spingarn Research Center, Washington, D.C.
DLC	Library of Congress, Washington, D.C.
DLC-Mu	Library of Congress, Daniel Murray Collection, Washington, D.C.*
DNLM	U.S. National Library of Medicine, Bethesda, Maryland
GAI	Interdenominational Theological Center, Atlanta, Georgia
GAU	Atlanta University, Atlanta, Georgia
ICCRL	Center for Research Libraries, Chicago, Illinois
ICHi	Chicago Historical Society, Chicago, Illinois
ICU	University of Chicago, Chicago, Illinois
In	Indiana State Library, Indianapolis, Indiana
KHi	Kansas State Historical Society, Topeka, Kansas
LNHT	Tulane University, Howard-Tilton Memorial Library New Orleans, Louisiana
MB	Boston Public Library, Boston, Massachusetts
MH	Harvard University, Cambridge, Massachusetts
MPB	Berkshire Athenaeum, Pittsfield, Massachusetts
MWA	American Antiquarian Society, Worcester, Massachusetts
MiU	University of Michigan, Ann Arbor, Michigan
N	New York State Library, Albany, New York
NHi	New-York Historical Society, New York City, New York
NIC	Cornell University, Ithaca, New York
NNG	General Theological Seminary of the Protestant Episcopal Church, New York City, New York
NN-Sch	Schomburg Center for Research in Black Culture, New York Public Library, Astor, Lenox and Tilden Foundations, New York City, New York

NR   Rochester Public Library, Rochester, New York
NRAB   American Baptist Historical Society, Rochester, New
                York
NcD   Duke University, Durham, North Carolina
NcSL   Livingstone College, Salisbury, North Carolina
OWibfU   Wilberforce University, Wilberforce, Ohio
PBA   *A. M. E. Zion Quarterly Review* Publication Office, Bed-
                ford, Pennsylvania
PLiL   Lincoln University, Lincoln University, Pennsylvania
PPHi   Historical Society of Pennsylvania, Philadelphia, Pennsyl-
                vania
ScCM-Wa   Medical University of South Carolina, Waring Historical
                Library, Charleston, South Carolina
TNF   Fisk University, Nashville, Tennessee
VHaI   Hampton Institute, Hampton, Virginia
VPV   Virginia State College, Petersburg, Virginia
VU   University of Virginia, Charlottesville, Virginia

*   The Daniel Murray Collection, organized at the Library of Congress in 1900
     as the Colored Author Collection, remained a separate, uncataloged body of
     materials until the early 1970s, when it was dispersed and items from it were
     added to appropriate divisions of the library.

A. M. E. Church Review

Title: *The A. M. E. Church Review*
First issue: July, 1884
Frequency: Quarterly
Place of publication: Philadelphia, Pa., July, 1884–July, 1908; Nash-
   ville, Tenn., October, 1908–October, 1909
Editors: Benjamin Tucker Tanner, July, 1884–April, 1888; Levi Jen-
   kins Coppin, July, 1888–April, 1896; Hightower T. Kealing, July,
   1896–April, 1912
Publisher: African Methodist Episcopal Church (A. M. E. Book Con-
   cern, July, 1884–July, 1908; Sunday School Union of the A. M. E.
   Church, October, 1908–October, 1909)
Price: $1.50 per year, July, 1884–April, 1896; $1.25 per year, July,
   1896–October, 1898; $1.00 per year, January, 1899–October, 1909
Circulation: 2,500 (*Ayer Directory of Newspapers and Periodicals*,
   1895, 1908)
Format: 100 or more pages per issue; 6 x 9 page size; 1 column per
   page; illustrations and advertisements

Publication history for extant issues through 1909 (102): I, No. 1, July, 1884–XXVI, No. 2, October, 1909

Notes: The *A. M. E. Church Review* has been published regularly from its founding until the present day.

Availability:

DLC   I, No. 1–XX, No. 4

GAI   I, No. 1–IV, No. 4; V, Nos. 1–3; IX, Nos. 1, 3, 4; X, No. 1–XI, No. 4; XII, Nos. 2–4; XIII, Nos. 2–4; XIV, No. 2; XV, No. 4; XVI, No. 3; XVII, No. 1; XVIII, Nos. 1, 2; XIX, Nos. 2, 4; XXII, No. 3; XXIII, No. 3; XXIV, Nos. 1, 4; XXV, Nos. 1–4

NN-Sch   I, No. 1–XXVI, No. 2

OWibfU   I, No. 1–XXVI, No. 2

Title listed in *ULS*; *NUC, Pre-1956*; *Microforms in Print, 1980*

A. M. E. Zion Quarterly Review

Title: *The A.M.E. Zion Church Quarterly*, 1890–December, 1894; *The A. M. E. Zion Quarterly Review*, April, 1895, to date

First issue: 1890

Frequency: Quarterly

Place of publication: Pittsburgh, Pa., 1890–July, 1891; Wilmington, N.C., October, 1892–December, 1894; Salisbury/Wilmington, N.C., April, 1895–October/January, 1895/96; Charlotte, N.C., July/October, 1896–1909

Editors: George Wylie Clinton, 1890–July, 1892; John Campbell Dancy, October, 1892–1912

Publisher: African Methodist Episcopal Zion Church

Price: Varied from $1.00 to $1.50 per year

Format: Varied in length from 34 to 174 pages, but generally at least 100 pages; 6 x 9 page size; 1 and 2 columns per page; illustrations and advertisements

Publication history for extant issues through 1909 (40): This periodical was irregular in publication and there were numerous discrepancies in the numbering of volumes and issues; therefore no attempt is made here to list the issues by volume, issue number, and date.

Notes: *The A. M. E. Zion Quarterly Review* has continued publication to the present day.

Availability:

Cty-D   15 issues, July, 1891–April, 1897

DLC-Mu   7 issues, July/October, 1896–July, 1899
NcSL   8 issues, July, 1892–October/November/December,
         1909
PBA   20 issues, 1891–1909
Title listed in *ULS*; *NUC, Pre-1956*

Advance

Title: *Advance*
First issue: 1902
Frequency: Monthly
Place of publication: Pittsburgh, Pa.
Editor and publisher: Oliver G. Waters
Publication history for extant issues: No issues located
Notes: Information about this periodical appeared in the Washington
   (D.C.) *Colored American*, June 7, 1902.

Afric-American Repository

Title: *Afric-American Repository*
First issue: Proposed in 1854; evidence of actual publication not found
Notes: The establishment of this quarterly periodical was recommended at the first convention of the National Emigration Convention of Colored People, held in Cleveland in 1854. The magazine
   was to be edited by James Monroe Whitfield and published by the
   Afric-American Printing Company. *Proceedings of the National Emigration Convention of Colored People . . . 1854* (Pittsburgh: A. A.
   Anderson, 1854), 12, 28–31; Toronto *Provincial Freeman*, November
   25, 1856, p. 62.

African Methodist Episcopal Church Magazine

Title: *African Methodist Episcopal Church Magazine*
First issue: September, 1841
Frequency: Monthly
Place of publication: Brooklyn, N.Y.
Editor: Not stated
Publisher: "Published by Geo. Hogarth, general book steward for the
   African Methodist Episcopal Church"
Price: $1.00 per year

Circulation: In May, 1844, Hogarth reported "213 cash subscribers" and the printing of 1,000 to 1,500 copies for each issue. *African Methodist Episcopal Church Magazine*, II (August, 1844), 57–58.

Format: 32 pages per issue; 6 x 9 page size; 1 column per page; illustrations and advertisements

Publication history for extant issues (24):

I, Nos. 1–12, September, October, 1841, May, August, December, 1842, April, July, September, November, 1843, January, March, May, 1844

II, Nos. 1–6, June, August, September, December, 1844, February, April, 1845

?, Nos. ?, August, September, October, 1845, January, September, 1846, August, 1847

Availability:

GAI   I, Nos. 3, 6; II, Nos. 1, 2, 5, 6
NHi   I, Nos. 7, 12
OWibfU   II, Nos. 1–4; ?, Nos. ?, August, September, October, 1845, January, September, 1846, August, 1847
TNF   I, Nos. 1–12

Title listed in *ULS*; *NUC, Pre-1956*

Afro-American Budget

Title: *The Afro-American Budget: A Monthly Magazine Devoted to the Practical Problems of the African Race in All Parts of the World*

First issue: May, 1889

Frequency: Monthly

Place of publication: Evanston, Ill., May, 1889–August, 1890; Decatur, Ill., October, 1890–February, 1891

Editor and publisher: Jesse S. Woods

Price: 75¢ per year, May, 1889–February, 1890; $1.00 per year, August, 1890–February, 1891

Circulation: 4,400 (*Remington Brothers' Newspaper Manual*, 1891)

Format: 32 pages per issue; 6 x 9 and 7 x 10 page size; 1 column per page; illustrations and advertisements

Publication history for extant issues (9):

I, Nos. 2–5, 7, 8, 10, 11, June, July, October, November, 1889, January, February, August, October, 1890

II, No. 2, February, 1891

Notes: I, No. 4, was dated "October, 1889" on the cover and "September, 1889" on the inside masthead. An advertisement for the *Afro-American Budget* appeared in the *A. M. E. Church Review*, VIII (April, 1892), unpaged.
Availability:
    DHU-Mo   I, Nos. 4, 5, 7, 8, 10, 11; II, No. 2
    NN-Sch   I, Nos. 2, 3

Afro-American Churchman

Title: *Afro-American Churchmcn: A Monthly Magazine Devoted to the Work of the Church Among Afro-American People*
First issue: 1886
Frequency: Semimonthly, 1886–August ?, 1887; monthly, September, 1887–September, 1890
Place of publication: Norfolk, Va.
Editor and publisher: George Freeman Bragg, Jr.
Price: 50¢ per year
Format (as a monthly): 8 pages per issue; 6 x 9 page size; 2 columns per page
Publication history for extant issues, as a monthly (7):
    IV, Nos. 2, 5, July, October, 1889
    VI [*sic*], No. 6, November/December, 1889
    V, Nos. 1–4, May, June, July, September, 1890
Notes: The *Afro-American Churchman* was published in the interest of the Protestant Episcopal Church.
Availability:
    VPV   IV, V, VI, as listed above

Afro-American Review

Title: *Afro-American Review: A Bimonthly Journal Devoted to the Religious, Educational, Social, and Economic Interests of the African Race in All Parts of the World*
First issue: 1899?
Frequency: Bimonthly
Place of publication: Mattoon, Ill.
Editor and publisher: Jesse S. Woods
Publication history for extant issues: No issues located

Notes: Information on this periodical appeared in the Indianapolis *Freeman*, January 28, February 4, April 22, 1899.

Alexander's Magazine

Title: *Alexander's Magazine*, May, 1905–March, 1907; *Alexander's Magazine and the National Domestic*, April–October, 1907; *Alexander's Magazine*, November, 1907–March/April, 1909
First issue: May, 1905
Frequency: Monthly
Place of publication: Boston, Mass.
Editors: Charles Alexander, May, 1905–August, 1907, December, 1907–March/April, 1909; Archibald H. Grimké, September–November, 1907
Publisher: Charles Alexander
Price: $1.00 per year
Circulation: 5,000 (*Ayer Directory of Newspapers and Periodicals*, 1908)
Format: 48 pages per issue; 6 x 9 page size; 2 columns per page, illustrations and advertisements
Publication history for extant issues (47):
    I, Nos. 1–12, May, 1905–April, 1906
    II, Nos. 1–6, May–October, 1906
    III, Nos. 1–6, November, 1906–April, 1907
    IV, Nos. 1–6, May–October, 1907
    V, Nos. 1–6, November, 1907–April, 1908
    VI, Nos. 1–6, May–October, 1908
    VII, Nos. 1–4, 5/6, November, 1908–February, March/April, 1909
Notes: The dating of the issues sometimes included the day of the month—*e.g.*, May 15, 1905. In April, 1907, *Alexander's Magazine* absorbed the *National Domestic* periodical (see listing below), which had been published in Indianapolis, Ind. The following work is a selective index of *Alexander's Magazine*, indexing significant items relating to social change and reform: Rose Bibliography (Project), American Studies Program, George Washington University, *Analytical Guide and Indexes to Alexander's Magazine, 1905–1909* (Westport, Conn.: Greenwood Press, 1974).
Availability:
CL   I, No. 1–VII, No. 5/6

DLC   I, No. 1–VII, No. 5/6
Title listed in *ULS; NUC, Pre-1956; Reprints, 1980; Microforms in Print, 1980*

Alumni Journal (Hampton Institute)

Title: *Alumni Journal*
First issue: 1881; suspended in 1895; resumed in 1904
Place of publication: Hampton, Va.
Editors: William M. Reid, 1881–?; George W. Davis, ?–?; Frank D. Banks, ?–1895; William Taylor Burwell Williams, 1904–?
Publisher: Hampton Alumni Association
Price: 50¢ per year
Publication history for extant issues through 1909: No issues located
Notes: Information about this periodical appeared in the *Southern Workman*, X (July, 1881), 77; XIII (January, 1884), 9; XXXIII (March, 1904), 137–38.

Alumni Magazine (Lincoln University, Pennsylvania)

Title: *The Alumni Magazine*
Motto: "The night is far spent: the day is at hand."
First issue: November, 1884
Frequency: Quarterly
Place of publication: Philadelphia, Pa.
Editors: Nathan Francis Mossell, William W. Still, and J. P. Williams, editors and managers, November, 1884–May, 1885; Nathan Francis Mossell, editor, and William W. Still, J. P. Williams, associate editors, November, 1885.
Publisher: Alumni Association of Lincoln University, Pa.
Price: $1.00 per year
Format: 28 to 34 pages per issue; 7 x 10 page size; 2 columns per page; no illustrations; advertisements
Publication history for extant issues (4):
I, Nos. 1–3, 5, November, 1884, February, May, November, 1885
Notes: The August, 1885, issue of the *Alumni Magazine* was reviewed in the *A. M. E. Church Review*, II (October, 1885), 208, 211–12. The first number of the second volume reportedly was issued in the spring of 1886. Horace Mann Bond, *Education for Freedom: A His-*

tory of Lincoln University, Pennsylvania (N.p.: Lincoln University, 1976), 341.
Availability:
PLiL   I, Nos. 1–3, 5

American Magazine

Title: *The American Magazine*
First issue: May, 1905
Frequency: Monthly
Place of publication: New York City, N.Y.
Editor: Not stated, May, 1905; Junius C. Ayler, June/July, 1905
Publishers: American Publishing Company, May, 1905; Afro-American News Company, June/July, 1905
Price: 25¢ per year
Format: 6 and 14 pages per issue; 6 x 9 page size; 1 and 2 columns per page; illustrations and advertisements
Publication history for extant issues (2):
[I, No. 1], May, 1905; I, No. 2, June/July, 1905
Notes: The *American Magazine* was superseded by the *Union Magazine* (see listing below). Jesse W. Watkins, who had been associated with the *Colored American Magazine*, was one of the promoters of these two publications.
Availability:
DLC-Mu   I, Nos. 1, 2

Anglo-African Magazine

Title: *The Anglo-African Magazine*
Motto: " 'et nigri Memnonis arma.' VIRG."
First issue: January, 1859
Frequency: Monthly
Place of publication: New York City, N.Y.
Editor: Not stated
Publisher: Thomas Hamilton
Price: $1.00 per year
Format: 32 pages per issue; 7 x 10 page size; 2 columns per page; illustrations and advertisements
Publication history for extant issues (15):

I, Nos. 1–12, January–December, 1859
II, Nos. 1–3, January–March, 1860
Availability:
DLC   I, No. 1–II, No. 3
MWA   I, No. 2–II, No. 3
MiU   I, No. 1–II, No. 3
NN-Sch   I, Nos. 1–12; II, No. 2
VHaI   I, No. 8–II, No. 3
Title listed in *ULS*; *NUC, Pre-1956*; *Reprints, 1980*; *Microforms in Print, 1980*

Brock's Magazine

Title: *Brock's Magazine*
First issue: 1894?
Place of publication: New York City, N.Y.
Editor and publisher: Edward Elmore Brock
Publication history for extant issues: No issues located
Notes: Information on this periodical appeared in Indianapolis *Freeman*, June 23, 1894, July 17, 1897; Augustus M. Hodges, "Edward Elmore Brock," *Colored American Magazine*, II (January, 1901), 197–98.

Church Advocate

Title: *Church Advocate*
First issue: 1894
Frequency: Weekly, February, 1891–February, 1898; monthly, March, 1898–May, 1934
Place of publication: Norfolk, Va., 1891; Baltimore, Md., 1891–May, 1934
Editor and publisher: George Freeman Bragg, Jr.
Price: 50¢ per year
Format (as a monthly): 4 pages per issue; 11 x 16 page size; 4 columns per page; illustrations and advertisements
Publication history, as a monthly, for extant issues through 1909 (218):
IX, No. 1–X, No. 12, November, 1899–October, 1901
XII, No. 1–XIX, No. 2, November, 1902–December, 1909
Notes: Receipt of the initial issue of the *Church Advocate* was men-

tioned in the Indianapolis *Freeman*, February 14, 1891. The periodical was published in the interest of the Protestant Episcopal Church.
Availability:

NNG   XVI, No. 3, January, 1907; XVI, No. 7–XIX, No. 2, May,
       1907–December, 1909

VPV   IX, No. 1–X, No. 12; XII, No. 1–XIX, No. 2, as listed above

Title listed in *ULS*

Church and Society World

Title: *Church and Society World*
First issue: 1902
Frequency: Monthly
Place of publication: Atlanta, Ga.
Editor: Thomas Hamilton Beb Walker
Format: 64 pages per issue; illustrations
Publication history for extant issues: No issues located
Notes: Sources of information on this periodical include *Who's Who of the Colored Race, 1915*, 274–75; *Who's Who in Colored America, 1941–44*, 535. The title is listed in *NUC, Pre-1956* for the Library of Congress, but it is no longer available in that library.

Citizen

Title: *The Citizen*
First issue: December 1, 1909
Frequency: "Published every now and then"
Place of publication: Washington, D.C.
Publisher: The Citizens' Committee (Napoleon B. Marshall, president; James L. Neill, secretary; S. E. Lacey, manager of the *Citizen*)
Price: Free
Format: 4 pages per issue; 8 x 11 page size; 3 columns per page; no illustrations; advertisements
Publication history for extant issues (4):

[No. 1], December 1, 1909; Nos. 2–4, January, May, July, 1910

Availability:

DHU-Mo   Nos. 1–4 (in Daniel Alexander Payne Murray Collection)

Colored American Journal

Title: *The Colored American Journal*
First issue: 1882
Frequency: Monthly
Place of publication: Palestine, Tex.
Editor: C. W. Porter
Publisher: Colored American Journal Company (W. R. Carson, president)
Price: $1.50 per year
Format: 24 pages; 6 x 9 page size; 1 column per page; no illustrations; advertisements
Publication history for extant issues (1):
I, No. 3, January, 1883
Availability:
   OWibfU   I, No. 3 (in the Benjamin W. Arnett Papers)
Title listed in *NUC, Pre-1956*

Colored American Magazine

Title: *The Colored American Magazine*
First issue: May, 1900
Frequency: Monthly
Place of publication: Boston, Mass., May, 1900–May, 1904; New York City, N.Y., June, 1904–November, 1909
Editors: Walter W. Wallace, May, 1900–March, 1903 (managing editor); Pauline Elizabeth Hopkins, May/June, 1903–April, 1904 (literary editor); Frederick Randolph Moore, June, 1904–April, 1909; George W. Harris, May–November, 1909
Publisher: Colored Co-operative Publishing Company, May, 1900–August, 1904; Moore Publishing and Printing Company, September, 1904–November, 1909
Price: $1.50 per year, May, 1900–February, 1904; $1.00 per year, March, 1904–November, 1909
Circulation: 17,840 (*Ayer Directory of Newspapers and Periodicals,* 1903–1908); 12,500 (*Ayer Directory of Newspapers and Periodicals,* 1910)
Format: 64 to 80 pages of text, plus several unnumbered pages of advertisements per issue; 6 x 9 and 7 x 10 page size; 2 columns per page; illustrations and advertisements

Publication history for extant issues (108):

I, Nos. 1–5, May, June, August–October, 1900

II, Nos. 1–6, November, December, 1900, January–April, 1901

III, Nos. 1–6, May–October, 1901

IV, Nos. 1–5, November, December, 1901, January/February, March, April, 1902

V, Nos. 1–6, May–October, 1902

VI, Nos. 1–12, November, December, 1902; January–March, May/June, July–December, 1903

VII, Nos. 1–12, January–December, 1904

VIII, Nos. 1–6, January–June, 1905 [March, 1905, actually numbered IX, No. 3]

IX, Nos. 1–6, July–December 1905 [July, 1905, actually numbered VIII, No. 7]

X, Nos. 1–6, January–June, 1906

XI, Nos. 1–6, July–December, 1906

XII, Nos. 1–6, January–June, 1907

XIII, Nos. 1–6, July–December, 1907

XIV, Nos. 1, 3–10, January, March–July, September–November, 1908

XV, Nos. 1–3, January–March, 1909

XVI, Nos. 4–6, April–June, 1909

XVII, Nos. 1–5, July–November, 1909

Notes: The editor was not named in the May, 1904, issue. After June 1907, Moore was not listed as editor; but advertisements in the magazine indicate that he was editor through April, 1909. During the Boston period of publication, the *Colored American Magazine* was the official journal of the Constitutional Rights Association of the United States, the Loyal Legion of Labor, and the Colored American League. During the New York period, the magazine served as a medium of communication for the National Negro Business League. The following work is a selective index of the *Colored American Magazine*, indexing significant items relating to social change and reform: Rose Bibliography (Project), American Studies Program, George Washington University, *Analytical Guide and Indexes to the Colored American Magazine, 1900–1909* (2 vols.; Westport, Conn.: Greenwood Press, 1974).

Availability:

Libraries with extensive holdings of original issues of the *Colored*

American Magazine include: DHU, DLC, TNF, VHaI
Title listed in *ULS; NUC, Pre-1956; Reprints, 1980; Microforms in Print, 1980*

Colored Catholic

Title: *Colored Catholic*
First issue: 1909
Frequency: Monthly
Place of publication: Baltimore, Md.
Editor and publisher: Charles Marcellus Dorsey
Price: $1.00 per year
Format: 4 pages per issue; 11 x 16 page size
Publication history for extant issues: No issues located
Notes: Information on the *Colored Catholic* appeared in the *Ayer Directory of Newspapers and Periodicals*, 1910, 1911.

Colored Home Journal

Title: *The Colored Home Journal: A Monthly Magazine Devoted to Literature, Science, Art, and Traditions of the Negro Race*
First issue: February, 1903
Frequency: Monthly
Place of publication: Pittsburgh, Pa.
Editors: Thomas S. Ewell and Joseph Garner
Publisher: Home Publishing Company
Price: $1.50 per year
Format: 64 pages; 7 x 10 page size; 2 columns per page; illustrations and advertisements
Publication history for extant issues (1):
    I, No. 1, February, 1903
Notes: The *Colored Home Journal* was listed in the Pittsburgh city directory from 1903 to 1906.
Availability:
    DLC-Mu   I, No. 1

Colored Teacher

Title: *The Colored Teacher*
First issue: 1906

Frequency: Monthly, from September to June
Place of publication: New Orleans, La.
Editor and publisher: John F. Guillaume
Price: $1.00 per year
Format: 20 pages per issue; 6 x 9 page size; 2 columns per page; illustrations and advertisements
Publication history for extant issues (4):
  II, Nos. 1, 3–5, September, November, December, 1907, January, 1908
Notes: The *Colored Teacher* served as the official journal of the Louisiana State Colored Teachers' Association. In 1908 the *Horizon* noted that the periodical had suspended "for lack of patronage." *Horizon,* III (April, 1908), 18.
Availability:
  CtY-Be   II, No. 1
  VHaI   II, Nos. 3–5
  Title listed in *NUC, Pre-1956*

Colored Woman's Magazine

Title: *Colored Woman's Magazine*
First issue: December, 1907
Frequency: Monthly
Place of publication: Topeka, Kansas
Editor: Mrs. C. M. Hughes
Publisher: Colored Woman's Magazine Publishing Company
Price: 75¢ per year
Publication history for extant issues through 1909: No issues located
Notes: Sources of information on this periodical include Indianapolis *Freeman,* January 25, April 11, 1908; *Ayer Directory of Newspapers and Periodicals,* 1916–20; Rashey B. Moten, Jr., "The Negro Press of Kansas" (M.A. thesis, University of Kansas, 1938), 107–108.

Dollar Mark

Title: *The Dollar Mark*
First issue: June, 1906
Frequency: Quarterly
Place of publication: Newport News, Va.

Editor: Edward C. Brown
Publisher: E. C. Brown, Incorporated
Price: Free
Format: 24 pages; 6 x 9 page size; 2 columns per page; illustrations
and advertisements
Publication history for extant issues (1):
I, No. 1, June, 1906
Notes: Advertisements for the *Dollar Mark* appeared in the Indi-
anapolis *Freeman*, July 7–September 15, 1906; and in the New York
Age, June 27–October 3, 1907, and February 6, 1908.
Availability:
ATT   I, No. 1

Douglass' Monthly

Title: *Douglass' Monthly*
Motto: " 'Open thy mouth for the dumb, in the cause of all such as
are appointed to destruction; open thy mouth, judge righteously,
and plead the cause of the poor and needy.'—1st Eccl. xxxi, 8, 9."
(The issues of August, 1861, through August, 1863, gave the source
of this verse as "Proverbs xxxi, 8, 9.")
First issue: June, 1858?
Frequency: Monthly
Place of publication: Rochester, N.Y.
Editor and publisher: Frederick Douglass
Price: 5 shillings per year to British subscribers; beginning August,
1860, $1.00 per year to American subscribers
Format: 16 pages per issue; 10 x 14 page size; 3 columns per page; no
illustrations; advertisements
Publication history for extant issues (48):
I, Nos. 8–12, January–May, 1859
II, Nos. 1–3, 5–7, 11, June–August, October–December, 1859, April,
1860
III, Nos. 1–12, June–December, 1860, January–May, 1861
IV, Nos. 1–12, June–December 1861, January–May, 1862
V (had erratic numbering):

No. 2, July 1862	No. 6, January, 1863
No. 3, August, 1862	No. 6, February, 1863
No. 3, September, 1862	No. 6, March, 1863

No. 5, October, 1862   No. 6, April, 1863
No. 5, November, 1862   No. 6, June, 1863
No. 6, December, 1862   No. 10, August, 1863

Notes: An index for *Douglass' Monthly*, compiled by Elma Marietta Stewart, is included with the microfilm of this periodical issued by the Kraus-Thomson Organization.

Availability:

ICHi	August–December, 1860; January–March, May, July–October, December, 1861; January, February, April, May, July–December, 1862; January–April, June, August, 1863
ICU	July–November, 1862; January–April, June, August, 1863
MWA	July, 1859; November, 1860; March, July–December, 1861; January–May, 1862
NHi	January, April, 1861; June, August, November, 1861
NR	April, May, 1859; July, August, 1862

Title listed in *ULS*; *NUC, Pre-1956*; *Reprints, 1980*; *Microforms in Print, 1980*

Ebony

Title: *Ebony: The Journal of "The Three P's."*
First issue: April, 1906
Frequency: Monthly
Place of publication: Philadelphia, Pa.
Editor and publisher: Thomas Wallace Swann
Price: $1.00 per year
Format: 54 pages; 5 x 6 page size; 1 column per page; illustrations and advertisements
Publication history for extant issues (1):
  I, No. 1, April, 1906
Notes: *Ebony* was printed by the Society of "The Three P's."
Availability:

ATT	I, No. 1
DHU-Mo	I, No. 1

Educational Era

Title: *Educational Era*
First issue: 1892

Place of publication: Baltimore, Md.
Editor: William Ashbie Hawkins
Publisher: Maryland State Teachers' Association
Publication history for extant issues: No issues located
Notes: Information relative to this periodical appeared in Indianapolis
Freeman, March 26, April 2, 1892; *Who's Who of the Colored Race,
1915,* 132–33; *Who's Who in Colored America, 1930–32,* 201.

Educator (Alabama)

Title: *The Educator: Devoted to Educational, Industrial, and General
Improvement of the Negro*
First issue: February, 1899
Frequency: Monthly
Place of publication: Huntsville, Ala.
Editor: Robert D. Hunt
Publisher: Not stated
Price: 50¢ per year, February–December, 1899; 75¢ per year, Febru-
ary, 1900–December, 1909
Format: 8 pages per issue; 11 x 16 page size; 4 columns per page;
illustrations and advertisements
Publication history for extant issues (127):
    I, Nos. 1–11, February–December, 1899
    II, Nos. 1–12, February–December, 1900, January, 1901
    III, Nos. 1–12, February–December, 1901, January, 1902
    IV, Nos. 1–6, February–July, 1902
    V, Nos. 7–11, August–December, 1902
    VI, Nos. 1–4, 6–12, February–May, July–December, 1903, January,
        1904
    VII, Nos. 1–12, February–December, 1904, January, 1905
    VIII, Omitted in numbering
    IX, Nos. 1–12, February–December, 1905, January, 1906
    X, Nos. 1–12, February–December, 1906, January, 1907
    XI, Nos. 1–12, February–December, 1907, January, 1908
    XII, Nos. 1–12, February–November, 1908, January, February,
        1909
    XIII, Nos. 1–10, March–December, 1909
Notes: The *Educator* was listed in the *Ayer Directory of Newspapers
and Periodicals* as late as 1915. This periodical was endorsed by the

Alabama State Teachers' Association as its official journal.
Availability:
DHEW   I, No. 1–XIII, No. 10, as listed above
Title listed in *ULS*; *NUC, Pre-1956*

Educator (North Carolina)

Title: *The Educator*
First issue: November, 1898
Frequency: Bimonthly
Place of publication: Kittrell, N.C.
Editor and publisher: John Russell Hawkins
Price: 50¢ per year
Format: 48 pages; 6 x 9 page size; 1 column per page; illustrations;
  no advertisements
Publication history for extant issues (1):
  I, No. 1, November, 1898
Notes: The *Educator* was the journal of the educational department
  of the African Methodist Episcopal Church.
Availability:
MWA   I, No. 1

Freedman's Torchlight

Title: *The Freedman's Torchlight*
Motto: " 'If God be for us, who can be against us?'—Rom. 8:31."
First issue: December, 1866
Frequency: Monthly
Place of publication: Brooklyn, N.Y.
Editor: Rufus Lewis Perry
Publisher: African Civilization Society
Price: 50¢ per year
Format: 4 pages; 11 x 16 page size; 4 columns per page; no illustra-
  tions or advertisements
Publication history for extant issues (1):
  I, No. 1, December, 1866
Availability:
CtHT-W   I, No. 1
DLC-Mu   I, No. 1
Title listed in *ULS*

Freeman

Title: *The Freeman: A Magazine of Opinion*
First issue: 1908
Frequency: Monthly
Place of publication: New York City, N.Y.
Editor: Not stated
Publisher: Timothy Thomas Fortune
Price: $1.00 per year
Format: 16 pages; 9 x 12 page size; 2 columns per page; no illustrations; advertisements
Publication history for extant issues (1):
    I, No. 8, May, 1908
Notes: Prior to May, 1908, this publication was issued weekly, under the title *Fortune's Freeman. Freeman*, I (May, 1908), 8.
Availability:
    DLC-Mu   I, No. 8

Future State

Title: *The Future State: A Monthly Journal of Negro Progress*
First issue: 1891
Frequency: Monthly
Place of publication: Kansas City, Mo.
Editors: Carrie A. Bannister and Ernest D. Lynwood
Publisher: Ernest D. Lynwood
Price: $1.00 per year
Circulation: 2,500 (*Ayer Directory of Newspapers and Periodicals*, 1898)
Format: 24 pages; 8 x 11 page size; 2 columns per page; illustrations and advertisements
Publication history for extant issues (1):
    III, No. 3/4, March/April, 1895
Notes: In the *Ayer Directory of Newspapers and Periodicals, Future State* was recorded as a weekly (established in 1891) in the 1893/94 edition and as a monthly in the 1895–98 editions.
Availability:
    NN-Sch   III, No. 3/4

Gazetteer and Guide

Title: *The Gazetteer and Guide*
First issue: November 15, 1901
Frequency: Monthly
Place of publication: Buffalo, N.Y.
Editor: James Alexander Ross
Publisher: Gazetteer and Guide Publishing Company
Price: $1.50 per year, 1901; $1.00 per year, 1904–1908
Circulation: 7,500 (*Ayer Directory of Newspapers and Periodicals,* 1905, 1908)
Format: 40 pages per issue (1901, 1904), 24 pages (1906, 1908); 7 x 10 page size (1901, 1904), 11 x 16 (1906, 1908); 2 columns per page (1901, 1904), 4 columns (1906, 1908); illustrations and advertisements
Publication history for extant issues through 1909 (6):
    I, Nos. 1, 2, November 15, December 15, 1901
    ?, Nos. ?, June, October, 1904
    V, No. 8, August, 1906
    VIII, No. 2, December 25, 1908
Notes: The *Gazetteer and Guide* was published for the National Colored Men's Railroad Association of America, the Head and Side Waiters' National Association, and the "higher Masonic colored bodies and auxiliaries." It was issued under various titles after 1909, including *American Caterer and Gazetteer and Guide* and *Caterer, Gazetteer and Guide*. The latest issue located has the title *For You, and Gazetteer and Guide*, L, No. 2, January 25, 1948.
Availability:
    DHU-Mo   VIII, No. 2
    DLC-Mu   I, Nos. 1, 2; ?, Nos. ?, June, October, 1904
    NN-Sch   V, No. 8
    Title listed in *ULS*; *NUC, Pre-1956*

Helper

Title: *The Helper: Published Monthly in the Interest of Child Saving*
First issue: 1899?
Frequency: Monthly
Place of publication: Harvey, Ill.

Editor: Amanda Berry Smith
Publisher: Amanda Smith Industrial Home
Price: 50¢ per year
Format: 12 pages; 9 x 12 page size; 3 columns per page; illustrations
and advertisements
Publication history for extant issues (1):
IX, No. 10, November, 1907
Availability:
DHU-Mo   IX, No. 10

Horizon

Title: *The Horizon: A Journal of the Color Line*
Motto: "Seeking the seldom sort."
First issue: January, 1907
Frequency: Monthly
Place of publication: Washington, D.C., 1907; Alexandria, Va., 1908;
Washington, D.C., 1909–10
Editors and publishers: William Edward Burghardt Du Bois, Lafa-
yette McKeene Hershaw, and Freeman Henry Morris Murray. 1907–
1908: "Owned by W. E. B. Du Bois, F. H. M. Murray, and L. M.
Hershaw, who write it, type it, and print it." 1909–10: "Edited by
W. E. Burghardt Du Bois, assisted by L. M. Hershaw and F. H. M.
Murray."
Price: 50¢ per year, 1907–1908; $1.00 per year, 1909–10
Circulation: 500 (*Crisis*, V [November, 1912], 27)
Format:
1907–1908: 24 pages per issue; 5 x 6 page size; 1 column per page;
no illustrations; advertisements
1909–10: 12 pages per issue; 8 x 11 page size; 2 columns per page;
illustrations; no advertisements
Publication history for extant issues (31):
I, Nos. 1–6, January–June, 1907
II, Nos. 1–6, July–December, 1907
III, Nos. 1–6, January–June, 1908
IV, Nos. 1–4, 5/6, July–October, November/December, 1908
V, Nos. 1–6, November, December, 1909, January–March, May,
1910
VI, Nos. 1, 2, June, July, 1910

Notes: The *Horizon* was published under the patronage of the Niagara Movement. Chronological listings of Du Bois's writings in the *Horizon* are given in: Herbert Aptheker, *Annotated Bibliography of the Published Writings of W. E. B. Du Bois* (Millwood, N.Y.: Kraus-Thomson, 1973), 109–20; and in Paul G. Partington, *W. E. B. Du Bois: A Bibliography of His Published Writings* (Whittier, Calif.: Penn Lithographics, Inc., 1977), 2–9.

Availability:

ATT	I, No. 1–IV, No. 5/6
DHU-Mo	I, No. 1–VI, No. 2
VHaI	II, No. 4; III, Nos. 1–3, 5, 6; IV, Nos. 1–4, 5/6; V, Nos. 2, 4, 6; VI, Nos. 1, 2

Title listed in *ULS*; *NUC, Pre-1956*; *Microforms in Print, 1980*

Hospital Herald

Title: *The Hospital Herald: A Monthly Journal Devoted to Hospital Work, Nurse Training, Domestic and Public Hygiene*

First issue: December, 1898

Frequency: Monthly

Place of publication: Charleston, S.C.

Editor: Alonzo Clifton McClennan

Publisher: Not stated

Price: 50¢ per year

Format: 16 pages average per issue; 6 x 9 page size; 2 columns per page; illustrations and advertisements

Publication history for extant issues (15):

I, Nos. 2–12, January–November, 1899
II, Nos. 1–4, January–March, May, 1900

Notes: The issue for January, 1899, which would be Vol. I, No. 2, is erroneously numbered Vol. II, No. 1. The *Hospital Herald* was established in the interest of the Hospital and Training School for Nurses in Charleston. It also became the official journal of the Association of Colored Physicians of South Carolina (later renamed the Palmetto Association of Physicians, Pharmaceutists, and Dentists of South Carolina).

Availability:

DNLM	I, No. 3–II, No. 4
ScCM-Wa	I, Nos. 2, 3, 5, 6, 8, 11, 12; II, No. 1

Howard's American Magazine

Title: *Howard's American Magazine: Devoted to the Educational, Religious, Industrial, Social, and Political Progress of the Colored Race*
First issue: 1895
Frequency: Monthly
Place of publication: Harrisburg, Pa., November, 1899–October, 1900; New York City, N.Y., March–July, 1901
Editor: Thomas Wallace Swann, November, 1899, March, April, September, 1900; editor not stated in other issues examined
Publishers: James H. W. Howard; Thomas Ayres Church and George T. Knox also listed as publishers, March–July, 1901
Price: $2.00 per year, 1899–1900; $1.00 per year, 1901
Format: 40 to 80 pages per issue; 6 x 9 and 7 x 10 page size; 1 and 2 columns per page; illustrations and advertisements
Publication history for extant issues (11):
  IV, Nos. 3, 4, 8, 9, October, November, 1899, March, April, 1900
  V, Nos. 2, 3, September, October, 1900
  VI, Nos. 8–12, March–July, 1901
Availability:
  DHU-Mo   IV, Nos. 4, 8, 9; V, No. 3; VI, Nos. 8, 11
  DLC   IV, Nos. 4, 9; V, Nos. 2, 3; VI, Nos. 9–12 (Nos. 10 and 12 are in the Mary Church Terrell Papers, in Manuscript Division)
  VHaI   IV, Nos. 3, 4; VI, Nos. 8, 9
  Title listed in *ULS*; *NUC, Pre-1956*

Howard's Negro-American Magazine

Title: *Howard's Negro-American Magazine: A Monthly Journal Devoted to All Questions Pertaining to the Educational, Religious, Social, and Political Advancement of the Negroes of America*
First issue: 1889
Frequency: Monthly
Place of publication: Harrisburg, Pa.
Editor and publisher: James H. W. Howard; Reuben Hanson Armstrong also listed as editor during 1890
Price: 10¢ and 15¢ per copy
Circulation: 2,000 (*Remington Brothers' Newspaper Manual*, 1891)

Format: 36 pages per issue; 6 x 9 page size; 1 column per page; illustrations and advertisements
Publication history for extant issues (4):
　I, No. 7, January, 1890
　II, Nos. 1, 4?, 5, July, October, December, 1890
Availability:
　CtY-Be　　II, No. 1
　DHU-Mo　　II, No. 4?
　DLC　　　　I, No. 7
　LNHT　　　II, No. 5
　Title listed in *ULS*; *NUC, Pre-1956* (under *Howard's American Magazine*)

Impending Conflict

Title: *The Impending Conflict*
First issue: July, 1903
Frequency: Monthly
Place of publication: New York City, N.Y.
Editor: John Edward Bruce
Publisher: Melvin Jack Chisum
Publication history for extant issues: No issues located
Notes: Information on this periodical appeared in the Washington, (D.C.) *Colored American*, July 18, 1903.

Jewel

Title: *Jewel*
First issue: January, 1891
Frequency: Monthly
Place of publication: St. Paul, Minn.
Editor and publisher: Lewis Charles Sheafe
Publication history for extant issues: No issues located
Notes: Information on this periodical appeared in the St. Paul *Appeal*, January 24, June 20, 1891.

Ladies' Magazine

Title: *Ladies' Magazine*
First issue: Proposed in 1880; evidence of actual publication not found

Notes: Recommendations for the publication of this periodical are recorded in African Methodist Episcopal Church, General Conference,
*Journal of the Seventeenth Session and Sixteenth Quadrennial Ses-
sion . . . 1880* (Xenia, Ohio: Torchlight Printing Company, 1882),
66–67, 112–13, 283.

L'Album Littéraire

Title: *L'Album Littéraire: Journal des Jeunes Gens, Amateurs de Lit-
térature*
Motto: "Homo doctus in se sempter divitias habet."
First issue: April, 1843
Frequency: Monthly, July, 1843; Semimonthly, August, 1843
Place of publication: New Orleans, La.
Editor: Not stated
Publisher: Not stated
Price: "60 sous par mois"
Format: 24 pages per issue; 6 x 9 page size; 1 column per page; no
illustrations or advertisements
Publication history for extant issues (3):
I, Nos. 4?, 5, 6, July, August 1, August 15, 1843
Notes: Armand Lanusse, a free man of color, was probably the pro-
moter of this periodical. Edward Larocque Tinker, *Les Écrits de
Langue Française en Louisiane au XIX*^e *Siècle: Essais Biographiques
et Bibliographiques* (Paris: Librairie Ancienne Honoré Champion,
1932), 298. All of the contents of the periodical were in French.
Availability:
MWA   I, Nos. 4?, 5, 6

Living Age

Title: *The Living Age*
First issue: 1891
Frequency: Monthly
Place of publication: Denison, Tex., 1891–?; Langston, Okla. Terr.,
?–1904
Editors and publishers: S. Douglass Russell and E. H. Garland, 1891;
S. Douglass Russell and son, 1904
Price: $1.00 per year, 1891; 50¢ per year, 1904
Format: 24 pages; 6 x 9 page size; illustrations

Publication history for extant issues: No issues located

Notes: Information on the *Living Age* appeared in St. Paul *Appeal*, August 8, 1891; Indianapolis *Freeman*, August 8, October 17, 1891, March 5, April 9, 1892; *Ayer Directory of Newspapers and Periodicals*, 1905.

Lowery's Religious Monthly

Title: *Colored Preacher*, 1897–99; *Lowery's Religious Monthly*, 1899–1900?

First issue: 1897

Frequency: Monthly

Place of publication: Spartanburg, S.C.

Editors and publishers: Irving E. Lowery and his son Warren Scott Lowery

Price: $1.00 per year

Format: 38 pages; 6 x 9 page size

Publication history for extant issues: No issues located

Notes: Information on this periodical appeared in Washington (D.C.) *Colored American*, May 7, 1898; Indianapolis *Freeman*, February 25, December 30, 1899; *Rowell's American Newspaper Directory*, 1900.

Lunar Visitor

Title: *The Lunar Visitor*

Motto: "A little one shall become a thousand, and a small one a strong nation."

First issue: January, 1862

Frequency: Monthly

Place of publication: San Francisco, Calif.

Editor: John Jamison Moore

Publisher: Not stated

Price: 25¢ per copy

Format: 4 pages per issue; 10 x 12 page size; 4 columns per page; no illustrations or advertisements

Publication history for extant issues (2):

I, Nos. 2, 6, February, June, 1862

Availability:

CU-B   I, No. 2

NIC   I, No. 6
Title listed in *ULS*

Lynk's Magazine

Title: *Lynk's Magazine*
First issue: 1898
Frequency: Monthly
Place of publication: Jackson, Tenn.
Editor: Miles Vandahurst Lynk
Publisher: M. V. Lynk Publishing House
Publication history for extant issues: No issues located
Notes: Information on this periodical appeared in Washington (D.C.)
    Colored American, May 7, July 30, 1898; Indianapolis *Freeman*,
    February 12, November 5, December 10, 1898.

McConico's Monthly Magazine

Title: *McConico's Monthly Magazine*
First issue: July, 1909
Frequency: Monthly
Place of publication: Birmingham, Ala.
Editor and Publisher: John F. A. McConico
Price: $1.00 per year
Format: 40 and 64 pages; 6 x 9 page size; 1 and 2 columns per page;
    illustrations and advertisements
Publication history for extant issues (2):
    I, Nos. 1, 6, July, December, 1909
Availability:
    CtY-Be   I, No. 1
    DLC-Mu   I, No. 6
    Title listed in *ULS*; *NUC, Pre-1956*

McGirt's Magazine

Title: *McGirt's Magazine: Art, Science, Literature and of General
    Interest* [*sic*]
First Issue: 1903
Frequency: Monthly, 1903–August, 1908; quarterly, January–Decem-
    ber, 1909
Place of publication: Philadelphia, Pa.

Editor: James Ephraim McGirt
Publishers: James Ephraim McGirt, 1903–December, 1905; McGirt Publishing Company, November, 1906–December, 1909
Price: $1.00 per year, 1903–August, 1908; 50¢ per year, 1909
Format: 32 to 40 pages per issue; 6 x 9 and 7 x 10 page size; 2 columns per page; illustrations and advertisements
Publication history for extant issues (17):
I, No. 2, September, [1903]
II, Nos. 6, 9–11, 14, January, April, June, July, October, 1904
II, No. 8 [sic], May, 1905
III, No. 3, December, 1905
V, Nos. 1. 7, 12, November, 1906, May, October, 1907
VI, Nos. 1, 2, 7, 9, November, December, 1907, May, August, 1908
I, Nos. 1, 4 [new series], January/February/March, October/November/December, 1909
Notes: *McGirt's Magazine* served as the official journal for the Constitutional Brotherhood of America.
Availability:
DHU-Mo   I, No. 2; II, Nos. 6, 9–11; III, No. 3; V, Nos. 1, 7; VI, No. 1
DLC-Mu   II, No. 14; V, No. 12; VI, Nos. 2, 7
GAU   I, No. 2; I, Nos. 1, 4, n.s.
NN-Sch   II, No. 8; V, No. 7; VI, No. 9

Medical and Surgical Observer

Title: *The Medical and Surgical Observer: Devoted to the Interests of Medicine, Dentistry, and Pharmacy*
First issue: December, 1892
Frequency: Monthly
Place of publication: Jackson, Tenn.
Editor and publisher: Miles Vandahurst Lynk
Price: $2.00 per year, December, 1892–May, 1893; $1.00 per year, June, 1893–January, 1894
Format: 16 pages average per issue; 6 x 9 page size; 1 column per page; illustrations and advertisements
Publication history for extant issues (14):
I, Nos. 1–12, December, 1892–November, 1893
I, No. 12 [sic], December, 1893
II, No. 1, January, 1894

Availability:
  DNLM   I, No. 1–II, No. 1
  ICCRL   I, No. 1–II, No. 1
  Title listed in *ULS*; *NUC, Pre-1956*

Mirror of Liberty

Title: *The Mirror of Liberty*
Motto: "Liberty is the word for me—above all, liberty."
First issue: July, 1838
Frequency: Quarterly
Place of publication: New York City, N.Y.
Editor and publisher: David Ruggles
Price: $1.00 per year
Format: 9 x 12 page size; 2 columns per page; no illustrations or advertisements
Publication history for extant issues (5):
  I, No. 1, July, 1838   (8 pages)
  I, No. 1, August, 1838   (16 pages)
  I, No. 2, January, 1838   (20 pages)
  I, No. 3, August, 1840   (16 pages)
  "Extra," July, 1841   (4 pages)
Notes: Eight pages of the August, 1838, issue were mainly a reprinting of the July, 1838, issue. The fourth number of volume I was probably the May, 1841, issue mentioned in the *Liberator*, August 13, 1841. The *Mirror of Liberty* was a medium of communication for the New York Committee of Vigilance and the American Reform Board of Disfranchised Commissioners.
Availability:
  MPB   I, No. 1, August, 1838
  MWA   I, No. 1, July, 1838; I, Nos. 2, 3, January, 1838, August, 1840
  N   "Extra," July, 1841
  NHi   I, No. 1, August, 1838; I, No. 2, January, 1838
  Title listed in *ULS*; *NUC, Pre-1956*

Monthly Review

Title: *The Monthly Review*
First issue: March, 1894

Frequency: Monthly
Place of publication: Boston, Mass., March, 1894–July, 1895; Philadel-
   phia, Pa., January–July, 1896?
Editor and publisher: Charles Alexander
Price: $1.00 per year
Format: 24 to 48 pages per issue; 6 x 9 and 7 x 10 page size; 1 and 2
   columns per page; illustrations and advertisements
Publication history for extant issues (14):
   I, Nos. 1–6, March–August, 1894
   II, Nos. 1/2, 3–6, September/October, November, December, 1894,
      January, February, 1895.
   III, Nos. 1, 3, 5, March, May, July, 1895
Notes: Publication of the *Monthly Review* in Philadelphia in 1896 was
   mentioned by the *National Baptist Magazine*, III (July, 1896), 223,
   but no Philadelphia issues have been located.
Availability:
   CL   I, No. 1–II, No. 6
   DHU-Mo   I, No. 1; III, Nos. 1, 5
   DLC-Mu   I, No. 4; III, No. 3

Mouth-Piece

Title: *The Mouth-Piece*
First issue: 1887
Frequency: Monthly
Place of publication: Chicago, Ill.
Editor: Thomas W. Henderson
Publisher: Mouth-Piece Company
Publication history for extant issues: No issues located
Notes: Information on this periodical appeared in *A. M. E. Church
   Review*, IV (October, 1887), 221; Cleveland *Gazette*, June 25, 1887.

Musical Advance

Title: *Musical Advance*
First issue: 1907?
Place of publication: Richmond, Va.
Editor: J. H. Carter
Price: 50¢ per year
Publication history for extant issues: No issues located

Notes: An advertisement for *Musical Advance* appeared in *Alexander's Magazine*, IV (June, 1907), 73, and IV (August, 1907), 184.

Musical Messenger

Title: *The Musical Messenger: Devoted to Music, Literature, and Art*
First issue: 1886
Frequency: Monthly
Place of publication: Montgomery, Ala., 1886–?; Washington, D.C. 1888–89
Editor: Amelia L. Tilghman
Publisher: Not stated
Price: 75¢ per year
Format: 4 pages per issue; 9 x 12 page size; 3 columns per page; no illustrations; advertisements
Publication history for extant issues (2):
  I, No. 11, May, 1889
  II, No. 1, July, 1889
Availability:
  DLC   I, No. 11; II, No. 1
  Title listed in *ULS*

National Afro-American

Title: *National Afro-American*
First issue: 1890
Frequency: Monthly
Place of publication: Washington, D.C.
Editor and publisher: John Willis Menard
Publication history for extant issues: No issues located
Notes: Information on the *National Afro-American* appeared in the Indianapolis *Freeman*, October 11, November 22, 1890, January 17, February 14, 1891.

National Association Notes

Title: *The National Association Notes*
Motto: "Lifting as we climb"
First issue: 1897
Frequency: Monthly
Place of publication: Tuskegee, Ala.
Editor: Margaret Murray Washington (Mrs. Booker T. Washington)

Publisher: National Association of Colored Women
Price: 25¢ per year
Format: 4 pages per issue; 6 x 9 and 11 x 16 page size; 2 and 4 columns per page; generally no illustrations; advertisements. The July, 1904, number was a special illustrated issue of 48 pages.
Publication history for extant issues through 1909 (22):

I, Nos. 2, 3, 7, May 15, June 15, September, 1897
II, Nos. 4, 8, 10–12, September, 1898, January, March–May, 1899
III, Nos. 1, 2, 5–8, 10–12, June, August, November, December, 1899; January, February, April, May, December, 1900
III, No. 10 [*sic*], November, 1900
IV, Nos. 1, 6, January, May, 1901
VII, No. 11, July, 1904
XII, No. 4, October, 1908

Notes: This periodical is currently published as a quarterly journal.
Availability:

ATT   VII, No. 11; XII, No. 4
DLC   I–IV, as listed above (in Mary Church Terrell Papers, in Manuscript Division)

Title listed in *ULS*; *NUC, Pre-1956*
(The archives of the National Association of Colored Women in Washington, D.C., were not accessible to the author during the time this study was being prepared.)

National Baptist Magazine

Title: *The National Baptist Magazine*
First issue: January, 1894
Frequency: Quarterly, January, 1894–April, 1898; monthly, June 1898–October/November, 1901
Place of publication: Washington, D.C., January, 1894–May, 1899; Nashville, Tenn., July–November/December, 1899; Washington, D.C., November, 1900–October/November, 1901
Editor: William Bishop Johnson
Publisher: American National Baptist Convention, January, 1894–July, 1895; National Baptist Convention, October, 1895–October/November, 1901
Price: $1.25 per year, 1894–99; $1.00 per year, 1900–1901
Circulation: 1,500 (*Ayer Directory of Newspapers and Periodicals*, 1905, 1908)

Format: Number of pages varied considerably, but averaged 70 pages
for the quarterly issues and 20 pages for the monthly issues; 6 x 9
page size; 1 column per page; illustrations and advertisements
Publication history for extant issues (37):
    I, Nos. 1–4, January, April, July, October, 1894
    II, Nos. 1–4, January, April, July, October, 1895
    III, Nos. 1–3, January, April, July, 1896
    IV, No. 4/V, no. 1, October, 1896/January, 1897 (one issue)
    V, Nos. 2–4, April, July, October, 1897
    VI, Nos. 1–3, 4/6, 11, 12, April, June, July, August/October, 1898,
    April, May, 1899
    VII, Nos. 1, 2, 3/4, 5/6, 7–12, July, August, September/October,
    November/December, 1899, November, December, 1900, Jan-
    uary–April, 1901
    VIII, Nos. 1–5, 6/7, May–September, October/November, 1901
Notes: The *National Baptist Magazine* was recorded in the *Ayer Directory of Newspapers and Periodicals* as late as 1908, with Johnson
as editor and Washington, D.C., as the place of publication.
Availability:
    NRAB   I–VIII, as listed above
    Title listed in *ULS*; *NUC, Pre-1956*

National Capital Searchlight

Title: *The National Capital Searchlight: A Monthly Journal Devoted
to Education Among Colored People*
First issue: February, 1901
Frequency: Monthly
Place of publication: Washington, D.C.
Editor: M. Grant Lucas
Publisher: Not stated
Price: $1.00 per year, for 10 issues
Format: 32 pages per issue; 7 x 10 page size; 2 columns per page;
illustrations and advertisements
Publication history for extant issues (2):
    I, Nos. 1, 2, February, March, 1901
Availability:
    DHU-Mo   I, No. 1
    DLC-Mu   I, Nos. 1, 2
    MWA   I, No. 1

Title listed in *ULS*; *NUC, Pre-1956*

National Domestic

Title: *The National Domestic*
First issue: 1905?
Frequency: Monthly
Place of publication: Indianapolis, Ind.
Editor: Not stated
Publisher: Coachmen and Butlers' Guide Publishing Company (Archibald Greathouse, president; John Dalphin Howard, secretary and manager)
Price: $1.00 per year
Format: 48 pages per issue; 7 x 10 page size; 2 columns per page; illustrations and advertisements
Publication history for extant issues (2):
I, No. 7, March, 1960
II, No. 3, November, 1906
Notes: John Dalphin Howard was identified as the founder and editor of the *National Domestic* in the Indianapolis *Freeman*, April 6, 1907. In April, 1907, the *National Domestic* was absorbed by *Alexander's Magazine* (see listing above).
Availability:
DHU-Mo   I, No. 7; II, No. 3

National Medical Association Journal

Title: *Journal [of the] National Medical Association: A Quarterly Publication Devoted to the Interest of the National Medical Association and Allied Professions of Medicine, Surgery, Dentistry and Pharmacy*
First issue: January/March, 1909
Frequency: Quarterly
Place of publication: Tuskegee, Ala.
Editor: Charles Victor Roman
Publisher: National Medical Association
Price: Free to members of the association; 50¢ per year to nonmembers
Format: 68 pages average per issue; 7 x 10 page size; 2 columns per page; illustrations and advertisements

Publication history for extant issues through 1909 (4):
I, Nos. 1–4, January/March–October/December, 1909
Notes: This periodical has continued publication to the present day; it is now issued monthly.
Availability:
DNLM   I, Nos. 1–4
ICCRL   I, Nos. 1–3
Title listed in *ULS; NUC, Pre-1956*

National Pilot

Title: *National Pilot*
First issue: 1888
Place of publication: Petersburg, Va.
Editor and publisher: Charles Benjamin William Gordon
Notes: Contemporary sources indicate that the *National Pilot* began publication in 1888 as a monthly, became a quarterly by 1890, and by 1900 was being published as a weekly newspaper. No issues of the *National Pilot* as a monthly or quarterly periodical have been located.

National Reformer

Title: *National Reformer*
Motto: " 'God hath made of one blood all nations of men for to dwell on all the face of the earth.'—Acts, xvii, 26."
First issue: September, 1838
Frequency: Monthly
Place of publication: Philadelphia, Pa.
Editor: William Whipper
Publisher: American Moral Reform Society
Price: $1.00 per year
Format: 16 pages per issue; 6 x 9 page size; 2 columns per page; no illustrations; generally no advertisements
Publication history for extant issues (12):
I, Nos. 1–12, September, 1838–April, 1839, September–December, 1839
Availability:
GAU   I, Nos. 1–12
PPHi   I, Nos. 1–12
Title listed in *NUC, Pre-1956*

Negro

Title: *The Negro: A Monthly Publication Devoted to Critical Discussions of Race Problems Involved in the Mental, Moral, Social, and Material Condition of the Negroes in the United States*
First issue: July, 1886
Frequency: Monthly
Place of publication: Boston, Mass.
Editor: Not stated
Publisher: Not stated
Price: $1.00 per year
Format: 32 pages per issue; 6 x 9 page size; 1 column per page; illustrations and advertisements
Publication history for extant issues (2):
  I, Nos. 1, 2, July, August, 1886
Notes: The editorship of this magazine was attributed to William Hannibal Thomas by his contemporary, John Edward Bruce. John E. Bruce, "The Critic Revealed; or, The Deadly Parallel," *Howard's American Magazine*, VI (April, 1901), 366; Bruce Grit [John E. Bruce], "He Defames the Race," Washington (D.C.) *Colored American*, February 2, 1901.
Availability:
  DHU-Mo   I, No. 1
              I, Nos. 1, 2, in author's personal collection
  Title listed in *ULS; NUC, Pre-1956*

Negro Agriculturist

Title: *The Negro Agriculturist: A Journal for the Farm*
First issue: February, 1909
Frequency: Monthly
Place of publication: Sandy Spring, Md.
Editor and publisher: "Edited and published by the Faculty of Maryland Normal and Agricultural Institute, George H. C. Williams, Principal"
Price: 50¢ per year
Format: 4 pages per issue; 8 x 11 page size; 3 columns per page; no illustrations; advertisements
Publication history for extant issues (6):
  I, Nos. 1–4, 5/6, 7/8, February–May, June/July, August/September, 1909

Availability:
  DA   I, No. 1, 7/8
  DLC-Mu   I, Nos. 1–4, 5/6, 7/8

Negro-American

Title: *The Negro-American: A Monthly Publication, Devoted to the Interests of the Race*
First issue: January, 1887
Frequency: Monthly
Place of publication: Boston, Mass.
Editors and publishers: Thomas T. Symmons and John Edward Bruce
Price: $1.00 per year
Format: 16 pages; 6 x 9 page size; 2 columns per page; no illustrations or advertisements
Publication history for extant issues (1):
  I, No. 1, January, 1887
Availability:
  NN-Sch   I, No. 1
              I, No. 1, in author's personal collection
  Title listed in *ULS*

Negro Business League Herald

Title: *The Negro Business League Herald*
First issue: April, 1909
Frequency: Monthly
Place of publication: Washington, D.C.
Editor: Not stated
Publisher: Negro Business League Herald Publishing Company (William Sidney Pittman, president)
Price: $1.00 per year
Format: 12 pages per issue; 9 x 12 page size; 3 columns per page; illustrations and advertisements
Publication history for extant issues (8):
  I, Nos. 1–8, April, May 15–October 15, November, 1909
Notes: The *Herald* was the official journal of the Washington Negro Business League and served as a channel of communication for the National Negro Business League.
Availability:
  DLC-Mu   I, Nos. 1–8
  Title listed in *NUC, Pre-1956*

Negro Educational Journal

Title: *The Negro Educational Journal*
First issue: November, 1894
Frequency: Monthly
Place of publication: Cartersville, Ga., November, 1894–January/February, 1895; Athens, Ga., May–September/October, 1895
Editors and publishers: Floyd Grant Snelson and William Baxter Matthews, 1894; Floyd Grant Snelson and his wife, Waterloo B. Snelson, 1895
Price: $1.00 per year
Circulation: 1,000 (*Negro Educational Journal*, I [June, 1895], unpaged)
Format: 14 to 32 pages per issue; 9 x 12 page size; 3 columns per page; illustrations and advertisements
Publication history for extant issues (7):
I, Nos. 1, 2, 3/4, 7, 8, 10, 11/12, November, December, 1894, January/February, May, June/July, August, September/October, 1895
Notes: *The Negro Educational Journal* was the official publication for the State Teachers' Association of Georgia, and it was also adopted by the Alabama Teachers' Association as a medium of communication.
Availability:
DHEW   I, as listed above
Title listed in *ULS*

Negro Educational Review

Title: *The Negro Educational Review*
First issue: November, 1904
Frequency: Monthly
Place of publication: Vincennes, Ind.
Editor: David V. Bohannon
Publisher: Negro Educational Review Press
Price: $1.50 per year
Format: 32 to 56 pages per issue; 6 x 9 page size; 2 columns per page; illustrations and advertisements
Publication history for extant issues (7):
I, Nos. 1–4, 8, 11, 12, November, 1904, January–March, July, October, November, 1905
Notes: An advertisement for the *Negro Educational Review* appeared

regularly from June 17, 1905, through March 2, 1907, in the *Tuskegee Student*, a weekly publication issued at Tuskegee Institute.
Availability:

ATT   I, Nos. 8, 11, 12
DHEW   I, Nos. 1–4
DHU-Mo   I, No. 3
Title listed in *ULS*; *NUC, Pre-1956*

Negro Music Journal

Title: *The Negro Music Journal: A Monthly Magazine Devoted to the Educational Interest of the Negro Race in Music*
First issue: September, 1902
Frequency: Monthly
Place of publication: Washington, D.C.
Editor: J. Hillary Taylor
Publisher: Not stated
Price: $1.00 per year
Format: 24 pages per issue; 6 x 9 and 7 x 10 page size; 1 and 2 columns per page; illustrations and advertisements
Publication history for extant issues (15):
    I, Nos. 1–2, September, 1902–August, 1903
    II, Nos. 13–15, September–November, 1903
Notes: Beginning October, 1903, the periodical was designated as the official journal of the newly established Washington Conservatory of Music.
Availability:

DHU-Mo   I, Nos. 5, 9, 10
DLC   I, No. 1–II, No. 15
Title listed in *ULS*; *NUC, Pre-1956*; *Reprints, 1980*; *Microforms in Print, 1980*

New Citizen

Title: *The New Citizen: A Magazine of Politics, Literature, and Current Events*
First issue: December, 1904
Frequency: Monthly
Place of publication: Columbia, S.C.
Editor: I. Nathaniel Nesbitt
Publisher: New Citizen Company

Price: $1.00 per year
Format: 24 pages; 6 x 9 page size; 1 column per page; no illustrations; advertisements
Publication history for extant issues (1):
I, No. 1, December, 1904
Availability:
DLC-Mu   I, No. 1

New Republic and Liberian Missionary Journal

Title: *New Republic and Liberian Missionary Journal*
First issue: December, 1856
Frequency: Monthly
Place of publication: Harrisburg, Pa.
Editor and publisher: John Wolff
Price: $1.00 per year
Publication history for extant issues: No issues located
Notes: Information relative to this periodical appeared in *Colonization Herald* (Pennsylvania Colonization Society), n.s., No. 66 (December, 1855), 258; *New York Colonization Journal*, VI (December, 1856), 3; *African Repository* (American Colonization Society), XXXIII (January, 1857), 13–15.

Our Women and Children

Title: *Our Women and Children*
First issue: August, 1888
Frequency: Monthly
Place of publication: Louisville, Ky.
Editor: William J. Simmons
Publisher: National Publishing Company (Charles H. Parrish, president)
Price: $1.50 per year
Circulation: 960 (*Remington Brothers' Newspaper Manual*, 1890)
Format: 32 pages per issue; 8 x 12 page size
Publication history for extant issues: No issues located
Notes: Sources of information on this periodical include *Rowell's American Newspaper Directory*, 1889, 1890; *Ayer Directory of Newspapers and Periodicals*, 1890; *A. M. E. Church Review*, V (October, 1888), 187–88, VI (October, 1889), 254; Washington *Bee*, August 18, 1888; Indianapolis *Freeman*, January 5, February 9, May 11, June 8, July 13, 1889.

"PI."

Title: *The "PI.": A Journal of the Printing Fraternity*
First issue: April, 1895
Frequency: Monthly
Place of publication: Tuskegee, Ala.
Editor: Not stated
Publisher: "Mann & Thornton"
Price: 50¢ per year
Format: 24 pages; 6 x 9 page size; 2 columns per page; illustrations
and advertisements
Publication history for extant issues (1):
I, No. 1, April, 1895
Availability:
DHU-Mo   I, No. 1

Paul Jones Monthly Magazine

Title: *The Paul Jones Monthly Magazine*
First issue: October, 1907
Frequency: Monthly
Place of publication: Topeka, Kansas
Editor: Paul Jones
Publisher: Paul Jones Publishing Company (George S. Oliver, president)
Price: $1.00 per year, October, November, 1907, January, 1908; $1.50
per year, July–October, 1908
Format: 32 to 48 pages per issue; 2 columns per page; illustrations
and advertisements
Publication history for extant issues through 1909 (6):
I, Nos. 1, 2, 4, 7, 9, 10, October, November, 1907, January, July,
September, October, 1908
Availability:
KHi   I, as listed above (the latest issue in this file is XXII, No. 5
July, 1936)
Title listed in *ULS*

Progressive Educator

Title: *Progressive Educator*
First issue: 1888?

Frequency: Monthly
Place of publication: Raleigh, N.C.
Editors: Charles N. Hunter and Simon Green Atkins
Publisher: North Carolina State Teachers' Association
Circulation: 860 (*Remington Brothers' Newspaper Manual*, 1890)
Publication history for extant issues: No issues located
Notes: Information about this periodical appeared in *A. M. E. Church Review*, V (April, 1888), 448; *North Carolina Teachers' Record*, I (January, 1930), 11.

Prospect

Title: *Prospect*
First issue: April, 1898
Frequency: Monthly
Place of publication: "near Greater New York"
Editor: Phil H. Brown
Price: 10¢ per copy
Format: 64 pages
Publication history for extant issues: No issues located
Notes: The initial issue of *Prospect* was reviewed in the Washington D.C.) *Colored American*, April 26, 1898.

Pulpit and Desk

Title: *Pulpit and Desk*
First issue: April, 1887
Frequency: Quarterly
Place of publication: Chicago, Ill.
Editor and publisher: J. Bird Wilkins
Publication history for extant issues: No issues located
Notes: Information on the periodical appeared in St. Paul *Western Appeal*, April 16, 23, 1887.

Railroad Porters and Hotel Waiters Magazine

Title: *Railroad Porters and Hotel Waiters Magazine*
First issue: 1902
Place of publication: Philadelphia Pa., 1902–?; Chicago, Ill., ?–?
Editor: George Waldo Chivis
Format: 50 pages; illustrations and advertisements
Publication history for extant issues: No issues located

Notes: Sources of information on this periodical include Washington (D.C.) *Colored American,* October 4, 1902; Indianapolis *Freeman,* September 3, 1904; Seattle *Republican,* October 19, 1906; National Negro Business League, *Report, Fifth Annual Convention, 1904,* Appendix, 27.

Repository of Religion and Literature and of Science and Art

Title: *Repository of Religion and Literature and of Science and Art*
First issue: April, 1858
Frequency: Quarterly, April, 1858–October, 1861; monthly, January, 1862–January, 1863
Place of publication: Indianapolis, Ind., April, 1858–January, 1860; Philadelphia, Pa., January–October, 1861; Baltimore, Md., January, 1862–January, 1863
Editors: Chief editor: Daniel Alexander Payne, April, 1858–January, 1863. Executive editors: Molliston Madison Clark, April ?, July, 1858; Elisha Weaver, October, 1858–October, 1859; Aneas McIntosh, January, 1860; John Mifflin Brown, January, 1861–January, 1863
Publisher: "The Literary Societies under the Baltimore, Indiana, and Missouri Conferences of the African Methodist Episcopal Church," April, 1858–January, 1860; "The Literary Societies under the Baltimore, Indiana, Missouri, Philadelphia, and New England Conferences of the African Methodist Episcopal Church," January–October, 1861; "all the Literary Societies that will contribute the annual sum of $24 for its support," January, 1862–January, 1863
Price: $1.00 per year, 1858–1861; 60¢ per year, 1862; $1.00 per year, 1863
Format: 48 pages per issue, 1858–61, 20 pages per issue, 1862, 24 pages, January, 1863; 6 x 9 page size; 2 columns per page; illustrations and advertisements
Publication history for extant issues (26):
    I, Nos. 1–4, April, July, October, November, 1858
    II, Nos. 1–4, January, April, July, October, 1859
    III, No. 1, January, 1860
    III [*sic*], Nos. 1–4, January, April, July, October, 1861
    IV, Nos. 1–12, January–December, 1862
    V, No. 1, January, 1863

Availability:
DHU-Mo   IV, Nos. 1–12
In   I, No. 1–III, No. 4
MH   IV, Nos. 1–3, 10, 11; V, No. 1
OWibfU   I, Nos. 2, 3; IV, No. 4
VU   IV, Nos. 1–12
Title listed in *ULS*; *NUC, Pre-1956*

Ringwood's Afro-American Journal of Fashion

Title: *Ringwood's Afro-American Journal of Fashion*, 1891–92?; *Ringwood's Home Magazine*, 1893?–95?
First issue: 1891
Frequency: Monthly
Place of publication: Cleveland, Ohio
Editor and publisher: Julia Ringwood Coston
Price: $1.25 to $2.00 per year
Circulation: 7,000 (*Ayer Directory of Newspapers and Periodicals*, 1895)
Format: 16 pages; 10 x 13 page size; illustrations
Publication history for extant issues: No issues located
Notes: Sources of information on this periodical include *A. M. E. Church Review*, IX (July, 1892), 111; Indianapolis *Freeman*, July 2, 9, 1892; *Ayer Directory of Newspapers and Periodicals*, 1892, 1893/1894, 1895. An advertisement for the magazine appeared in the Cleveland *Gazette*, October 24, 1891–January 23, 1892.

Russell's Review

Title: *Russell's Review*
First issue: 1898
Frequency: Monthly
Place of publication: Kingfisher, Okla. Terr., 1898; Guthrie, Okla. Terr., 1899–?
Editor and publisher: S. Douglass Russell
Price: $1.00 per year, 1898–?; 50¢ per year, 1901–1904
Format: 32 pages; 6 x 9 page size; illustrations
Publication history for extant issues: No issues located
Notes: Information on this periodical appeared in Washington (D.C.)

Colored American, July 30, 1898, November 4, 1899; *Ayer Directory of Newspapers and Periodicals,* 1899, 1901, 1904.

School Teacher

Title: *The School Teacher*
Motto: " 'The best is none too good for our children.'—James F. Oyster."
First issue: September, 1909
Frequency: Monthly, for the ten months of the school year
Place of publication: Washington, D.C.
Editor: Not stated
Publisher: School Teacher Company
Price: $1.00 per year, for 10 issues
Format: 30 to 40 pages of text, plus several pages of advertising, per issue; 5 x 6 page size; 1 column per page; generally no illustrations
Publication history for extant issues (11):
    I, Nos. 1–5, September–December, 1909, January, 1910
    II, Nos. 1–5, February–June, 1910
    III, No. 1, September, 1910
Availability:
    DHEW   I, No. 1–II, No. 5
    DHU-Mo   I, No. 5; II, Nos. 2, 3
    DLC   I, No. 1–III, No. 1
Title listed in *ULS; NUC, Pre-1956*

Small's Illustrated Monthly

Title: *Small's Illustrated Monthly*
First issue: 1905
Frequency: Monthly
Place of publication: New York City, N.Y.
Editor and publisher: Thomas Frederick Small
Publication history for extant issues: No issues located
Notes: Information relative to this periodical appeared in *Who's Who of the Colored Race, 1915,* 246.

Small's Negro Trade Journal

Title: *Small's Negro Trade Journal*
First issue: 1906

Place of publication: New York City, N.Y.
Editor and publisher: Thomas Frederick Small
Publication history for extant issues: No issues located
Notes: Sources of information on this periodical include *Negro Year Book, 1912*, 186; *Who's Who of the Colored Race, 1915*, 246.

Southern Educator

Title: *The Southern Educator*
First issue: 1895?
Frequency: Monthly
Place of publication: Hawkinsville, Ga.
Editor: S. Timothy Tice
Publisher: Southern Colored Teachers' Association
Price: $1.00 per year
Publication history for extant issues: No issues located
Notes: An advertisement for the *Southern Educator* appeared in the *Monthly Review*, III (July, 1895), unpaged.

Southern Teachers' Advocate

Title: *The Southern Teachers' Advocate: A Negro Journal of Education.*
First issue: June, 1905
Frequency: Monthly, from September to June
Place of publication: Lexington, Ky.
Editor: Chapman C. Monroe
Publisher: Mary B. Monroe, June–November, 1905; Monroe and Monroe, December, 1905–May, 1906
Price: $1.00 per year, for 10 issues
Format: 26 to 58 pages per issue; 7 x 10 page size; 2 columns per page; illustrations and advertisements
Publication history for extant issues (10):
    I, Nos. 1–10, June, September–December, 1905, January–May, 1906
Notes: The *Southern Teachers' Advocate* served as the medium of communication for the Kentucky State Colored Teachers' Association
Availability:
    DHEW   I, Nos. 1, 3–10
    Title listed in *ULS*
    OWibfU   I, No. 2 (in William S. Scarborough Papers)
    Title listed in *ULS*

Southland

Title: *The Southland*
First issue: February, 1890
Frequency: Monthly, February–June, 1890; quarterly, January, April,
    1891
Place of publication: Salisbury, N.C., February–June, 1890; Winston,
    N.C., January, April, 1891
Editor: Simon Green Atkins
Publisher: Southland Publishing Company
Price: $2.50 per year, 1890; $1.50 per year, 1891
Format: 72 to 130 pages per issue; 6 x 9 page size; 1 column per page;
    illustrations and advertisements
Publication history for extant issues (5):
    I, Nos. 1, 3, 4, February, May, June, 1890
    II, Nos. 1, 2, January, April, 1891
Notes: The *Southland* was founded by Joseph Charles Price, president
    of Livingstone College in Salisbury.
Availability:
    DHU-Mo   II, No. 2
    DLC   I, Nos. 3, 4; II, No. 2
    MWA   I, No. 1
    NN-Sch   I, No. 3; II, No. 1
    NcD   I, No. 4
    Title listed in *ULS*; *NUC, Pre-1956*

Students' Repository

Title: *The Students' Repository*
First issue: July, 1863
Frequency: Quarterly
Place of publication: Spartanburg, Ind.
Editors: Samuel H. Smothers; James Buckner also listed as editor
    October, 1863–April, 1864; Samuel Peters also listed as editor July,
    October 1, 1864
Publishers: Samuel S. Smothers; J. E. Beverly also listed as publisher
    October, 1863–April, 1864
Price: 50¢ per year, July, 1863–July, 1864; $1.00 per year, October 1,
    1864
Format: 32 pages per issue; 6 x 9 page size; 2 columns per page; no
    illustrations; advertisements

Publication history for extant issues (6):
I, Nos. 1–4, July, October, 1863, January, April, 1864
II, Nos. 1, 2, July, October 1, 1864
Notes: The *Students' Repository* was issued at the Union Literary Institute, a manual training school operated by the Union Literary Society.
Availability:
NHi   I, No. 2–II, No. 2
NcD   I, No. 1–II, No. 2
Title listed in *ULS*; *NUC, Pre-1956*

Sylvester Russell's Review

Title: *Sylvester Russell's Review*
First issue: January, 1906
Frequency: Monthly
Place of publication: Orange, N.J., 1906; Hazleton, Pa., 1907
Editor: Sylvester Russell
Publisher: Sylvester Russell Publishing Company
Price: $1.00 per year, 1906; 50¢ per year, 1907
Publication history for extant issues: No issues located
Notes: Advertisements and news items relative to this periodical appeared in the Indianapolis *Freeman*, December 2, 16, 1905, January 20, June 2, 1906, April 13, May 4, November 9, 1907.

Theological Institute

Title: *Theological Institute*
First issue: 1909
Frequency: Monthly
Place of publication: Atlanta, Ga.
Editors: James Walker Hood, of the African Methodist Episcopal Zion Church; Lucius Henry Holsey, of the Colored Methodist Episcopal Church; and Henry McNeal Turner, of the African Methodist Episcopal Church
Publisher and editor-in-chief: Henry McNeal Turner
Price: 90¢ per year
Format: 16 to 20 pages per issue; 9 x 12 page size; 3 columns per page; no illustrations; advertisements
Publication history for extant issues (1):
III, No. 4, May, 1911

Notes: The *Theological Institute* was listed in the *Ayer Directory of Newspapers and Periodicals*, 1910–12.
Availability:
DHU-Mo   III, No. 4

Thornton's Magazine

Title: *Thornton's Magazine*
First issue: 1907
Frequency: Monthly
Place of publication: Wilmington, Del.
Editor and publisher: Montrose William Thornton
Publication history for extant issues: No issues located
Notes: Information on this periodical appeared in the *A. M. E. Church Review*, XXIII (April, 1907), 377.

Union Magazine

Title: *The Union Magazine: The Working People's Friend*
First issue: 1905
Frequency: Monthly
Place of publication: New York City, N.Y.
Publisher: Afro-American News Company
Price: 50¢ per year
Publication history for extant issues: No issues located
Notes: The *Union Magazine*, a continuation of the *American Magazine* (see listing above), was advertised in the Richmond (Va.) *Planet*, October 21, 1905–January 13, 1906. Jesse W. Watkins, who had been associated with the *Colored American Magazine*, was one of the promoters of these two magazines.

Voice of the Negro

Title: *The Voice of the Negro*, January, 1904–October, 1906; *The Voice*, November, 1906–October, 1907
First issue: January, 1904
Frequency: Monthly
Place of publication: Atlanta, Ga., January, 1904–September, 1906; Chicago, Ill., October, 1906–October, 1907
Editors: John Wesley Edward Bowen, editor, January, 1904–October, 1906. Jesse Max Barber, managing editor, January, February, 1904; editor, March, 1904–October, 1907

Publishers: J. L. Nichols & Company, Atlanta, Ga., January–April, 1904; Hertel, Jenkins & Company, Atlanta, Ga., May, 1904–July, 1906; Voice Publishing Company, Atlanta, Ga., August, September, 1906, and Chicago, Ill., October-December, 1906; Voice Company, Chicago, Ill., January/February–October, 1907

Price: $1.00 per year

Circulation: 13,000 (*Ayer Directory of Newspapers and Periodicals*, 1907); 15,000 (*Voice of the Negro*, III [September, 1906], 627; *Voice*, IV [May, 1907], 196)

Format: 48 to 72 pages for most of the issues; 7 x 10 page size; 2 columns per page; illustrations; advertisements

Publication history for extant issues (42):

    I, Nos. 1–12, January–December, 1904

    II, Nos. 1–12, January–December, 1905

    III, Nos. 1–12, January–December, 1906

    IV, Nos. 1, 2, 5–7, 10, January/February, March, May–July, October, 1907 (These 6 issues have continuous pagination without omissions.)

Notes: This periodical served as a medium of communication for the Niagara Movement. The following work is a selective index of the periodical, indexing significant items relating to social change and reform: Rose Bibliography (Project), American Studies Program, George Washington University, *Analytical Guide and Indexes to the Voice of the Negro, 1904–1907* (Westport, Conn.: Greenwood Press, 1974).

Availability:

DHU-Mo	Nos. 1, 2, 4–12; II, Nos. 1–12; III, Nos. 1–7, 10; IV, Nos. 1, 2, 5–7, 10
DLC	I, No. 1–III, No. 12
GAU	I, No. 1–IV, No. 10
VHaI	I, No. 1–III, No. 12

    Title listed in *ULS*; *NUC, Pre-1956*; *Reprints, 1980*; *Microforms in Print, 1980*

Western Lever

Title: *The Western Lever*

First issue: September, 1908

Frequency: Monthly

Place of publication: Des Moines, Iowa

Editor and publisher: Julius Dean Pettigrew
Price: $1.00 per year
Format: 20 pages per issue; 9 x 12 page size; 3 columns per page; no
    illustrations; advertisements
Publication history for extant issues (3):
    I, Nos. 2–4, October, 1908, January/February, March, 1909
Notes: The *Western Lever* was the official publication of the Colored
    Co-operative League (of which Pettigrew was the founder and
    president).
Availability:
    DHU-Mo   I, Nos. 2–4

Woman's Era

Title: *The Woman's Era*
First issue: March 24, 1894
Frequency: Monthly
Place of publication: Boston, Mass.
Editors and publishers: Josephine St. Pierre Ruffin and her daughter,
    Florida Ruffin Ridley
Price: $1.00 per year
Format: 16 to 24 pages per issue; 9 x 12 page size; 2 and 3 columns
    per page; illustrations; advertisements
Publication history for extant issues (24):
    I, Nos. 1–6, 8, 9, 11, March 24, May 1, June 1, July, August, Sep-
        tember, November, December, 1894, February, 1895
    II, Nos. 1–7, 9, 10, 12, April–August, October, November, 1895,
        January, February, May, 1896
    III, Nos. 2, 2 [*sic*], 3–5, June, July, August/September, October/
        November, 1896, January, 1897
Notes: The *Woman's Era* was the journal of the Woman's Era Club in
    Boston. It also served as a medium of communication for the Na-
    tional Federation of Afro-American Women and the National Asso-
    ciation of Colored Women.
Availability:
    DLC   I, Nos. 8, 9, 11; II, Nos. 2–7, 9, 12; III, Nos. 2, 2 [*sic*],
                4 (in Mary Church Terrell Papers, in Manuscript
                Division)
    MB   I, Nos. 1–6, 8, 9; II, Nos. 1–5, 7, 9, 10, 12; III, Nos. 2,
                2 [*sic*], 3–5
    Title listed in *ULS*

Woman's World

Title: *Woman's World*
First issue: 1900
Frequency: Monthly
Place of publication: Fort Worth, Tex.
Editor: Jay W. Taylor
Publisher: World Publishing Company
Price: $1.00 per year
Format: 16 pages per issue; 11 x 16 page size; illustrations
Publication history for extant issues: No issues located
Notes: Information on this periodical appeared in *Ayer Directory of Newspapers and Periodicals*, 1901–1905; *Remington's Annual Newspaper Directory*, 1907; *Colored American Magazine*, III (July, 1901), unpaged; Washington (D.C.) *Colored American*, March 2, 1901, March 8, 1902.

Zion Trumpet and Homiletic Magazine

Title: *The Zion Trumpet and Homiletic Magazine*
Motto: "Holiness to the Lord"
First issue: 1905?
Frequency: Bimonthly
Place of publication: New Haven, Conn.
Editor and publisher: Eli George Biddle
Price: 50¢ per year
Format: 16 pages; 6 x 9 page size; 2 columns per page; illustrations; no advertisements
Publication history for extant issues (1):
  XIV, No. 3, May/June, 1909
Availability:
  GAU   XIV, No. 3

Chronology of the Periodicals

This listing gives the year and the location in which each of the periodicals was first issued. The year only is given for periodicals that were proposed but not published. Titles under the same year are listed alphabetically.

1838
Mirror of Liberty. New York City, New York
National Reformer. Philadelphia, Pennsylvania

1841
African Methodist Episcopal Church Magazine. Brooklyn, New York

1843
L'Album Littéraire. New Orleans, Louisiana

1854
Afric-American Repository.

1856
New Republic and Liberian Missionary Journal. Harrisburg, Pennsylvania

1858
Douglass' Monthly. Rochester, New York

Repository of Religion and Literature and of Science and Art. Indianapolis, Indiana

1859
Anglo-African Magazine. New York City, New York

1862
Lunar Visitor. San Francisco, California

1863
Students' Repository. Spartanburg, Indiana

1866
Freedman's Torchlight. Brooklyn, New York

1880
Ladies' Magazine

1881
Alumni Journal (Hampton Institute). Hampton, Virginia

1882
Colored American Journal. Palestine, Texas

1884
A. M. E. Church Review. Philadelphia, Pennsylvania
Alumni Magazine (Lincoln University). Philadelphia, Pennsylvania

1886
Afro-American Churchman. Norfolk, Virginia
Musical Messenger. Montgomery, Alabama
Negro. Boston, Massachusetts

1887
Mouth-Piece. Chicago, Illinois
Negro-American. Boston, Massachusetts
Pulpit and Desk. Chicago, Illinois

1888
National Pilot. Petersburg, Virginia
Our Women and Children. Louisville, Kentucky
Progressive Educator. Raleigh, North Carolina

1889
Afro-American Budget. Evanston, Illinois
Howard's Negro-American Magazine. Harrisburg, Pennsylvania

1890
A. M. E. Zion Quarterly Review. Pittsburgh, Pennsylvania
  (First published as *A. M. E. Zion Church Quarterly*)
National Afro-American. Washington, D.C.
Southland. Salisbury, North Carolina

1891
Church Advocate. Norfolk, Virginia
Future State. Kansas City, Missouri
Jewel. St. Paul, Minnesota
Living Age. Denison, Texas
Ringwood's Afro-American Journal of Fashion. Cleveland, Ohio

1892
Educational Era. Baltimore, Maryland
Medical and Surgical Observer. Jackson, Tennessee

1894
Brock's Magazine. New York City, New York
Monthly Review. Boston, Massachusetts
National Baptist Magazine. Washington, D.C.
Negro Educational Journal. Cartersville, Georgia
Woman's Era. Boston, Massachusetts

1895
Howard's American Magazine. Harrisburg, Pennsylvania
"PI." Tuskegee, Alabama
Southern Educator. Hawkinsville, Georgia

1897
Lowery's Religious Monthly. Spartanburg, South Carolina

(First published as *Colored Preacher*)
National Association Notes. Tuskegee, Alabama

1898

Educator. Kittrell, North Carolina
Hospital Herald. Charleston, South Carolina
Lynk's Magazine. Jackson, Tennessee
Prospect. "near Greater New York", New York
Russell's Review. Kingfisher, Oklahoma Territory

1899

Afro-American Review. Mattoon, Illinois
Educator. Huntsville, Alabama
Helper. Harvey, Illinois

1900

Colored American Magazine. Boston, Massachusetts
Woman's World. Fort Worth, Texas

1901

Gazetteer and Guide. Buffalo, New York
National Capital Searchlight. Washington, D.C.

1902

Advance. Pittsburgh, Pennsylvania
Church and Society World. Atlanta, Georgia
Negro Music Journal. Washington, D.C.
Railroad Porters and Hotel Waiters Magazine. Philadelphia, Pennsylvania

1903

Colored Home Journal. Pittsburgh, Pennsylvania
Impending Conflict. New York City, New York
McGirt's Magazine. Philadelphia, Pennsylvania

1904

Negro Educational Review. Vincennes, Indiana
New Citizen. Columbia, South Carolina
Voice of the Negro. Atlanta, Georgia

1905

Alexander's Magazine. Boston, Massachusetts
American Magazine. New York City, New York
National Domestic. Indianapolis, Indiana
Small's Illustrated Monthly. New York City, New York
Southern Teachers' Advocate. Lexington, Kentucky
Union Magazine. New York City, New York
Zion Trumpet and Homiletic Magazine. New Haven, Connecticut

1906

Colored Teacher. New Orleans, Louisiana
Dollar Mark. Newport News, Virginia
Ebony. Philadelphia, Pennsylvania
Small's Negro Trade Journal. New York City, New York
Sylvester Russell's Review. Orange, New Jersey

1907

Colored Woman's Magazine. Topeka, Kansas
Horizon. Washington, D.C.
Musical Advance. Richmond, Virginia
Paul Jones Monthly Magazine. Topeka, Kansas
Thornton's Magazine. Wilmington, Delaware

1908

Freeman. New York City, New York
Western Lever. Des Moines, Iowa

1909

Citizen. Washington, D.C.
Colored Catholic. Baltimore, Maryland
McConico's Monthly Magazine. Birmingham, Alabama
National Medical Association Journal. Tuskegee, Alabama
Negro Agriculturist. Sandy Spring, Maryland
Negro Business League Herald. Washington, D.C.
School Teacher. Washington, D.C.
Theological Institute. Atlanta, Georgia

Geography of the Periodicals

This listing is arranged alphabetically by state and then by city. Under the cities, the titles are given chronologically by the year in which the periodical was first issued in that location. If a periodical was published in more than one place, it is listed under each locality. Places of publication after 1909 have not been indicated. Titles that were proposed but never published are not included in this appendix.

ALABAMA
  Birmingham
    McConico's Monthly Magazine. 1909
  Huntsville
    Educator. 1899
  Montgomery
    Musical Messenger. 1886
  Tuskegee
    "PI." 1895
    National Association Notes. 1897
    National Medical Association Journal. 1909

CALIFORNIA
  San Francisco
    Lunar Visitor. 1862

CONNECTICUT
  New Haven
    Zion Trumpet and Homiletic Magazine. 1905

DELAWARE
Wilmington
  Thornton's Magazine. 1907

DISTRICT OF COLUMBIA
Washington
  Musical Messenger. 1888 (Founded 1886 in Montgomery, Alabama)
  National Afro-American. 1890
  National Baptist Magazine. 1894
  National Capital Searchlight. 1901
  Negro Music Journal. 1902
  Horizon. 1907
  Citizen. 1909
  Negro Business League Herald. 1909
  School Teacher. 1909

GEORGIA
Athens
  Negro Educational Journal. 1895 (Founded 1894 in Cartersville, Georgia)
Atlanta
  Church and Society World. 1902
  Voice of the Negro. 1904
  Theological Institute. 1909
Cartersville
  Negro Educational Journal. 1894
Hawkinsville
  Southern Educator. 1895

ILLINOIS
Chicago
  Mouth-Piece. 1887
  Pulpit and Desk. 1887
  Railroad Porters and Hotel Waiters Magazine. 1904 (Founded 1902 in Philadelphia, Pennsylvania)
  Voice of the Negro (Published as the *Voice*). 1906 (Founded 1904 in Atlanta, Georgia)
Decatur

Afro-American Budget. 1890 (Founded 1889 in Evanston, Illinois)
Evanston
Afro-American Budget. 1889
Harvey
Helper. 1899
Mattoon
Afro-American Review. 1899

INDIANA
Indianapolis
Repository of Religion and Literature and of Science and Art. 1858
National Domestic. 1905
Spartanburg
Students' Repository. 1863
Vincennes
Negro Educational Review. 1904

IOWA
Des Moines
Western Lever. 1908

KANSAS
Topeka
Colored Woman's Magazine. 1907
Paul Jones Monthly Magazine. 1907

KENTUCKY
Lexington
Southern Teachers' Advocate. 1905
Louisville
Our Women and Children. 1888

LOUISIANA
New Orleans
L'Album Littéraire. 1843
Colored Teacher. 1906

MARYLAND
Baltimore
Repository of Religion and Literature and of Science and Art.

1862 (Founded 1858 in Indianapolis, Indiana)
Church Advocate. 1891 (Founded 1891 in Norfolk, Virginia)
Educational Era. 1892
Colored Catholic. 1909
Sandy Spring
Negro Agriculturist. 1909

MASSACHUSETTS
Boston
Negro. 1886
Negro-American. 1887
Monthly Review. 1894
Woman's Era. 1894
Colored American Magazine. 1900
Alexander's Magazine. 1905

MINNESOTA
St. Paul
Jewel. 1891

MISSOURI
Kansas City
Future State. 1891

NEW JERSEY
Orange
Sylvester Russell's Review. 1906

NEW YORK
Brooklyn
African Methodist Episcopal Church Magazine. 1841
Freedman's Torchlight. 1866
Buffalo
Gazetteer and Guide. 1901
New York City
Mirror of Liberty. 1838
Anglo-African Magazine. 1859
Brock's Magazine. 1894
Howard's American Magazine. 1901 (Founded 1895 in Harrisburg, Pennsylvania)

Impending Conflict. 1903

Colored American Magazine. 1904 (Founded 1900 in Boston, Massachusetts)

American Magazine. 1905

Small's Illustrated Monthly. 1905

Union Magazine. 1905

Small's Negro Trade Journal. 1906

Freeman. 1908

Rochester

Douglass' Monthly. 1858

"Near Greater New York"

Prospect. 1898

NORTH CAROLINA

Charlotte

A. M. E. Zion Quarterly Review. 1896 (Founded 1890 in Pittsburgh, Pennsylvania)

Kittrell

Educator. 1898

Raleigh

Progressive Educator. 1888

Salisbury

A. M. E. Zion Quarterly Review. 1895 (Founded 1890 in Pittsburgh, Pennsylvania)

Southland. 1890

Wilmington

A. M. E. Zion Quarterly Review. 1892 (Founded 1890 in Pittsburgh, Pennsylvania)

Winston

Southland. 1891 (Founded 1890 in Salisbury, North Carolina)

OHIO

Cleveland

Ringwood's Afro-American Journal of Fashion. 1891

OKLAHOMA TERRITORY

Guthrie

Russell's Review. 1899 (Founded 1898 in Kingfisher, Oklahoma Territory)

Kingfisher

Russell's Review. 1898
Langston
  Living Age. 1904 (Founded 1891 in Denison, Texas)

PENNSYLVANIA
  Harrisburg
  New Republic and Liberian Missionary Journal. 1856
  Howard's Negro-American Magazine. 1889
  Howard's American Magazine. 1895
  Hazleton
  Sylvester Russell's Review. 1907 (Founded 1906 in Orange, New
    Jersey)
  Philadelphia
  National Reformer. 1838
  Repository of Religion and Literature and of Science and Art.
    1861 (Founded 1858 in Indianapolis, Indiana)
  A. M. E. Church Review. 1884
  Alumni Magazine (Lincoln University). 1884
  Monthly Review. 1896 (Founded 1894 in Boston, Massachusetts)
  Railroad Porters and Hotel Waiters Magazine. 1902
  McGirt's Magazine. 1903
  Ebony. 1906
  Pittsburgh
  A. M. E. Zion Quarterly Review (First published as *A. M. E.
    Zion Church Quarterly*). 1890
  Advance. 1902
  Colored Home Journal. 1903

SOUTH CAROLINA
  Charleston
  Hospital Herald. 1898
  Columbia
  New Citizen. 1904
  Spartanburg
  Lowery's Religious Monthly (First published as *Colored Preacher*).
    1897

TENNESSEE
  Jackson

Medical and Surgical Observer. 1892

Lynk's Magazine. 1898

Nashville

National Baptist Magazine. 1899 (Founded 1894 in Washington, D.C.)

A. M. E. Church Review. 1908 (Founded 1884 in Philadelphia, Pennsylvania)

TEXAS

Denison

Living Age. 1891

Fort Worth

Woman's World. 1900

Palestine

Colored American Journal. 1882

VIRGINIA

Alexandria

Horizon. 1908 (Founded 1907 in Washington, D.C.)

Hampton

Alumni Journal (Hampton Institute). 1881

Newport News

Dollar Mark. 1906

Norfolk

Afro-American Churchman. 1886

Church Advocate. 1891

Petersburg

National Pilot. 1888

Richmond

Musical Advance. 1907

Notes

CHAPTER ONE

1. U.S. Bureau of the Census, *Negro Population, 1790–1915* (Washington, D.C.: Government Printing Office, 1918), 33, 51, 53, 55.
2. U.S. Census Office, *Return of the Whole Number of Persons Within the Several Districts of the United States, 1st Census, 1790* (Philadelphia: Printed by Childs and Swaine, 1791), 23, 36, 37, 45, 47; U.S. Census Office, *Census for 1820* (Washington, D.C.: Printed by Gales & Seaton, 1821), 31; U.S. Census Office, *Sixth Census; or, Enumeration of the Inhabitants of the United States, as Corrected at the Department of State, in 1840* (Washington, D.C.: Printed by Blair and Rives, 1841), 256; U.S. Census Office, *Population of the United States in 1860, Compiled from the Original Returns of the Eighth Census* (Washington, D.C.: Government Printing Office, 1864), 185, 194–95, 214, 225, 328, 335.
3. Leon F. Litwack, *North of Slavery: The Negro in the Free States, 1790–1860* (Chicago: University of Chicago Press, 1961), 75.
4. Benjamin Quarles, *The Negro in the Making of America* (Rev. ed.; New York: Macmillan, 1969), 148.
5. U.S. Bureau of Education, *Illiteracy in the United States in 1870 and 1880*, Circular of Information 1884, no. 3 (Washington, D.C.: Government Printing Office, 1884), 74–75; U.S. Bureau of the Census, *Negro Population*, 404.
6. U.S. Bureau of the Census, *Negro Population*, 33, 93; Warren S. Thompson and P. K. Whelpton, *Population Trends in the United States* (New York: McGraw-Hill, 1933), 77; U.S. Bureau of the Census, *Urban Population in the United States from the First Census (1790) to the Fifteenth Census (1930)* (N.p., 1939), 1.
7. U.S. Bureau of the Census, *Negro Population*, 33.
8. "Apology. (Introductory.)," *Anglo-African Magazine*, I (January, 1859), 1, 3.
9. Henry Highland Garnet, *The Past and the Present Condition and the Destiny of the Colored Race: A Discourse Delivered at the Fifteenth Anniversary of the Female Benevolent Society of Troy, N.Y., Feb. 14, 1848* (Troy, N.Y.: Steam Press of J. C. Kneeland and Company, 1848), 19.

CHAPTER TWO

1. "Apology. (Introductory.)," *Anglo-African Magazine,* I (January, 1859), 3.
2. "The Obstacles in the Way of the Education of the Present Generations of Our People," *Lunar Visitor,* I (June, 1862), unpaged.
3. "The *Anglo-African Magazine,*" *Douglass' Monthly,* I (February, 1859), 20.
4. "Apology. (Introductory.)," 4; "The *Anglo-African Magazine* for 1860," *Anglo-African Magazine,* I (December, 1859), 400.
5. Edward Larocque Tinker, *"Les Cenelles*: Afro-French Poetry in Louisiana," *Colophon,* No. 3 (1930), unpaged.
6. Edward Larocque Tinker, *Les Écrits de Langue Française en Louisiane au XIXe Siècle: Essais Biographiques et Bibliographiques* (Paris: Librairie Ancienne Honoré Champion, 1932), 298.
7. R. L. Desdunes, *Nos Hommes et Notre Histoire* (Montréal: Arbour & Dupont, 1911), 17–32; Charles B. Rousseve, *The Negro in Louisiana: Aspects of His History and His Literature* (New Orleans: Xavier University Press, 1937), 63–65, 67–70, 120; Tinker, *Les Écrits de Langue Française,* 272–73; Tinker, *"Les Cenelles,"* unpaged.
8. *Proceedings of the National Emigration Convention of Colored People . . . 1854* (Pittsburgh: Printed by A. A. Anderson, 1854), 12, 28–31.
9. *Arguments, Pro and Con, on the Call for a National Emigration Convention To Be Held in Cleveland, Ohio, August, 1854, by Frederick Douglass, W. J. Watkins, & J. M. Whitfield* (Detroit: M. T. Newson, 1854), 7–11, 16–17.
10. "Afric-American Quarterly Repository," Toronto *Provincial Freeman,* November 25, 1856, p. 62.
11. "Advertisement, Afric-American Printing Company," in Jas. Theo. Holly, *A Vindication of the Capacity of the Negro Race for Self-Government, and Civilized Progress* (New Haven: Published for the Afric-American Printing Company; William H. Stanley, Printer, 1857), 47–48.
12. "The *New Republic and Liberian Missionary Journal,*" *Colonization Herald,* n.s., no. 66 (December, 1855), 258; "A New Journal Cooperating," *New York Colonization Journal,* VI (December, 1856), 3; *African Repository,* XXXIII (January, 1857), 13–15.
13. Philip M. Montesano, "Some Aspects of the Free Negro Question in San Francisco, 1849–1870," (M.A. thesis, University of San Francisco, 1967), 12; Rudolph M. Lapp, *Blacks in Gold Rush California* (New Haven: Yale University Press, 1977), 49–50, 94–103, 166–67, 238; Robert W. O'Brien, "Victoria's Negro Colonists, 1858–1866," *Phylon,* III (First Quarter, 1942), 15–18.
14. William J. Walls, *The African Methodist Episcopal Zion Church: Reality of the Black Church* (Charlotte, N.C.: A. M. E. Zion Publishing House, 1974), 164–65, 199–200, 360, 576–77; Montesano, "Some Aspects of the Free Negro Question in San Francisco," 54–58; *Frederick Douglass' Paper,* January 13. 1854; *Pacific Appeal,* September 26, October 17, 1863.
15. "The Obstacles in the Way of the Education of the Present Generation of Our People," unpaged; "The Want of Unity Among the Colored People," *Lunar Visitor,* I (February, 1862), unpaged.
16. Emma Lou Thornbrough, *The Negro in Indiana: A Study of a Minority* ([Indianapolis]: Indiana Historical Bureau, 1957), 173–77, 374–75; "Union Literary Institute," *North Star,* November 10, 1848.
17. "Preamble and Constitution of the Union Literary Society," quoted in *Students' Repository,* I (July, 1863), 18–19.

18. "Apology, (Introductory)," *Students' Repository*, I (July, 1863), 1.
19. *North Star*, February 1, 1850.
20. The main source of information on the life of David Ruggles is the research of Dorothy B. Porter: "David Ruggles, an Apostle of Human Rights," *Journal of Negro History*, XXVIII (January, 1943), 23–50; "David Ruggles, 1810–1849: Hydropathic Practitioner," *National Medical Association Journal*, XLIX (January, 1957), 67–72, and *ibid.*, XLIX (March, 1957), 13–34; "The Water Cures," in *The Northampton Book: Chapters from 300 Years in the Life of a New England Town, 1654–1954* (Northampton, Mass.: Tercentenary Committee, 1954), 121–26. See also Benjamin Quarles, *Black Abolitionists* (New York: Oxford University Press, 1969), 25, 150–53, 163.
21. *Freedom's Journal*, May 9, 1828, and March 21, 1829.
22. *Colored American*, June 16, 1838.
23. *Mirror of Liberty*, "Extra" (July, 1841), 4; *National Anti-Slavery Standard*, October 14, 1841.
24. *Colored American*, July 10, 1841; *Liberator*, July 9, July 23, 1841; *National Anti-Slavery Standard*, July 29, 1841.
25. *Mirror of Liberty*, I (January, 1839), 30.
26. *Ibid.*
27. The essays by Ruggles, "Appeals to the Colored Citizens of New York and Elsewhere in Behalf of the Press," appeared in the *Emancipator*, January 13, 20, 27, February 3, 10, 17, 1835. They are reprinted in Dorothy Porter (ed.), *Early Negro Writing, 1760–1837* (Boston: Beacon Press, 1971), 637–55.
28. William Wells Brown, *The Rising Son; or, The Antecedents and Advancement of the Colored Race* (Boston: A. G. Brown and Company, 1874), 434–35; *Mirror of Liberty*, I (August, 1838), 2; *ibid.*, I (July, 1838), 1.
29. New-Lisbon (Ohio) *Aurora* and Wheeling (Virginia) *Gazette*, quoted in *Mirror of Liberty*, I (January, 1839), back cover.
30. *Mirror of Liberty*, I (January, 1839), 35.
31. *National Anti-Slavery Standard*, December 10, 1840; *Liberator*, August 20, 1841; *North Star*, February 1, 1850.
32. William Still, *The Underground Rail Road* (Philadelphia: Porter & Coates, 1872), 735; Brown, *The Rising Son*, 493–95.
33. Henry M. Minton, *Early History of Negroes in Business in Philadelphia* (Nashville: A. M. E. Sunday School Union, n.d.), 10, 17; William F. Worner, "The Columbia Race Riots," in *Historical Papers and Addresses of the Lancaster County (Pa.) Historical Society*, XXVI (October 6, 1922), 176–77, 185–87; Louis C. Jones, "A Leader Ahead of His Times," *American Heritage*, XIV (June, 1963), 59, 83.
34. William Whipper to William Still, December 4, 1871, quoted in Still, *The Underground Rail Road*, 735, 736, 739, 740.
35. *Freedom's Journal*, June 20, 1828; *Sketches of the Higher Classes of Colored Society in Philadelphia, by a Southerner* (Philadelphia: Merrihew and Thompson, Printers, 1841), 97–100; Dorothy B. Porter, "The Organized Educational Activities of Negro Literary Societies, 1828–1846," *Journal of Negro Education*, V (October, 1936), 557–59.
36. Howard Holman Bell, "A Survey of the Negro Convention Movement, 1830–1861" (Ph.D. dissertation, Northwestern University, 1953), 18, 277.
37. *Minutes of the Fourth Annual Convention for the Improvement of the Free People of Colour ... 1834* (New York: Published by order of the Convention, 1834), 35; *Minutes of the Fifth Annual Convention for the Improve-*

ment of the Free People of Colour . . . 1835 (Philadelphia: Printed by William P. Gibbons, 1835), 5, 8, 10, 32. The documents of this American Moral Reform Society do not indicate that it had any official connection with the American Moral Reform Society that had been organized among white people during 1833–34 and had published the *Journal of Public Morals.* For the society established in 1833–34, see American Moral Reform Society, *The Third Annual Report . . . May, 1838* (New York: Printed by Martin, Lambert & Company, 1838), 15, 21.

38. Bell, "A Survey of the Negro Convention Movement," 56.
39. *Colored American*, September 9, 1837.
40. *National Reformer*, I (February, 1839), 83; *ibid.,* I (September, 1838), 1–2.
41. "To Our Readers," *ibid.,* I (December, 1839), 177–78; William Whipper to the Editor, *Colored American*, July 18, 1840.
42. Daniel A. Payne, *The Semi-Centenary and the Retrospection of the African Meth. Episcopal Church in the United States of America* (Baltimore: Sherwood & Company, 1866), 41; Daniel A. Payne, *History of the African Methodist Episcopal Church* (Nashville: A. M. E. Sunday School Union, 1891), 136.
43. *Centennial Encyclopedia of the African Methodist Episcopal Church*, ed. Richard R. Wright, Jr. (Philadelphia: Book Concern of the A. M. E. Church, 1916), 114; Payne, *History of the African Methodist Episcopal Church*, 57, 114, 252–53.
44. Payne, *History of the African Methodist Episcopal Church*, 297–305.
45. M. M. Clark, "The Condition of Our People," *African Methodist Episcopal Church Magazine*, II (February, 1845), 147–49.
46. Daniel A. Payne, *Recollections of Seventy Years* (Nashville: A. M. E. Sunday School Union, 1888), 74–77; Payne, *History of the African Methodist Episcopal Church*, 168–69.
47. Payne, *The Semi-Centenary*, 42, 75.
48. George Hogarth, "Prospectus," *African Methodist Episcopal Church Magazine*, I (September, 1841), 1–3; "Editorial," *ibid.,* I (May, 1842), 1; George Hogarth, "Finance Report of the General Book Steward," *ibid.,* I (September, 1843), 180; George Hogarth, "General Book Steward's Financial Report," *ibid.,* II (August, 1844), 57.
49. M. M. Clark to George Hogarth, January, 1845, quoted in *ibid.,* II (February, 1845), 139–40; [First annual report of the general book agent, M. M. Clark], quoted in Payne, *History of the African Methodist Episcopal Church*, 192.
50. Payne, *History of the African Methodist Episcopal Church*, 152–53.
51. Payne, *Recollections*, 138; [Prospectus], bound with African Methodist Episcopal Church, Conferences, Indiana, *Nineteenth Annual Conference of the Indiana District . . . 1858* (N.p., n.d. [title page missing]).
52. "Prospectus," *Repository of Religion and Literature and of Science and Art*, IV (February, 1862), unpaged.
53. "Financial Report to the Bishop and Conference of the Indiana District," *ibid.,* II (October, 1859), 186–87; "An Appeal to Our Patrons and Friends," *ibid.,* IV (January, 1862), 17–19; African Methodist Episcopal Church, Conferences, Baltimore, *Proceedings of the Forty-Seventh Session of the Baltimore Annual Conference . . . 1864* (Washington, D.C.: Gibson Brothers, Printers, 1864), 31.
54. Information on Payne's life and his contributions to the church can be found

in Josephus R. Coan, *Daniel Alexander Payne, Christian Educator* (Philadelphia: A. M. E. Book Concern, 1935), and in Payne's own writings: *Recollections, The Semi-Centenary,* and *History of the African Methodist Episcopal Church.*

55. Benjamin T. Tanner, *An Apology for African Methodism* (Baltimore: A. M. E. Book Depository, 1867), 175–76, 309–11; Alexander W. Wayman, *Cyclopedia of African Methodism* (Baltimore: Methodist Episcopal Book Depository, 1882), 102, 177.

56. William J. Simmons, *Men of Mark: Eminent, Progressive and Rising* (Cleveland: Geo. M. Rewell & Company, 1887), 1113–18; *Centennial Encyclopedia of the African Methodist Episcopal Church,* 47; R. R. Wright, Jr., *The Bishops of the African Methodist Episcopal Church* (Nashville: A. M. E. Sunday School Union, 1963), 111–14; *Dictionary of American Biography,* III, 138–39.

57. "Natural Science," *Repository of Religion and Literature and of Science and Art,* I (July, 1858), 83–84.

58. D. A. P. [Daniel A. Payne], "Artists and the Fine Arts Among Colored People: Robert Seldon Duncanson," *ibid.,* III (January, 1860), 2.

59. W. H. Gibson, "Music," *ibid.,* I (July, 1858), 83; Thomas Strother, "Concerning Instrumental Music," *ibid.,* I (November, 1858), 184.

60. E[lisha] W[eaver], "To Our Subscribers," *ibid.* I (October, 1858), 192.

61. The main sources used in this study for biographical data on Frederick Douglass are: Frederick Douglass, *Narrative of the Life of Frederick Douglass, an American Slave, Written by Himself,* ed. Benjamin Quarles (1845; reprint ed., Cambridge: Belknap Press of Harvard University Press, 1960); Frederick Douglass, *My Bondage and My Freedom* (New York: Miller, Orton & Company, 1857); Frederick Douglass, *Life and Times of Frederick Douglass . . . Written by Himself* (Rev. ed., 1892; reprint ed., New York: Collier Books, 1962); Benjamin Quarles, *Frederick Douglass* (Washington, D.C.: Associated Publishers, 1848); Philip S. Foner, *Frederick Douglass: A Biography* (New York: Citadel Press, 1964).

62. Douglass, *Narrative,* 142–45.

63. Douglass, *My Bondage and My Freedom,* 388–89.

64. "Prospectus," quoted in *National Anti-Slavery Standard,* September 30, 1847, and in *Ram's Horn,* November 5, 1847. The prospectus reprinted in the *Standard* gave Cleveland as the proposed site of publication rather than Rochester.

65. "Frederick Douglass' Paper," *Anti-Slavery Reporter,* 3rd ser., VI (October, 1858), 238.

66. Frederick Douglass, "Valedictory," August 16, 1863 (included with *Douglass' Monthly,* August, 1863).

67. Detailed analysis of *Douglass' Monthly* is given in P. Dolores Brewington Perry, "Frederick Douglass: Editor and Journalist" (Ph.D. dissertation, University of North Carolina at Chapel Hill, 1972), 93–113, 298–300.

68. *Douglass' Monthly,* I (March, 1859), 35.

69. "Letter from Bishop Payne to the Ministers of the A. M. E. Church," *ibid.,* III (April, 1861), 441.

70. Rochester (N.Y.) *Union and Advertiser,* October 14, 1861; New York (State), Secretary of State, *Manual for the Use of the Legislature of the State of New York for the Year 1862* (Albany: Weed, Parsons and Company, 1862), 337; Amy Hanmer-Croughton, "Anti-Slavery Days in Rochester," *Publications of*

the *Rochester Historical Society*, XIV (1936), 147–48; John Hope Franklin, *A Southern Odyssey: Travelers in the Antebellum North* (Baton Rouge: Louisiana State University Press, 1976), 244–48.

71. *Douglass' Monthly*, III (August, 1860), 314; *ibid.*, V (October, 1862), 723; Rochester (N.Y.) *Union and Advertiser*, October 25, 1861.

72. Douglass, "Valedictory."

73. The main sources of biographical data on members of the Hamilton family are: *Colored American*, October 30, 1841; San Francisco *Elevator*, July 14, 1865, June 8, 1872; I. Garland Penn, *The Afro-American Press and Its Editors* (Springfield, Mass.; Willey & Company, 1891), 83–88, 118–19, 364–66; John J. Zuille, *Historical Sketch of the New York African Society for Mutual Relief* (N.p., n.d.), 5–7, 43–44; Walls, *The African Methodist Episcopal Zion Church*, 45–52, 89–91, 138–44; Fifth Census of the United States, 1830, Records of the U.S. Bureau of the Census, Record Group 29, National Archives Microfilm Publication M19, roll 98, frame 293; Eighth Census of the United States, 1860, Records of the U.S. Bureau of the Census, Record Group 29, National Archives Microfilm Publication M653, roll 763, frame 102. Further information and insight regarding this family were gained through interviews on August 27, 1977, with Olyve Jeter Haynes (Mrs. George Edmund Haynes), granddaughter of Thomas Hamilton, and Julia Saunders McLeveighn (Mrs. Joseph McLeveighn), great-great granddaughter of Thomas Hamilton.

74. "Apology. (Introductory)," *Anglo-African Magazine*, I (January, 1859), 1.

75. William Hamilton to John Jay, March 8, 1796, quoted in *Journal of Negro History*, XVII (October, 1932), 493.

76. *Minutes of the Fourth Annual Convention for the Improvement of the Free People of Colour . . . 1834*, 6.

77. *Weekly Advocate*, January 7, 1837.

78. *Weekly Anglo-African*, July 23, 1859.

79. *Ibid.*, March 16, 1861.

80. *Ibid.*, November 16, 1861, March 29, April 5, 12, 1862; *North Star*, June 13, 1850.

81. *Weekly Anglo-African*, August 12, November 18, 1865; San Francisco *Elevator*, July 14, 1865.

82. *Anglo-African Magazine*, I (November, 1859), 368.

83. "Prospectus of the *Anglo-African Magazine*," *Liberator*, December 24, 1858.

84. "The Outbreak in Virginia," *Anglo-African Magazine*, I (November, 1859), 347; "The Nat Turner Insurrection," *ibid.*, I (December, 1859), 386.

85. "Ira Aldridge," *ibid.*, II (January, 1860), 31.

86. *Ibid.*, I (January, 1859), 21.

87. Floyd J. Miller, "Introduction," in *Blake; or, The Huts of America: A Novel by Martin R. Delany* (Boston: Beacon Press, 1970), xi–xii.

88. Brown, *The Rising Son*, 444–45.

89. Ethiop [William J. Wilson], "What Shall We Do with the White People?" *Anglo-African Magazine*, II (February, 1860), 43–45.

90. *Anglo-African Magazine*, II (March, 1860), unpaged. Discussions of the contents of the *Anglo-African Magazine* are included in: Vernon Loggins, *The Negro Author: His Development in America to 1900* (New York: Columbia University Press, 1931), 209–11; William Luther Moore, "The Literature of the American Negro Prior to 1865: An Anthology and a History" (4 vols.: Ed.D. dissertation, New York University, 1942), III, 954–56; Mary

Fair Burks, "A Survey of Black Literary Magazines in the United States, 1859–1940" (Ed.D. dissertation, Columbia University, Teachers College, 1975), 38–86.

CHAPTER THREE

1. John C. Dancy, "Report of the Editor of the *Quarterly Review*," in African Methodist Episcopal Zion Church, General Conference, *Official Journal of the Daily Proceedings of the Twenty-First Quadrennial Session . . . 1900* (York, Pa.: Dispatch Print., 1901), 211; "The *Horizon*," Horizon, IV (July, 1908), 3; "The New *Horizon*," *ibid.*, V (January, 1910), 1.
2. "Editorial and Publishers' Announcements," *Colored American Magazine*, I (May, 1900), 60.
3. "Publishers' Announcements," *ibid.*, VII (June, 1904), 458.
4. *Notable American Women*, II, 137–39.
5. J. Max Barber to Charles W. Chesnutt, September 3, 1904, in Charles Waddell Chesnutt Collection, Fisk University Library, Nashville, Tenn.; William Stanley Braithwaite to J. Max Barber, January 5, 1907, in Philip Butcher (ed.), *The William Stanley Braithwaite Reader* (Ann Arbor: University of Michigan Press, 1972), 244; Mary Church Terrell, *A Colored Woman in a White World* (Washington, D.C.: Ransdell, 1940), 223; James E. McGirt to Charles W. Chesnutt, November 5, 1906, in Chesnutt Collection; William Stanley Braithwaite, "Negro America's First Magazine," *Negro Digest*, VI (December, 1947), 24–25.
6. John T. Jenifer, *Centennial Retrospect: History of the African Methodist Episcopal Church* (Nashville: A. M. E. Sunday School Union, n.d.), 427; Dancy, "Report of the Editor of the *Quarterly Review*," 211–12; "An Appeal and An Offer," *National Baptist Magazine*, I (January, 1894), 61.
7. A circulation of 17,840 for the *Colored American Magazine* was recorded in the *Ayer Directory of Newspapers and Periodicals*, 1905–1908. The *Ayer Directory* for 1907 gave the *Voice* circulation as 13,000; the figure most frequently announced by the editors of the periodical was 15,000. *Voice of the Negro*, III (September, 1906), 627; *Voice*, IV (May, 1907), 196.
8. *Howard's American Magazine*, VI (April, 1901), unpaged.
9. "Editorial Briefs," *A. M. E. Zion Quarterly Review*, V (April, 1895), 88; *National Baptist Magazine*, VIII (August, 1901), 342; B. T. Tanner, "Report of the Managing Editor of the *A. M. E. Church Review*," in *Journal of the Nineteenth Session and Eighteenth Quadrennial Session of the General Conference of the African Methodist Episcopal Church . . . 1888* (Philadelphia: Published by Rev. James C. Embry, General Business Manager, n.d.), 210–11; "Bishop B. T. Tanner," *A. M. E. Church Review*, V (July, 1888), 5.
10. *Liberator*, October 15, 1841; George W. Clinton, "The Literature of the A. M. E. Zion Church," *A. M. E. Zion Quarterly Review*, V (October/January, 1895/96), 257–58; William J. Walls, *The African Methodist Episcopal Zion Church: Reality of the Black Church* (Charlotte, N.C.: A. M. E. Zion Publishing House, 1974), 333–36, 346–48.
11. A. B. Caldwell (ed.), *History of the American Negro: North Carolina Edition* (Atlanta: A. B. Caldwell Publishing Company, 1921), 9–14; *Dictionary of American Biography*, IV, 228–29; Walls, *The African Methodist Episcopal Zion Church*, 356–58, 584.
12. I. Garland Penn, *The Afro-American Press and Its Editors* (Springfield,

Mass.: Willey & Company, 1891), 197–200; Historical Records Survey, Michigan Project, *Calendar of the John C. Dancy Correspondence, 1898–1910* (Detroit: Historical Records Survey, Michigan Project, 1941), 1–2.

13. These statements appeared on the title page of the *Quarterly Review* during Clinton's editorship and Dancy's editorship, respectively.

14. "The Baptist Magazine: Its Needs" (leaflet included with *National Baptist Magazine*, January, 1896).

15. Penn, *The Afro-American Press*, 235–37; A. W. Pegues, *Our Baptist Ministers and Schools* (Springfield, Mass.: Willey & Company, 1892), 294–97.

16. "Our Bow," *National Baptist Magazine*, I (January, 1894), 58.

17. Bruce Grit [John E. Bruce], "He Defames the Race," Washington (D.C.) *Colored American*, February 2, 1901; John E. Bruce, "The Critic Revealed; or, The Deadly Parallel," *Howard's American Magazine*, VI (April, 1901), 366; William Hayes Ward to Booker T. Washington, March 21, 1901, in Louis R. Harlan (ed.), *The Booker T. Washington Papers* (15 vols.; Urbana: University of Illinois Press, 1972–), VI, 56.

18. [Bruce], "He Defames the Race"; Bruce, "The Critic Revealed"; Charles Chesnutt, "A Defamer of His Race," *Critic*, XXXVIII (April, 1901), 350–51; W. E. Burghardt Du Bois, "The Storm and Stress in the Black World," *Dial*, XXX (April 16, 1901), 262–64.

19. Cleveland *Gazette*, March 19, 1887; John Wesley Cromwell, "Sketch of John Edward Bruce," Indianapolis *Freeman*, April 4, 1903; New York *Times*, August 11, 1924, p. 13; Schomburg Center for Research in Black Culture, *Calendar of the Manuscripts in the Schomburg Collection of Negro Literature and History* (New York: Historical Records Survey, 1942), I, 162–66; Peter Gilbert (ed.), *The Selected Writings of John Edward Bruce, Militant Black Journalist*, (New York: Arno Press, 1971), 1–9.

20. Alexander Crummell to John E. Bruce, March 22, 1898, in John E. Bruce Collection, Schomburg Center for Research in Black Culture, New York Public Library, Astor, Lenox and Tilden Foundations.

21. John W. Parker, "James Ephraim McGirt: Poet of 'Hope Deferred,'" *North Carolina Historical Review*, XXXI (July, 1954), 321–35; John W. Parker, "James E. McGirt: Tar Heel Poet," *Crisis*, LX (May, 1953), 286–89.

22. James E. McGirt, "Black Hand," *McGirt's Magazine*, II (July, 1904), 21.

23. James E. McGirt to Charles W. Chesnutt, November 5, 1906, in Chesnutt Collection.

24. "The Constitutional Brotherhood of America," *McGirt's Magazine*, VI (August, 1908), 29–30.

25. *McGirt's Magazine*, II (April, 1904), 14.

26. *Who's Who of the Colored Race, 1915*, xxx; George P. Marks, III, *The Black Press Views American Imperialism, 1898–1900* (New York: Arno Press, 1971), 209.

27. *Ebony*, I (April, 1906), 1–2.

28. Washington (D.C.) *Colored American*, June 7, 1902.

29. *Who's Who of the Colored Race, 1915*, 143–44.

30. *A. M. E. Church Review*, VI (October, 1889), 254.

31. John Edward Bruce, "Negro Aristocracy!—A Myth," *Howard's American Magazine*, V (September, 1900), 84–85.

32. Indianapolis *Freeman*, June 23, 1894, July 17, 1897; Augustus M. Hodges, "Edward Elmore Brock," *Colored American Magazine*, II (January, 1901), 197–98.

33. Indianapolis *Freeman*, April 16, 1898; Washington (D.C.) *Colored American*, April 26, 1898, September 22, 1900.

34. Washington (D.C.) *Colored American*, July 18, 1903; *Who's Who of the Colored Race, 1915*, 64–65; Thelma D. Perry, "Melvin J. Chisum, Pioneer Newsman," *Negro History Bulletin*, XXXVI (December, 1973), 176–80; Harlan (ed.), *Booker T. Washington Papers*, VII, 219–20, 222–23.
35. *Who's Who of the Colored Race, 1915*, 246.
36. *Freeman*, I (May, 1908), 15–16.
37. Thomas V. Gibbs, "John Willis Menard: The First Colored Congressman-Elect," *A. M. E. Church Review*, III (April, 1887), 426–32; Indianapolis *Freeman*, November 22, 1890, January 17, February 14, November 14, 1891; Edith Menard, "100th Anniversary of the Election of the First Negro, John Willis Menard, Second Congressional District of the State of Louisiana to the United States House of Representatives, Fortieth Congress, November 3, 1868–November 3, 1968: A Centennial Documentary," *Negro History Bulletin*, XXXI (November, 1968), 10–11; U.S. Congress, *Biographical Directory of the American Congress, 1774–1971* (Washington, D.C.: U.S. Government Printing Office, 1971), 189.
38. "Our Policy," *New Citizen*, I (December, 1904), 1–2.
39. "Start a Magazine of Your Own," *McConico's Monthly Magazine*, I (July, 1909), unpaged.
40. *Evanston Directory*, 1884, pp. 29, 130, 1886, pp. 166, 176–77, 1888, p. 174; *Evanston and Wilmette Directory*, 1890, p. 201; Indianapolis *Freeman*, January 28, April 22, 1899; *A. M. E. Church Review*, VIII (April, 1892), unpaged; Evanston *Review*, April 14, 1955, November 10, 1960.
41. Frederick Douglass to Jesse S. Woods, June 5, 1889, in *Afro-American Budget*, I (June, 1889), 63; *ibid.*, I (October, 1889), 101; *ibid.*, I (November, 1889), 157.
42. Indianapolis *Freeman*, January 25, 1890.
43. *Future State*, III (March/April, 1895), unpaged.
44. "Editorial Comment: Appreciation," *Paul Jones Monthly Magazine*, I (November, 1907), 3.
45. *Colored American Journal*, I (January, 1883), 45, 63, 67.
46. Penn, *The Afro-American Press*, 267–69; *A. M. E. Church Review*, XVII (April, 1901), 390; Richmond (Va.) *Planet*, April 25, June 13, 1908; Indianapolis *Freeman*, August 14, 1909; *Negro Heritage*, XII (1973), 86–87, 97.
47. *American Newspapers, 1821–1936: A Union List of Files Available in the United States and Canada*, ed. Winifred Gregory (New York: H. W. Wilson Company, 1937), 568.
48. B. T. Tanner, "How the *A. M. E. Church Review* Came into Being," *A. M. E. Church Review*, XXV (April, 1909), 361; *ibid.*, I (July, 1884), unpaged.
49. "Editorial: One Year in Journalism," *ibid.*, VI (July, 1889), 110; African Methodist Episcopal Church, General Conference, *A. M. E. Church Review, Sixth Quadrennial Report of the A. M. E. Church Review to the Twenty-Third General Conference of the African Methodist Episcopal Church* (Philadelphia: A. M. E. Publishing House, 1908), 5–6.
50. William J. Simmons, *Men of Mark: Eminent, Progressive and Rising* (Cleveland: Geo. M. Rewell & Company, 1887), 985–88; New York *Times*, January 16, 1923, p. 21; *Dictionary of American Biography*, XVIII, 296; R. R. Wright, Jr., *The Bishops of the African Methodist Episcopal Church* (Nashville: A. M. E. Sunday School Union, 1963), 323–26.
51. "Lives of the Editors," *A. M. E. Church Review*, XXV (April, 1909), 377–78.
52. *Ibid.*, XXV (April, 1909), 381; *Who Was Who in America, 1951–60*, 184; Wright, *Bishops of the African Methodist Episcopal Church*, 146–50; Wil-

berforce University, Carnegie Library, *The Levi Jenkins Coppin Collection at Carnegie Library, Wilberforce University,* comp. Casper LeRoy Jordan (Wilberforce, Ohio: Author, 1957), iii.

53. "Editorial: One Year in Journalism,' 111; J. Albert Johnson, "An Estimate of Dr. Coppin as an Editor," *A. M. E. Church Review,* XXV (April, 1909), 388.

54. "Lives of the Editors," 383–84; *Who's Who of the Colored Race, 1915,* 166; *Centennial Encyclopedia of the African Methodist Episcopal Church,* ed. Richard R. Wright, Jr. (Philadelphia: Book Concern of the A. M. E. Church, 1916), 144.

55. "Lives of the Editors," 384.

56. *A. M. E. Church Review,* XIX (April, 1903), 779.

57. L. J. Coppin, "Was the Church Wise in Establishing the *A. M. E. Review?*" *ibid.,* XXV (April, 1909), 364.

58. Dorothy Holmes Cunningham, "An Analysis of the *A. M. E. Church Review,* 1884–1900" (M.A. thesis, Howard University, 1950), is a study of those articles in the *Review* that discussed the political, social, economic, and educational status of the Negro.

59. *A. M. E. Church Review,* XXI (October, 1904), 185.

60. Henry M. Turner to Benjamin T. Tanner, undated, in *ibid.,* I (July, 1884), 46–47.

61. Indianapolis *Freeman,* February 22, 1890; William Jacob Walls, *Joseph Charles Price, Educator and Race Leader* (Boston: Christopher Publishing House, 1943), *passim;* Walls, *The African Methodist Episcopal Zion Church,* 309–14, 504–506.

62. "Simon Green Atkins and the Winston-Salem Teachers' College," in N. C. Newbold (ed.), *Five North Carolina Negro Educators* (Chapel Hill: University of North Carolina Press, 1939), 1–32.

63. *Proceedings of the Third Oecumenical Methodist Conference Held in . . . London, September, 1901* (New York: Eaton & Mains, 1901), 209–10.

64. "Prospectus and Other Editorials," *Southland,* I (February, 1890), 1–2.

65. *Who's Who of the Colored Race, 1915,* 76; *Who's Who in Colored America, 1950,* 120; *Journal of Negro History,* XLIX (April, 1964), 149–50.

66. A. J. Cooper, "Prospectus to Our Woman's Department," *Southland,* I (May, 1890), 159–60; A. J. Cooper, "The Higher Education of Women," *ibid.,* II (April, 1891), 202.

67. John R. Lynch, "Should the Colored Vote Divide?" *ibid.,* I (May, 1890), 234, 238; John Mitchell, Jr., "Will a Division of the Negro Vote Help Toward the Solution of the Race Problem?" *ibid.,* I (May, 1890), 240.

68. "Prospectus and Other Editorials," *ibid.,* I (February, 1890), 1–2.

69. August Meier, "Booker T. Washington and the Negro Press, with Special Reference to the *Colored American Magazine,*" *Journal of Negro History,* XXXVIII (January, 1953), 68–73; Abby Arthur Johnson and Ronald M. Johnson, "Away from Accommodation: Racial Editors and Protest Journalism, 1900–1910," *ibid.,* LXII (October, 1977), 325–29.

70. R. S. Elliott, "The Story of Our Magazine," *Colored American Magazine* III (May, 1901), 45–47; *ibid.,* II (December, 1900), 157.

71. "Pauline E. Hopkins," *ibid.,* II (January, 1901), 218.

72. Information on this phase of Pauline Hopkins' life was found in documents in the Pauline E. Hopkins Collection, Fisk University Library, Nashville, Tenn. See also Ann Allen Shockley, "Pauline E. Hopkins: A Biographical Excursion into Obscurity," *Phylon,* XXXIII (Spring, 1972), 22–26.

73. Elliott, "The Story of Our Magazine," 48.

74. Braithwaite, "Negro America's First Magazine," 22–23.
75. Walter Wallace to Booker T. Washington, August 6, 1901, in Harlan (ed.), *Booker T. Washington Papers*, VI, 184.
76. Braithwaite, "Negro America's First Magazine," 24.
77. "Biographies of the Officers of the New Management of Our Magazine," *Colored American Magazine*, VI (May/June, 1903), 443–46; "Col. William H. Dupree," *ibid.*, III (July, 1901), 228–32; Maud Cuney Hare, *Negro Musicians and Their Music* (Washington, D.C.: Associated Publishers, 1936), 211; John Daniels, *In Freedom's Birthplace: A Study of the Boston Negroes* (Boston: Houghton Mifflin Company, 1914), 99.
78. "John F. Ransom," *Colored American Magazine*, IV (January/February, 1902), 247–48; *Negro Music Journal*, I (January, 1903), 67; Hare, *Negro Musicians*, 220.
79. "Biographies of the Officers," 447–48.
80. Braithwaite, "Negro America's First Magazine," 25.
81. "Editorial: Retrospection of a Year," *Colored American Magazine*, VIII (June, 1905), 342.
82. Washington (D.C.) *Colored American*, September 19, 1903; *Who's Who of the Colored Race, 1915*, 195–96; *Who's Who in Colored America, 1938–40*, 378; New York *Times*, March 3, 1943, p. 24; *Dictionary of American Biography*, Suppl. 3, 534–35.
83. Meier, "Booker T. Washington and the Negro Press," 70; New York *Times*, April 29, 1951, p. 88; George A. Sewell, *Mississippi Black History Makers* (Jackson: University Press of Mississippi, 1977), 101–104.
84. *Who's Who of the Colored Race, 1915*, 130; *Who's Who in Colored America, 1938–40*, 233; New York *Times*, March 28, 1948, p. 48.
85. *Colored American Magazine*, II (August, 1900), 189; "Constitutional Rights Association of the United States," *ibid.*, I (October, 1900), 309–11.
86. "The Loyal Legion of Labor," *ibid.*, V (June, 1902), 111–17.
87. "Publishers' Announcements," *ibid.*, VII (June, 1904), 458.
88. T. Thomas Fortune, "What A Magazine Should Be," *ibid.*, VII (June, 1904), 394. Discussions of the literary content of the *Colored American Magazine* are included in: Mary Fair Burks, "A Survey of Black Literary Magazines in the United States, 1859–1940" (Ed.D. dissertation, Columbia University Teachers College, 1975), 115–49; and in Johnson, "Away from Accommodation," 325–29.
89. H. S. Fortune, "Grand Opera As We See It," *Colored American Magazine*, I (June, 1900), 78.
90. Lester A. Walton, "Music and the Stage," *ibid.*, XIV (July, 1908), 409–10; *ibid.*, XVI (May, 1909), 308.
91. "Ernest Hogan: The Link Between the Old and the New," *ibid.*, IX (October, 1905), 587–90.
92. George W. Walker, "The Negro on the American Stage," *ibid.*, XI (November, 1906), 247–48.
93. J. Rosamond Johnson, "Why They Call American Music Ragtime," *ibid.*, XV (January, 1909), 636–39.
94. "Publishers' Announcements," *ibid.*, X (June, 1906), 434.
95. For Washington's relationships with the *Voice of the Negro* and Scott's appointment to the editorial board, see Meier, "Booker T. Washington and the Negro Press," 75; Harlan (ed.), *Booker T. Washington Papers*, VII, 328–29, 364–65, 370–71, 486–88; Johnson, "Away from Accommodation," 329–32; Louis R. Harlan, "Booker T. Washington and the *Voice of the Negro*, 1904–1907," *Journal of Southern History*, XLV (February, 1979), 45–62.

96. *Who's Who of the Colored Race, 1915,* 32; *The National Cyclopedia of the Colored Race,* ed. Clement Richardson (Montgomery: National Publishing Company, 1919), 491–93; *Who's Who in Colored America, 1930–32,* 49.
97. William Pickens, "Jesse Max Barber," *Voice,* III (November, 1906), 483–88.
98. *Who's Who of the Colored Race, 1915,* 19; Philadelphia *Tribune,* September 24, October 4, 1949; Allen H. Spear, *Black Chicago: The Making of a Negro Ghetto, 1890–1920* (Chicago: University of Chicago Press, 1968), 74. See also Grace T. Sherry, "J. Max Barber and the Prerequisites of Race Leadership" (M.A. thesis, Georgia State University, 1972).
99. "The Voice Publishing Company," *Voice of the Negro,* III (June, 1906), 399.
100. Chicago *Broad Ax,* February 8, 1908.
101. J. Max Barber, "Why Mr. Barber Left Atlanta," *Voice,* III (November, 1906), 470; "Shall the Press Be Free?" *Voice of the Negro,* III (October, 1906), 392.
102. Chicago *Broad Ax,* February 8, 1908. See also Emma L. Thornbrough, *T. Thomas Fortune: Militant Journalist* (Chicago: University of Chicago Press, 1972), 308–309, 312–13.
103. "The Healthful Growth of the Magazine," *Voice of the Negro,* II (June, 1905), 425. Analyses of the contents of this periodical are found in: Carolyn Walden, "An Analysis of the Black Experience as Reflected in the *Voice of the Negro,* 1904–1907" (M.A. thesis, Atlanta University, 1971); Burks, "A Survey of Black Literary Magazines," 151–56; Johnson, "Away from Accommodation," 329–32; and Penelope L. Bullock, "Profile of a Periodical: The 'Voice of the Negro,'" *Atlanta Historical Bulletin,* XXI (Spring, 1977), 102–13.
104. "Roosevelt on the Race Problem," *Voice of the Negro,* II (March, 1905,) 147.
105. *Voice of the Negro,* I (June, 1904), unpaged.
106. "The Moral Conflict in the South," *ibid.,* I (October, 1904), 25; "Anti-Southern? No!" *ibid.,* I (July, 1904), 309.
107. "Miss Jeanes' Donation," *Voice,* IV (June, 1907), 220.
108. "Discussion Not Crimination," *Voice of the Negro,* II (April, 1905), 272.
109. "The Macon Convention," *ibid.,* III (March, 1906), 163.
110. "The Vagrancy Problem," *ibid.,* II (September, 1905), 604.
111. "A New Sign of Progress," *ibid.,* III (June, 1906), 438.
112. John Hope, "Our Atlanta Schools," *ibid.,* I (January, 1904), 16.
113. Atlanta *Constitution,* June 23, 1902, p. 5.
114. *Ibid.;* James A. Porter, *Modern Negro Art* (New York: Dryden Press, 1943), 79.
115. J. Max Barber to Charles W. Chesnutt, January 4, 1904, in Chesnutt Collection.
116. "Negro Journalism," *Alexander's Magazine,* I (March, 1906), 19; *Who's Who of the Colored Race,* 1915, 3; Delilah L. Beasley, *The Negro Trail Blazers of California* (Los Angeles: N.p., 1919), 256, 262; *Monthly Review,* I (March, 1894), 8.
117. *National Baptist Magazine,* III (January, 1896), 70; *ibid.,* III (July, 1896), 223; Indianapolis *Freeman,* December 23, 1899.
118. Charles Alexander to John E. Bruce, June 28, 1896, in Bruce Collection.
119. G. F. Richings, *Evidences of Progress Among Colored People* (2nd ed.; Philadelphia: Geo. S. Ferguson Company, 1896), 357–58. Other complimentary notices on the *Review* appeared in *National Baptist Magazine,* III (January, 1896), 70; *Woman's Era,* I (September, 1894), 7; *A. M. E. Church*

Review, XI (October, 1894), 324; *ibid.*, XIII (July, 1896), 167–68; Indianapolis *Freeman*, December 30, 1899.

120. For the relationship of Booker T. Washington to journals edited by Charles Alexander, see: Meier, "Booker T. Washington and the Negro Press," 74–75; Harlan (ed.), *Booker T. Washington Papers*, IV, 445, VII, 404, 496, 524–25.

121. Chicago *Broad Ax*, September 22, 1923.

122. "Negro Journalism," 20.

123. *Monthly Review*, III (July, 1895), 157; Addison Gayle, Jr., *Oak and Ivy* (New York: Doubleday, 1971), 52–56; Sara S. Fuller, *The Paul Laurence Dunbar Collection: An Inventory to the Microfilm Edition* (Columbus: Ohio Historical Society, 1972), 14–17; *Notable American Women*, II, 614–15.

124. *Monthly Review*, III (March, 1895), unpaged; *ibid.*, I (March, 1894), 3–4.

125. *Voice*, IV (June, 1907), unpaged.

126. Walter F. Walker, "News About Liberia and Africa Generally," *Alexander's Magazine*, V (November, 1907), 17.

127. Walter F. Walker, "Liberia and Emigration," *ibid.*, VI (August, 1908), 162–65; Daniels, *In Freedom's Birthplace*, 138.

128. *Alexander's Magazine*, V (November, 1907), 36.

129. *Ibid.*, II (October, 1906), 11–15.

130. S. Laing Williams, "The New Negro," *ibid.*, VII (November, 1908), 18–20.

131. *Alexander's Magazine*, IV (September, 1907), 243; *Horizon*, II (October, 1907), 22.

132. Daniels, *In Freedom's Birthplace*, 103, 455; *Dictionary of American Biography*, VII, 632–33; Gerda Lerner, *The Grimké Sisters from South Carolina: Rebels Against Slavery* (Boston: Houghton Mifflin, 1967), 358–64.

133. Charles Alexander to John E. Bruce, April 11, 1896, in Bruce Collection; Beasley, *Negro Trail Blazers*, 262.

134. The major sources consulted for information on Du Bois's life were his autobiographical writings: *Darkwater: Voices from Within the Veil* (New York: Harcourt, Brace and Howe, 1920); *Dusk of Dawn: An Essay Toward an Autobiography of a Race Concept* (New York: Harcourt, Brace and Company, 1940); *The Autobiography of W. E. B. Du Bois: A Soliloquy on Viewing My Life from the Last Decade of Its First Century*, ed. Herbert Aptheker (New York: International Publishers, 1968). Articles on Du Bois's journalistic career include: Paul G. Partington, "The *Moon Illustrated Weekly* —The Precursor of the *Crisis*," *Journal of Negro History*, XLVIII (July, 1963), 206–16; Irene Diggs, "Du Bois—Revolutionary Journalist Then and Now, Part I," *Current Bibliography on African Affairs*, IV (March, 1971), 95–117; Dan S. Green, "W. E. B. Du Bois: His Journalistic Career," *Negro History Bulletin*, XL (March/April, 1977), 672–77.

135. Du Bois, *Darkwater*, 22.

136. *Crisis*, V (November, 1912), 27.

137. W. E. B. Du Bois (ed.), *The Negro in Business*, Atlanta University Publications, no. 4 (Atlanta: [Atlanta University Press], 1899), 77; W. E. B. Du Bois to Jacob Schiff, 1905, quoted in Du Bois, *Dusk of Dawn*, 82–83.

138. *Crisis*, V (November, 1912), 27; *Horizon*, V (May, 1910), 1; *Horizon*, IV (July, 1908), 2–4. Du Bois persuaded John E. Milholland and J. Max Barber to abandon plans they were formulating for a new periodical and invited them to join him in reestablishing the *Horizon*. W. E. B. Du Bois to the Guarantors of the *Horizon*, March 12, 1909, in Herbert Aptheker (ed.), *The Correspondence of W. E. B. Du Bois* (3 vols.; Amherst: University of Massachusetts Press, 1973–78), I, 144–45.

139. Charles Flint Kellogg, *NAACP: A History of the National Association for the Advancement of Colored People, Volume I, 1909–1920* (Baltimore: Johns Hopkins Press, 1967), 52.
140. "Our Policy," *Horizon*, V (November, 1909), 1.
141. "The New *Horizon*," *ibid.*, V (January, 1910), 1–2.

CHAPTER FOUR

1. "As to Necessity, Purpose and Policy," *Southern Teachers' Advocate*, I (June, 1905), 19.
2. *Freedman's Torchlight*, I (December, 1866), 3.
3. William J. Simmons, *Men of Mark: Eminent, Progressive and Rising* (Cleveland: Geo. M. Rewell & Company, 1887), 620–25; A. W. Pegues, *Our Baptist Ministers and Schools* (Springfield, Mass.: Willey & Company, 1892), 375–80; *Dictionary of American Biography*, XIV, 492.
4. *Freedman's Torchlight*, I (December, 1866), 2.
5. *Southern Workman*, X (July, 1881), 77; *ibid.*, XIII (January, 1884), 9; *ibid.*, XXXIII (March, 1904), 137–38. (The *Southern Workman*, a monthly magazine established at Hampton Institute in 1872, has not been included in this study because it was not edited by Negroes during this period.)
6. Horace Mann Bond, *Education for Freedom: A History of Lincoln University, Pennsylvania* (N.p.: Lincoln University, 1976), 338–40, 384, 394; Horace Mann Bond, " A Negro First," *Negro History Bulletin*, XXVI (November, 1962), 91.
7. T. H. Gray, "Biographical Sketch of Nathan F. Mossell," *Voice of the Negro*, III (February, 1906), 108–13; *Who's Who in Colored America, 1933–37*, 383–84; New York *Times*, October 29, 1946, p. 25; W. Montague Cobb, "Nathan Francis Mossell, M.D., 1856–1946," *National Medical Association Journal*, XLVI (March, 1954), 118–30.
8. Bond, *Education for Freedom*, 340; Bond, "A Negro First," 91.
9. *Who's Who of the Colored Race, 1915*, 132–33; *Who's Who in Colored America, 1930–32*, 201.
10. *Negro Education Journal*, I (June, 1895), 13.
11. E. R. Carter, *The Black Side* (Atlanta: N.p., 1894), 167–72; "A Prominent Churchman of Bermuda," *Colored American Magazine*, XIII (December, 1907), 465–67; *The Encyclopedia of the African Methodist Episcopal Church*, comp. R. R. Wright, Jr. (2nd ed.; Philadelphia: A. M. E. Book Concern, 1947), 601.
12. *Who's Who of the Colored Race, 1915*, 147; *Educator*, IX (October, 1905), 1.
13. *Colored Teacher*, II (September, 1907), 3.
14. *Monthly Review*, III (July, 1895), unpaged.
15. *National Capital Searchlight*, I (February, 1901), ii, 2.
16. *Negro Educational Review*, I (November, 1905), 30. The *Review* was also advertised in National Association of Teachers of Negro Youth, *Minutes of the First Annual Meeting . . . 1904* (Nashville: A. M. E. Sunday School Union, 1905), unpaged. This organization (later the National Association of Teachers in Colored Schools) initiated a monthly journal, *School News*, in October, 1910, under the editorship of J. R. E. Lee; the title was changed to *National Negro School News* the following year.
17. *Negro Educational Review*, I (February, 1905), 45.
18. New York *Age*, September 2, 1909; *Citizen*, January, 1910; Washington *Bee*, July 16, 1910.
19. *Citizen*, December 1, 1909; *ibid.*, January, 1910; Daniel Murray, "Economy the Watchword," *ibid.*, May, 1910.

20. John T. Jenifer, *Centennial Retrospect: History of the African Methodist Episcopal Church* (Nashville: A. M. E. Sunday School Union, n.d.), 350.

21. *Theological Institute*, III (May, 1911), 1; *A. M. E. Zion Quarterly Review*, XIV (First and Second Quarters, 1909), 62.

22. For Turner, see Simmons, *Men of Mark*, 805–19; R. R. Wright, Jr., *The Bishops of the African Methodist Episcopal Church* (Nashville: A. M. E. Sunday School Union, 1963), 329–41; *Dictionary of American Biography*, XIX, 65–66. For Holsey, see *Dictionary of American Biography*, IX, 176–77; John Brother Cade, *Holsey, the Incomparable* (New York: Pageant Press, [1963]), 119–24. For Hood, see *Dictionary of American Biography*, IX, 192–93.

23. Cleveland *Gazette*, June 25, 1887; *A. M. E. Church Review*, IV (October, 1887), 221; St. Paul *Western Appeal*, April 16, 23, 1887; St. Paul *Appeal*, January 24, June 20, 1891.

24. J. W. Hood, *One Hundred Years of the African Methodist Episcopal Zion Church* (New York: A. M. E. Zion Book Concern, 1895), 480–82; *Zion Trumpet and Homiletic Magazine*, XIV (May–June, 1909), 15.

25. Washington (D.C.) *Colored American*, July 11, 1903; *McGirt's Magazine*, II (January, 1904), 21; *A. M. E. Church Review*, XXIII (April, 1907), 377; *Encyclopedia of the African Methodist Episcopal Church*, 274.

26. *Who's Who of the Colored Race, 1915*, 93–94; *Ayer Directory of Newspapers and Periodicals*, 1910, 1911.

27. Indianapolis *Freeman*, February 14, 1891; *Church Advocate*, XVI (July, 1907), 2; George F. Bragg, Jr., *History of the Afro-American Group of the Episcopal Church* (Baltimore: Church Advocate Press, 1922), 99; *Who Was Who in America, 1951–60*, 97.

28. Indianapolis *Freeman*, March 30, 1889, December 13, 1890, January 24, 1891, March 5, 1892; I. Garland Penn, *The Afro-American Press and Its Editors* (Springfield, Mass.: Willey & Company, 1891), 194–96; *Ayer Directory of Newspapers and Periodicals*, 1893/94, 1895; *Remington Brothers' Newspaper Manual*, 1890, 1898; Samuel William Bacote (ed.), *Who's Who Among the Colored Baptists of the United States* (Kansas City, Mo.: Franklin Hudson Publishing Company, 1913), 211–13.

29. Washington (D.C.) *Colored American*, May 7, 1898; Indianapolis *Freeman*, February 25, December 30, 1899; *Rowell's American Newspaper Directory*, 1900.

30. *Who's Who of the Colored Race, 1915*, 274–75; *Who's Who in Colored America, 1941–44*, 535.

31. Amanda Smith, *An Autobiography: The Story of the Lord's Dealings with Mrs. Amanda Smith, the Colored Evangelist . . .* (Chicago: Meyer & Brother, Publishers, 1893).

32. *Helper*, IX (November, 1907), 2.

33. Chicago *Defender*, March 6, 1915; Julia A. Savage, "The Last Days of Sister Amanda Smith," *A. M. E. Church Review*, XXXI (April, 1915), 378–81; *Notable American Women*, III, 304–305.

34. African Methodist Episcopal Church, General Conference, *Journal of the Seventeenth Session and the Sixteenth Quadrennial Session . . . 1880* (Xenia, Ohio: Torchlight Printing Company, 1882), 66–67, 283; African Methodist Episcopal Church, *The Doctrines and Discipline of the African Methodist Episcopal Church* (20th rev. ed.: Philadelphia: A. M. E. Book Concern, 1892), 355.

35. Washington *Bee*, August 18, 1888; *A. M. E. Church Review*, V (October, 1888), 187–88.

36. Henry M. Turner, "Introduction," in Simmons, *Men of Mark*, 39–63; Penn, *Afro-American Press*, 120, 122; Pegues, *Our Baptist Ministers*, 439–53.
37. Simmons, *Men of Mark*, 1059–63; Pegues, *Our Baptist Ministers*, 357–63; *Who's Who in Colored America, 1930–32*, 326; Bacote, *Who's Who Among the Colored Baptists*, 36–37.
38. Penn, *Afro-American Press*, 407–10; *Notable American Women*, III, 565–67.
39. *A. M. E. Church Review*, V (October, 1888), 187–88; Indianapolis *Freeman*, February 9, 1889.
40. L. A. Scruggs, *Women of Distinction* (Raleigh: L. A. Scruggs, Publisher, 1893), 140–43; Washington (D.C.) *Colored American*, January 28, 1899.
41. M. A. Majors, *Noted Negro Women: Their Triumphs and Activities* (Chicago: Donohue & Henneberry, Printers, 1893), 251–58.
42. *A. M. E. Church Review*, IX (July, 1892), 111; Philadelphia *Times*, quoted in Majors, *Noted Negro Women*, 256.
43. *Ayer Directory of Newspapers and Periodicals*, 1901–1905; Washington (D.C.) *Colored American*, March 2, 1901, March 8, 1902; *Colored American Magazine*, III (July, 1901), unpaged.
44. Indianapolis *Freeman*, January 25, 1908; *Ayer Directory of Newspapers and Periodicals*, 1920; Rashey B. Moten, Jr., "The Negro Press of Kansas" (M.A. thesis, University of Kansas, 1938), 107–108.
45. Elizabeth Lindsay Davis (comp.), *Lifting as They Climb: National Association of Colored Women* (N.p., 1933), 19–21; Emma L. Fields, "The Women's Club Movement in the United States, 1877–1900" (M.A. thesis, Howard University, 1948), *passim*; Mary Church Terrell, "The History of the Club Women's Movement," *Aframerican Woman's Journal*, I (Summer–Fall, 1940), 34–38; Mary Church Terrell, *A Colored Woman in a White World* (Washington, D.C.: Ransdell, 1940), 148–51.
46. Davis, *Lifting as They Climb*, 77, 172; *National Notes*, n.s., XXVIII (January/February, 1947), 4.
47. Davis, *Lifting as They Climb*, 77, 171–72; *Who's Who of the Colored Race, 1915*, 278; Pittsburgh *Courier*, June 13, 1925; *Who's Who in Colored America, 1927*, 214–15.
48. "An Appeal," *Musical Messenger*, II (July, 1889), 2.
49. Penn, *Afro-American Press*, 401–405; Scruggs, *Women of Distinction*, 211–15.
50. "An Appeal," 2.
51. *Alexander's Magazine*, IV (June, 1907), 73; *ibid.*, IV (August, 1907), 184.
52. Indianapolis *Freeman*, May 4, 1907; William Henry Davis, "A Historic Account of Sylvester Russell," Indianapolis *Freeman*, January 1, 1910; Los Angeles *California News*, January 8, 1931.
53. "Medical History: Miles Vandahurst Lynk," *National Medical Association Journal*, XLIV (November, 1952), 475–76.
54. Quoted in W. Montague Cobb, "Medical History [Charles Victor Roman]," *National Medical Association Journal*, XLV (July, 1953), 301. (This quotation was attributed to Roman.)
55. *Who's Who of the Colored Race, 1915*, 233; *Who's Who in Colored America, 1933–37*, 367; Cobb, "Medical History," 301; *Journal of Negro History*, XX (January, 1935), 116–17.
56. *Who's Who of the Colored Race, 1915*, 167–68; *Who's Who in Colored America, 1933–37*, 306; *The National Cyclopedia of the Colored Race*, ed. Clement Richardson (Montgomery: National Publishing Company, 1919), 45.
57. "Salutatory," *National Medical Association Journal*, I (January/March, 1909), 37.
58. Washington (D.C.) *Colored American*, March 14, 1903, April 23, 1904;

Crisis, V (December, 1912), 67–68; "Biographical Note" in Register of the Alonzo Clifton McClennan Papers, Amistad Research Center, Dillard University, New Orleans, La.

59. A similar black periodical was probably published during this time in North Carolina. Passing references have been found to the "Sanitarium" or the "Southern Sanitarium," issued by the Raleigh physician Lawson A. Scruggs to promote the Pickford Sanitarium at Southern Pines, which he founded for the treatment of tubercular patients. Because of the lack of substantive evidence, the title has not been included in this survey.

60. Robert W. Carter, "A Worker and Organizer," New York *Age,* August 29, 1907.

61. New York *Age,* March 5, 1908; *ibid.,* September 5, 1907.

62. J. W. Watkins, "Will the Negro Race Unite?" *American Magazine,* I (June/July, 1905), 5; J. C. Ayler, "Solution of the Negro Problem," in *Guide-Lights: Lectures* ([Princeton]: Princeton Press, 1897), 27, 31.

63. *Dollar Mark,* I (June, 1906), unpaged; "Mr. E. C. Brown," *Alexander's Magazine,* IV (September, 1907), 261–62; Indianapolis *Freeman,* December 23, 1899; *Who's Who of the Colored Race, 1915,* 41.

64. New York *Age,* June 27, October 3, 1907, February 6, 1908; Indianapolis *Freeman,* July 7, September 15, 1906; "Millions in Amusements: The Afro-American Amusement Company," *Dollar Mark,* I (June, 1906), 11–13; *Who's Who in Colored America, 1927,* 26; Louis R. Harlan (ed.), *The Booker T. Washington Papers* (15 vols.; Urbana: University of Illinois Press, 1972–), VI, 498.

65. *Negro Year Book, 1913,* 288; *Who's Who of the Colored Race, 1915,* 246.

66. Washington (D.C.) *Colored American,* October 4, 1902; Indianapolis *Freeman,* September 3, 1904; Seattle *Republican,* October 19, 1906; National Negro Business League, *Report, Fifth Annual Convention, 1904,* Appendix, 27.

67. *Who's Who of the Colored Race, 1915,* 234; *Who's Who in Colored America, 1941–44,* 446; *Gazetteer and Guide,* I (November 15, 1901), 15; *For You, and Gazetteer and Guide,* XLVIII (August 25, 1946), 9; Harlan (ed.), *Booker T. Washington Papers,* VI, 32.

68. *Gazetteer and Guide,* I (November 15, 1901), unpaged, June, 1904, unpaged; *Ayer Directory of Newspapers and Periodicals,* 1905; *Negro Year Book, 1912,* 186.

69. Indianapolis *Freeman,* April 13, 1907; *Caterer, Gazetteer and Guide,* XXXIV (September 25, 1941), 8; *For You, and Gazetteer and Guide,* XLVIII (August 25, 1946), 9.

70. Indianapolis *Freeman,* November 8, 1902, June 25, 1904, April 6, 1907; *Who's Who of the Colored Race, 1915,* 144; *Crisis,* XIX (March, 1920), 281.

71. Harlan (ed.), *Booker T. Washington Papers,* III, 106.

72. "*Pl.*", I (April, 1895), 5.

73. William T. Thom, "The Negroes of Sandy Spring, Maryland: A Social Study," in U.S. Department of Labor, *Bulletin,* no. 32 (Washington, D.C.: Government Printing Office, 1901), 48–52; *Negro Agriculturist,* I (February, 1909), 1.

74. *Annals of Sandy Spring; or, Fourteen Years' History of a Rural Community in Maryland* (Baltimore: King Brothers, 1909), III, 452, 463–64; *Negro Agriculturist,* I (February, 1909), 2.

75. *Western Lever,* I (March, 1909), 70.

76. *Ibid.,* I (January/February, 1909), 55–57.

77. Helena (Montana) *Plaindealer,* July 5, October 18, 1907; Seattle *Republican,*

February 8, 1907; Butte (Montana) *New Age*, August 23, 1902.

78. *Western Lever*, I (January/February, 1909), 50.
79. M. V. Lynk, *Sixty Years of Medicine; or, The Life and Times of Dr. Miles V. Lynk, an Autobiography* (Memphis: Twentieth Century Press, 1951), *passim*.
80. *Ibid.*; *Who's Who in Colored America, 1950*, 348; "The M. V. Lynk Story: The Grand Old Man of Medical Science," *National Medical Association Journal*, XLVII (May, 1955), 206; Indianapolis *Freeman*, August 15, 1903.
81. Indianapolis *Freeman*, June 2, 1900.
82. Miles V. Lynk, "Preface," in *Afro-American School Speaker and Gems of Literature* (Jackson, Tenn.: The M. V. Lynk Publishing House, 1896), iii–v; Indianapolis *Freeman*, June 2, 1900.
83. Lynk, *Sixty Years of Medicine*, 33; "Salutatory," *Medical and Surgical Observer*, I (December, 1892), 14.
84. *Medical and Surgical Observer*, I (December, 1892), 15, *ibid.*, I (June, 1893), unpaged.
85. Lynk, *Sixty Years of Medicine*, 39.
86. Julia Ward Howe (ed.), *Representative Women of New England* (Boston: New England Historical Publishing Company, 1904), 335–39; Hallie Q. Brown, *Homespun Heroines and Other Women of Distinction* (Xenia, Ohio: Aldine Publishing Company, 1926), 151–54; *Notable American Women*, III, 206–208.
87. Boston *Evening Transcript*, January 10, 1922; Brown, *Homespun Heroines*, 182–93; *Notable American Women*, I, 86–88.
88. "The Woman's Era Club," *Woman's Era*, I (March 24, 1894), 4.
89. Josephine St. Pierre Ruffin, "Statement," November 17, 1897 (leaflet, in Rare Book Room, Boston Public Library).
90. "Editorial: Greeting," *Woman's Era*, I (March 24, 1894), 8; "Shall We Have a Convention of the Colored Women's Clubs, Leagues and Societies: What Prominent Women Have to Say," *ibid.*, I (June 1, 1894), 5.
91. "Our Young Men in Business," *ibid.*, I (June 1, 1894), 9.
92. Clarence A. Bacote, *The Story of Atlanta University: A Century of Service, 1865–1965* (Atlanta: Atlanta University, 1969), 111; "The Woman's Era Club," *Woman's Era*, I (March 24, 1894), 4.
93. "Advertise in the Woman's Era," *Woman's Era*, I (June 1, 1894), 9.
94. "Editorial: Greeting," 8.
95. *Negro Music Journal*, I (October, 1902), 32; *ibid.*, I (July, 1903), 235; Washington Conservatory of Music, *Announcement, 1903–1904*, in Washington Conservatory of Music Collection, Moorland-Spingarn Research Center, Howard University, Washington, D.C.
96. *Negro Music Journal*, I (September, 1902), 8.
97. Agnes Carroll, "Music as an Educator and Moral Builder," *ibid.*, I (September, 1902), 14–15; Agnes Carroll, "Music and Morals," *ibid.*, I (June, 1903), 198; J. Hillary Taylor, "A Musical Retrospection," *ibid.*, I (January, 1903), 68; J. Hillary Taylor, "A Child's Musical Education," *ibid.*, I (October, 1902), 21.
98. The contents of this periodical are analyzed in William E. Terry, "*The Negro Music Journal*: An Appraisal," *Black Perspectives in Music*, V (Fall, 1977), 146–60.
99. "Editorial: The Production of 'Aida,'" *Negro Music Journal*, I (June, 1903), 209–10.

100. "Editorial: An Opera House," *ibid.*, I (February, 1903), 111.
101. "Editorial: Our Musical Condition," *ibid.*, I (March, 1903), 138.
102. Harlan (ed.), *Booker T. Washington Papers*, II, 411, IV, 391; *Who's Who of the Colored Race, 1915*, 47.
103. *Who's Who in Colored America, 1941–44*, 460. Biographical data also received in letter to the author from Vincent E. Reed, Superintendent, Public Schools of the District of Columbia, March 9, 1978.
104. *Who's Who of the Colored Race, 1915*, 283; Washington *Star*, October 21, 1962; *Journal of Negro History*, LIV (July, 1969), 324–25; District of Columbia Public Library, "Dedication, Garnet C. Wilkinson Branch Library," January 29, 1978.
105. New York *Age*, September 2, 16, November 25, 1909; Washington *Bee*, September 25, 1909.
106. "Editorial: Promotional Examinations for Teachers," *School Teacher*, I (September 15, 1909), 23, 26.
107. Roscoe Conkling Bruce, "The Education and Training of the American Negro," *ibid.*, II (April 15, 1910), 81–84.
108. "Editorial: Elementary Manual Training, a Reform," *ibid.*, I (November, 1909), 93.
109. E. J. Josey, "Williams, Edward Christopher (1871–1929)," in Bohdan S. Wynar (ed.), *Dictionary of American Library Biography* (Littleton, Col.: Libraries Unlimited, 1978), 552–53.
110. Hallie E. Queen, "My School in Puerto Rico," *School Teacher*, II (February, 1910), 27–28.
111. "Editorial: A Boast and a Confession," *ibid.*, III (September, 1910), 27–28.
112. William Sidney Pittman to Booker T. Washington, October 31, 1893, in Harlan (ed.), *Booker T. Washington Papers*, III, 370.
113. "A Successful Architect," *Colored American Magazine*, XI (December, 1906), 424–25; "Men of the Month," *Crisis*, XII (September, 1916), 239; Richard K. Dozier, "A Historical Survey: Black Architects and Craftsmen," *Black World*, XXIII (May, 1974), 4–15; Harlan (ed.), *Booker T. Washington Papers*, II, 236–37. The author is also indebted to Roy L. Hill for material from his files, including interviews with Mrs. Portia Washington Pittman.
114. Washington *Bee*, October 16, 1909.
115. Booker T. Washington to the Editors of the *Negro Business League Herald*, February 11, 1909, in *Negro Business League Herald*, I (April, 1909), 9.
116. "To the Readers of This Magazine," *ibid.*, I (May 15, 1909), 5; "A Clear Case of Negligence," *ibid.*, II (April, 1909), 10.
117. "The Folly of Misspent Energy," *ibid.*, I (August 15, 1909), 23.
118. *Ibid.*, I (August 15, 1909), 10–11, 14–18; *ibid.*, I (October 15, 1909), 10; *ibid.*, I (November, 1909), 11.
119. *Ibid.*, I (May 15, 1909), 3; *ibid.*, I (July 15, 1909), unpaged; *ibid.*, I (August 15, 1909), 23; *ibid.*, I (September 15, 1909), 4–5.
120. Ruth Ann Stewart, *Portia: The Life of Portia Washington Pittman, the Daughter of Booker T. Washington* (Garden City, N.Y.: Doubleday and Company, 1977), *passim*; Washington *Post*, February 27, 1978, Sec. C, p. 3.

CHAPTER FIVE

1. Frank Luther Mott, *A History of American Magazines* (5 vols.; Cambridge: Belknap Press of Harvard University Press, 1938–68), I, 24, 71–77.

2. *Ibid.*, I, 13.
3. U.S. Bureau of the Census, *Negro Population, 1790–1915* (Washington, D.C.: Government Printing Office, 1918), 33; U.S. Bureau of the Census, *Urban Population in the United States from the First Census (1790) to the Fifteenth Census (1930)* (N.p., 1939), 1.
4. Mott, *A History of American Magazines*, IV, 6–7.
5. *Alexander's Magazine*, III (November, 1906), 6; *Colored American Magazine*, VII (March, 1904), unpaged; *A. M. E. Church Review*, XIII (October, 1896), 265; *Woman's Era*, II (February, 1896), 14; *Voice of the Negro*, I (May, 1904), unpaged.
6. "One Way to Help," *Voice*, IV (March, 1907), 96; "Our Name Changed," *ibid.*, III (November, 1906), 464.
7. "Apology. (Introductory.)," *Anglo-African Magazine*, I (January, 1859), 1, 3.
8. These newsletters were the *Southern Letter* and the *Tuskegee Student*. The name "Black Belt Magazine" was suggested by Victoria Earle Matthews as a title for the proposed periodical. See the letters of T. Thomas Fortune to Booker T. Washington, January 21, 1887, March 7, 1890, and March 13, 1896, in Louis R. Harlan (ed.), *The Booker T. Washington Papers* (15 vols.; Urbana: University of Illinois Press, 1972–), II, 327–28, IV, 130–31, 136–37.
9. Armistead Scott Pride, "A Register and History of Negro Newspapers in the United States, 1827–1950" (Ph.D. dissertation, Northwestern University, 1950), 417.
10. G. F. Richings, *Evidences of Progress Among Colored People* (2nd ed.; Philadelphia: Geo. S. Ferguson Company, 1896), 358.
11. *Mirror of Liberty*, "Extra," July, 1841; "The Want of Unity Among the Colored People," *Lunar Visitor*, I (February, 1862), unpaged; "Editorial," *Woman's Era*, II (April, 1895), 8–9; J. W. Watkins, "Will the Negro Unite?" *American Magazine*, I (June/July, 1905), 5; "Race Co-operation," *Negro Business League Herald*, I (May 15, 1909), 5; *Western Lever*, I (January/February, 1909), 55–56.
12. Mary Church Terrell, "Where Is the Conscience of the North?" *McGirt's Magazine*, II (June, 1904), 29.
13. "On Boycotting Street Cars," *Colored American Magazine*, IX (July, 1905), 398.
14. Daniel Murray, "The Industrial Problem of the United States and the Negro's Relation to It," *Voice of the Negro*, I (September, 1904), 407; "Strong Words on 'The Industrial Problem,'" *ibid.*, I (October, 1904), 489.
15. E. A. Johnson, "Negro Dolls for Negro Babies," *Colored American Magazine*, XIV (November, 1908), 583; "The Adams Pictures," *Voice of the Negro*, III (September, 1906), 622–23.
16. "Announcements for 1903," *Colored American Magazine*, VI (December, 1902), unpaged.
17. Corcoran Gallery of Art, *The Historic Photographs of Addison N. Scurlock* (Washington, D.C.: Corcoran Gallery of Art, 1976), *passim*.
18. *Mirror of Liberty*, I (July, 1838), 1; *Douglass' Monthly*, III (August, 1860), 305; *African Methodist Episcopal Church Magazine*, II (April, 1845), unpaged; *Weekly Anglo-African*, January 7, 1860; *Repository of Religion and Literature and of Science and Art*, IV (March, 1862), unpaged.
19. "Looking to the Future," *A. M. E. Church Review*, XIII (July, 1896), 175–76.
20. J. Max Barber, "The Morning Cometh," *Voice of the Negro*, I (January, 1904), 37–38.

Selected Bibliography on the Afro-American Periodical Press 1838–1909

Bond, Horace Mann. "A Negro First." *Negro History Bulletin*, XXVI (November, 1962), 91. [*Alumni Magazine*, Lincoln University, Pa.]

Braithwaite, William Stanley. "Negro America's First Magazine." *Negro Digest*, VI (December, 1947), 21–26. [*Colored American Magazine*]

Bullock, Penelope L. "The Negro Periodical Press in the United States, 1838–1909." Ph.D. dissertation, University of Michigan, 1971.

———. "Profile of a Periodical: The 'Voice of the Negro.'" *Atlanta Historical Bulletin*, XXI (Spring, 1977), 95–114.

Burks, Mary Fair. "The First Black Literary Magazine in American Letters." *CLA Journal*, XIX (March, 1976), 318–21. [*Anglo-African Magazine*]

———. "A Survey of Black Literary Magazines in the United States, 1859–1940." Ed.D. dissertation, Columbia University Teachers College, 1975.

Clinton, George W. "The Literature of the A. M. E. Zion Church." *A. M. E. Zion Quarterly Review*, V (October/January, 1895/96), 248–60.

"The Colored Magazine in America." *Crisis*, V (November, 1912), 33–35.

Cronin, Patricia M. "Negro Magazines in America, 1833–1950." M.A. thesis, University of Missouri, 1951.

Cunningham, Dorothy Holmes. "An Analysis of the *A. M. E. Church Review*, 1884–1900." M.A. thesis, Howard University, 1950.

Detweiler, Frederick G. *The Negro Press in the United States.* Chicago: University of Chicago Press, 1922.

Diggs, Irene. "Du Bois—Revolutionary Journalist Then and Now: Part I." *A Current Bibliography on African Affairs,* IV (March, 1971), 95–117.

Green, Dan S. "W. E. B. Du Bois: His Journalistic Career," *Negro History Bulletin,* XL (March/April, 1977), 672–77.

Hagins, John E. "Publications and Literature of the African Methodist Episcopal Church." *A. M. E. Church Review,* XIX (January, 1903), 596–604.

Hampton Institute. Huntington Library. *Black Periodicals and News-papers: Holdings of Seventy-Four Libraries in the State of Virginia.* African-American Materials Project. Compiled by Lucy B. Campbell. Hampton, Virginia: Hampton Institute, 1973.

Harlan, Louis R. "Booker T. Washington and the *Voice of the Negro,* 1904–1907." *Journal of Southern History,* XLV (February, 1979), 45–62.

Johnson, Abby Arthur, and Ronald M. Johnson. "Away from Accommodation: Radical Editors and Protest Journalism, 1900–1910." *Journal of Negro History,* LXII (October, 1977), 325–38.

———. *Propaganda and Aesthetics: The Literary Politics of Afro-American Magazines in the Twentieth Century.* Amherst: University of Massachusetts Press, 1979.

Johnson, Charles S. "The Rise of the Negro Magazine." *Journal of Negro History,* XIII (January, 1928), 7–21.

Joyce, Donald Franklin. "Magazines of Afro-American Thought on the Mass Market: Can They Survive?" *American Libraries,* VII (December, 1976), 678–83.

Loggins, Vernon. *The Negro Author: His Development in America.* New York: Columbia University Press, 1931.

Meier, August. "Booker T. Washington and the Negro Press, with Special Reference to the *Colored American Magazine.*" *Journal of Negro History,* XXXVIII (January, 1953), 67–90.

Miles, Frank W. "Negro Magazines Come of Age." *Magazine World,* June 1, 1946, pp. 12–13, 18, 21; July 1, 1946, pp. 12–13, 18–20.

Moore, William Luther. "The Literature of the American Negro Prior to 1865: An Anthology and a History." 4 vols. Ed.D. dissertation, New York University, 1942.

North Carolina Central University. School of Library Science. African-American Materials Project. *Newspapers and Periodicals By and*

About Black People: Southeastern Library Holdings. Boston: G. K. Hall, 1978.

Penn, I. Garland. *The Afro-American Press and Its Editors.* Springfield, Mass.: Willey & Company, 1891.

Perry, P. Dolores Brewington. "Frederick Douglass: Editor and Journalist." Ph.D. dissertation, University of North Carolina at Chapel Hill, 1972.

Perry, Patsy Brewington. "The Literary Content of *Frederick Douglass' Paper* through 1860." *CLA Journal,* XVII (December, 1973), 214–29.

Rose Bibliography (Project), American Studies Program, George Washington University. *Analytical Guide and Indexes to Alexander's Magazine, 1905–1909.* Westport, Conn.: Greenwood Press, 1974.

———. *Analytical Guide and Indexes to the Colored American Magazine, 1900–1909.* 2 vols. Westport, Conn.: Greenwood Press, 1974.

———. *Analytical Guide and Indexes to the Voice of the Negro, 1904–1907.* Westport, Conn.: Greenwood Press, 1974.

Sherry, Grace T. "J. Max Barber and the Prerequisites of Race Leadership." M.A. thesis, Georgia State University, 1972. [*Voice of the Negro*]

Terry, William E. "*The Negro Music Journal*: An Appraisal." *The Black Perspective in Music,* V (Fall, 1977), 146–60.

Walden, Carolyn. "An Analysis of the Black Experience as Reflected in the *Voice of the Negro, 1904–1907.*" M.A. Thesis, Atlanta University, 1971.

Wolseley, Roland E. *The Black Press, U.S.A.* Ames: Iowa State University Press, 1972.

Index